Caribbean Reasonings

Freedom, Power and Sovereignty:
The Thought of Gordon K. Lewis

Other Titles in the Caribbean Reasonings Series

After Man, Towards the Human: Critical Essays on Sylvia Wynter

Culture, Politics, Race and Diaspora: The Thought of Stuart Hall

George Padmore: Pan-African Revolutionary

The Thought of New World: The Quest for Decolonisation

The George Lamming Reader: The Aesthetics of Decolonisation

M. G. Smith: Social Theory and Anthropology in the Caribbean and Beyond

Caribbean Political Activism: Essays in Honour of Richard Hart

Caribbean Reasonings
Series Editors
Anthony Bogues
Rupert Lewis
Brian Meeks

Caribbean Reasonings

Freedom, Power and Sovereignty:
The Thought of Gordon K. Lewis

edited by
Brian Meeks
Jermaine McCalpin

IAN RANDLE PUBLISHERS
Kingston • Miami

First published in Jamaica, 2015 by
Ian Randle Publishers
11 Cunningham Avenue
Box 686
Kingston 6
www.ianrandlepublishers.com

Introduction and editorial material
© Centre for Caribbean Thought, University of the West Indies

ISBN 978-976-637-863-9 (pbk)

NATIONAL LIBRARY OF JAMAICA CATALOGUING-IN-PUBLICATION DATA

Freedom, power and sovereignty: the thought of Gordon K. Lewis / edited / by Brian Meeks, Jermaine McCalpin

   p. ; cm. – (Caribbean reasonings)
Bibliography: p. – Includes index
ISBN 978-976-637-863-9 (pbk)

1. Lewis, Gordon K. – Criticism and interpretation
2. Caribbean Area – Civilization
3. Caribbean Area – Politics and government
4. Caribbean Area – Social conditions
I. Meeks, Brian   II. McCalpin, Jermaine   III. Series

320.9   - dc 23

All rights reserved. While copyright in the selection and editorial material is vested in the Centre for Caribbean Thought, University of the West Indies, copyright in individual chapters belongs to their respective authors and no part of this publication may be reproduced, stored in a retrieval system or transmitted in any form or by any means electronic, photocopying, recording or otherwise, without the prior express permission of the author and publisher.

Cover Image: Gordon K. Lewis and Sybil Farrell Lewis. Photo courtesy of Lewis Family Estate Collection at University of Puerto Rico, Caribbean Collection, Faculty of Social Sciences, Rio Piedras Campus. Photo taken at Lewis Family Home in Trujillo Alto, Puerto Rico, Circa 1988.

Cover and book design by Ian Randle Publishers
Printed and bound in the United States of America

Table of Contents

Acknowledgements /vii

Introduction
    The Scholar as Optimist /ix
    Brian Meeks

PART 1
IN THE VANGUARD OF CARIBBEAN THOUGHT

1. Deciphering the Marx-Burke Counterpoint in Gordon K. Lewis's Work /1
   Anthony P. Maingot

2. Gordon Lewis and the Writing of Afro-Caribbean Political Thought /14
   Paget Henry

3. 'An Extended Debate with Europe?':
   G.K. Lewis, Denis Benn, Paget Henry, and the Epistemological Challenge in the Writing of Caribbean Political Thought /46
   Tennyson S.D. Joseph

4. A Lens of a Different Colour:
   Gordon K. Lewis, Postmodernity and Cuban Antislavery Narratives /69
   Claudette M. Williams

5. Opening the Canon:
   The Place of Theology in Caribbean Intellectual Thought /79
   Delroy A. Reid-Salmon

6. Toward Reconstituting Caribbean Identity Discourse from within the Dutch Caribbean Island of Curaçao /94
   Rose Mary Allen

PART 2
RETHINKING CARIBBEAN POLITICS

7. The 'Slums of Empire' and Gordon K. Lewis: Reflections on Decolonization and Sovereignty in the Caribbean   /**113**
   Jessica Byron

8. Some Perspectives on Gordon Lewis's Legacy in the Understanding of Regionalism   /**145**
   Edward Greene

9. The Reshaping of Freedom and Power in Puerto Rico: Community-based Social Change in the Era of Neoliberal Reforms   /**154**
   Rafael A. Boglio Martínez

10. Gordon Lewis and the Mass Suicide in Jonestown, Guyana 1978   /**177**
    Ralph Premdas

Bibliography   /**195**

Contributors   /**211**

Index   /**215**

Acknowledgements

I am thankful to my colleagues in the Centre for Caribbean Thought and fellow series editors Rupert Lewis and Anthony Bogues for their invaluable help and intellectual support extended over a decade in the hosting of numerous conferences and seven accompanying books in the 'Caribbean Reasonings' series. The critical interrogation and foregrounding of a selection of important Caribbean intellectuals has served, I hope, to place the discipline of Caribbean Thought on the front burner of anyone interested in the contemporary history of the region. Jermaine McCalpin gave unstinting support in the planning of the 2010 G.K. Lewis Conference and as co-editor of this volume. I offer a special word of thanks to David Lewis and the Lewis family who gave support throughout the planning of the conference and strongly encouraged us to get this volume in print. The cover photograph of Gordon and his wife Sybil Farrell Lewis is from their archive. Particular mention must be made of our conference co-sponsors, including the Research Institute for the Study of Man, The University of Puerto Rico, Brown University, The Caribbean Development Bank, Caribbean Airlines, The Jamaica Pegasus Hotel and the UWI Development and Endowment Fund. The G.K. Lewis Conference and this volume would not have been possible without their collective contribution. I am grateful to Beverly Sutherland Lewis and Eleanor Williams both of whom played central roles in the organisation of the conference and, before returning home to South Africa, Eleanor did her usual, difficult job of rounding up and copy-editing the work of contributors. This was completed by Carol Lawes who joined the editorial team late in the day, but brought her own energy and skills to the project. Thank you Carol! A final word of gratitude to Christine Randle from IRP who took over the risky remit passed on by Ian Randle and published, over a decade, the Caribbean Reasonings Series, against the tide of the typical book publishing currents in the region. These demand that, at best, only disciplinary specific, narrowly defined textbooks should appear. IRP has ignored this imperative and the result is this substantial body of work on Caribbean thought. Without vision, we perish and IRP has shown demonstrably, that it is not without vision.

Brian Meeks
Mona, May 2014

Introduction

The Scholar as Optimist

Brian Meeks

In September 2010 The Centre for Caribbean Thought at the University of the West Indies, Mona, hosted, along with Brown University and the University of Puerto Rico, Rio Piedras, the Seventh Caribbean Reasonings Conference, 'Freedom and Power in the Caribbean: the Work of Gordon K. Lewis.'[1] It turned out to be the final in a series of captivating 'Caribbean Reasonings' that honoured, for seven consecutive years, outstanding, if insufficiently heralded Caribbean intellectuals including, in order of appearance, Sylvia Wynter, George Lamming, Stuart Hall, the New World Group, Richard Hart and M.G. Smith, the latter posthumously.[2] The Seventh Conference was noteworthy not only because it recognized Lewis's significant, indeed promethean contributions to Caribbean political thought and science, but also in that it was the only event in the series to honour someone who was neither of Caribbean birth nor heritage. Yet, as was evident from the many testimonials and remembrances throughout the three days, Gordon Lewis, with his long sojourn in Puerto Rico, intimate connection with people from all walks of life throughout the archipelago and sensitive, exhaustive studies of the Caribbean condition, was as Caribbean a citizen as any.

Born into a family of teachers in 1919 in the post-War destitution of Southern Wales, the young Lewis grew to understand the world in a time of unrest and uprising. There was intense agitation among the coal miners in Wales, strikes for better living conditions and in support of the nascent Soviet state throughout the United Kingdom and myriad uncertainties surrounding the future of Ireland and the resolution of the Irish Question. So while his early formation didn't expose him to the peculiarities of the Caribbean situation, it grounded him nonetheless in an understanding of class and its dynamics, the effects of marginalization, as was the Welsh experience at the periphery of the Kingdom, and the many implications of colonialism and the resistance to it, as was evident in nearby Ireland.[3]

Lewis graduated from University College, Cardiff, in 1940 with a BA in modern English and European history, then spent five years in the British Army, before going up to Oxford, where he read politics, economics and philosophy, obtaining his MA in 1947. Next, he travelled to the United States where he lectured at the University of Chicago, then the University of California, Los Angeles, before enrolling at Harvard for his PhD. His dissertation, completed in 1954, was on 'The Christian Socialist Movement in Nineteenth Century Britain.' Shortly before finishing in 1952, he visited Puerto Rico as part of an interdisciplinary team of social scientists working on the island's new constitution that would determine the form of her peculiar arrangement of Commonwealth associated status with the United States. The island, and the Caribbean generally, made a profound impression on him and two years later, after receiving his doctorate, he returned to take up a position in the Department of Political Science at the University of Puerto Rico, Rio Piedras. There he laid his bed, eventually marrying his love and future intellectual partner, the Trinidadian-born Sybil Farrell, raising with her five children and leading an extraordinarily productive, scholarly life until his untimely death in 1991 at the age of 72.

When Gordon Lewis arrived in the Caribbean he was already a maturing scholar with significant publications in politics and political theory. Yet, it was in the Caribbean of the 1950s, with its differing experiences of colonialism, burgeoning political movements, numerous language groupings and polyphonic island cultures that he found his muse and reason to write. Between his first arrival and his passing, Lewis published numerous articles and seven major books[4] of which four, I suggest, are most influential and together demarcate him as a Caribbean thinker of the first order.

The first of these, *Puerto Rico: Freedom and Power in the Caribbean*,[5] was published in 1962 and sought to explain modern Puerto Rico's political history and to explicate the peculiarity of her Commonwealth Status. In a severe critique of the arrangement and of United States policy, Lewis also engaged in a deft and multi-disciplinary attempt to grasp the nuances of Puerto Rican politics, culture and the national personality. *Freedom and Power*, a tour de force of some 650 pages, initiated, certainly for Caribbean social sciences, a novel style of writing which moved with alacrity from empirical data to literary reference, interspersed with memorable sketches of individual players. Among the most outstanding was that of Luis Muñoz Marín, who played an extraordinary role as architect of much of the island's political and economic programme and whose policies became a model for a generation of emerging political leaders throughout the region.

In *The Growth of the Modern West Indies*,[6] first published in 1968, Lewis engaged with the new politics of the Anglophone Caribbean, where, in the wake of the 1961 collapse of the West Indies Federation, individual territories, beginning with Jamaica and Trinidad in August 1962, were embarking on the first phase of their independence experiment. In a richly descriptive and insightful survey, yet to be replicated for its comprehensive approach to the region, he both appreciated the rich cultural and political heritage, and, presciently, identified the potentially grim future that faced resource-poor mini-states in an unforgiving world economy. However, in typically optimistic fashion, Lewis concluded that, inevitably, the islands for their own survival would have to come together in some form, which, he suggested, might be

> ...the starting point for a massive revolution which would give to a region so long renowned for its natural beauty a social beauty it has hitherto not known.[7]

It is in the third of these four volumes, however, that Lewis – already at the height of his powers – produced his most outstanding work, with the appearance in 1983 of *Main Currents in Caribbean Thought*.[8] Sub-titled 'The Historical Evolution of Caribbean Society in its Ideological Aspects 1492 – 1900,' *Main Currents* is the first consistent attempt to identify and define Caribbean Thought as a distinct stream within modern scholarship. Lewis carefully sifts through the pro- and anti-slavery literature and the emerging nationalist writings of the nineteenth century as well as their colonialist antinomies to arrive at the conclusion that Caribbean Thought is to be located at the intersection of the clashing of civilizations and the effervescent struggle for freedom against unspeakable barbarities. The Caribbean may not as yet have overcome all of these confining social and political ideas and their accompanying institutions, but the hope, he asserted, is to be found in the role the region has played, far beyond its diminutive scale, in generating some of the leading ideas associated with freedom and liberation in the modern world as well as producing many of the outstanding intellectual and political leaders. There are, of course, notable lacunae in his analysis, including, as captured in this volume, the absence of any discussion of African philosophical notions and the general paucity of reference to subaltern ideas; but it is to Lewis's credit that he stakes out a foundation on which these contemporary critiques and debates can flourish.

The final of these four and the last to appear in his lifetime,[9] was *Grenada: the Jewel Despoiled*.[10] Published in 1987, some four years after the tragic collapse of the Grenada Revolution, he sought to row against the growing conservative current of the time and rescue a place for progressive ideas and politics, which is captured in his proposals for a democratic socialism. If the first three volumes were written in what can be considered moments of optimism associated with the long post-War economic boom and the prospects of independence, then *Jewel*, in the wake of Walter Rodney's assassination and the Jonestown suicides in Guyana, the defeat of the Manley government in the bloody 1980 elections in Jamaica and the Grenada tragedy, was written in an atmosphere, certainly from the perspective of the left, of cynicism and despair. Distancing himself philosophically from a certain stream of authoritarian socialism, he was nonetheless able to recognize the profound effects of the revolution in energizing Grenada and raising people's sense of self-worth:

> ...any account of the Grenada Revolution must end by remembering it. For all that it did wrong, the PRG leadership was able to mobilize a mass enthusiasm for the revolution that no other Caribbean country save Cuba has managed to do...Somehow or another, in Grenada, a spark seems to have been touched that enabled a whole populace to engage itself in refurbishing its house.[11]

Three decades later, despite the 2008 worldwide recession and its deleterious effects on Caribbean economies, which many have traced directly to the growing power and dangerous overreach of finance capitalism, there is, as yet, no sign of a radical revival. However, were such a renaissance, on whatever novel foundations, to occur in the future, it is to Lewis's credit that he, in unequivocal terms, has powerfully advocated for the road down which it should not travel.

INTRODUCTION

The chapters in this volume, all initially presented at the 2010 conference, while not attempting to do the impossible in comprehensively addressing Lewis's oeuvre, nonetheless capture the flavour of his interests and passions. In Part One 'In the Vanguard of Caribbean Thought' six essays explore Lewis's ideas in *Main Currents* and his other works. Tony Maingot, his former student and close friend, elaborates in chapter 1 on the seeming contradiction between Lewis's self-identification with Marxism and his lifelong fascination with conservative talisman Edmund Burke. Maingot concludes that both Marx and Burke are seamlessly woven into the tapestry of G.K. Lewis's own brand of humanist and democratic socialism. In chapter 2, Paget Henry proposes that while *Main Currents*, in setting the cornerstones for Caribbean Thought is certainly a classic, it fails to address in any comprehensive fashion the African contribution to Caribbean Thought. Henry suggests in the remainder of his essay some of the ideas, institutions and historical figures that should be included in order to correct this perceived flaw. In chapter 3, Tennyson Joseph's starting point is to critique, inter alia, both Lewis and Henry. He argues that neither Lewis in *Main Currents*, Henry in his well-received volume *Caliban's Reason: Introducing Afro-Caribbean Philosophy*,[12] nor Denis Benn in his survey of Caribbean intellectuals,[13] appreciates the existence of what he considers to be an entirely different cultural and epistemological universe to be found in African thought and in the African Diaspora. Correcting this failure, he suggests, will have to be an intellectual labour of the future. In chapter 4, Claudette Williams borrows from Gordon Lewis's compelling methodology in which he takes literary sources seriously as sites of social investigation. She engages with a number of Cuban anti-slavery narratives in order to better understand the dynamics of Caribbean slavery, as well as the formation of ideologies of domination and resistance in nineteenth century Cuba. In chapter 5, Delroy Reid-Salmon stakes out a different claim in his proposal that Caribbean intellectual thought has paid insufficient attention to theology. Despite Lewis's recognition and critique of ecclesiastical scholars, Reid-Salmon suggests and develops his argument that theology itself is worthy of greater scholarly recognition. The final chapter in this section, by Rose Mary Allen, is of a different form, as she engages in a brief exploratory survey of social and political thought in the Dutch Caribbean. Taking Lewis's invocation seriously, that one cannot claim to be a full practitioner of Caribbean studies until one writes on the Caribbean as a whole,[14] Allen seeks to remedy this by introducing the Dutch Caribbean to an English-speaking audience that is largely ignorant of the important intellectual traditions that have emerged in that sub-region.

In Part Two, as the title 'Rethinking Caribbean Politics' suggests, a variety of essays develop themes and issues in Caribbean politics that concerned Gordon Lewis. In chapter 7, Jessica Byron draws liberally on a variety of Lewis's texts to explore contemporary definitions of sovereignty and to suggest its limitations as well as possible openings for its exercise in the contemporary Caribbean. In chapter 8, Eddie Greene, agreeing undoubtedly with Lewis's more optimistic proposals that regional integration might provide a better future for the Caribbean, describes some of the positive steps that CARICOM has taken towards this end and further urgent tasks that are necessary if such a vision is not to be squandered. Rafael Boglio Martínez in chapter 8 returns to the Puerto Rican matrix in exploring the role of NGOs and the nature of democracy in contemporary Puerto Rico. In an analysis redolent with many of the themes raised in *Freedom and Power*, Boglio Martínez concludes with a sceptical assessment of the ubiquitous NGO industry and a gloomy perspective on the state of democracy in Puerto Rico. In the final chapter, Ralph Premdas, working through arguments first mooted in Lewis's text, *Gather With the Saints at the River: The Jonestown Guyana Holocaust of 1978*,[15] explores the terrible events in Guyana in 1978 when 918 Americans, members of Jim Jones's People's Temple committed mass suicide in their hinterland commune. Premdas suggests that Lewis, in parallel fashion to his later study on Grenada, delved into the authoritarianism and absence of democracy in Jones's so-called socialist experiment in order to suggest, as counterpoint, what a democratic and humanist socialism might look like in the Caribbean context.

If tragedy, then, as exemplified in the Jonestown events and of course in Grenada, is a recurring theme in Gordon Lewis's later work, it might also be useful to conclude by remembering that there is another stream of hope and optimism that runs through it all. In *Freedom and Power, Growth, Main Currents* and *Jewel*, there is everywhere a genuine empathy and appreciation of the strengths inherent in the Caribbean people, who despite the ravages of history, ethnic differences and poverty, have found the wherewithal to live in peace and relative harmony with each other, have generated some of the leading ideas of the modern world and continue to make an inordinately great mark on global culture. All of these, he suggests,

> ...have added to constitute the never-ending fascination felt by travellers and visitors to the region. They are the elements and the promise of Caribbean life. The future of the Caribbean lies within the capacity and the willingness of these elements to fulfil and indeed enlarge that promise.[16]

This sentiment lies at the heart of Gordon K. Lewis's remarkable work and one that we hope, above all others, is captured in this memorial volume.

Notes

1. An interesting anecdote surrounds the staging of the conference itself. It was initially scheduled for early June 2010, but was postponed due to the intercession of the 'Dudus' events in Kingston. After much vacillation over many months on a US request for the extradition of notorious inner-city 'Don' Christopher 'Dudus' Coke, the JLP government eventually conceded to the request. Dudus, however, had other ideas and barricaded himself and his supporters in his Tivoli Gardens stronghold. The subsequent shooting of police officers and burning to the ground of a police station, led to a major military/police assault on Tivoli and the frightening tragedy of more than 70 deaths. The conference was rescheduled for September – in the hurricane season – and as luck would have it, a few days before the event, a storm skirted Jamaica with accompanying high winds and rain. Despite this and the inevitably reduced attendance, it was successfully staged. Gordon Lewis, I think, would have appreciated that two features so typical of the Caribbean he knew, interfered with his memorial event – both social and meteorological upheaval!
2. The Centre for Caribbean Thought (CCT) launched in 2001, functioned effectively for 11 years until it was shuttered due to cutbacks and new priorities at UWI Mona. During that period, it not only staged the seven Caribbean Reasonings conferences, but also co-sponsored with the UWI St Augustine separate conferences in honour of C.L.R. James and George Padmore; a Seminar on African thought with the University of Cape Town and Brown University, in Cape Town; a two-stage conference on Black Power with University College, London; a conference on Walter Rodney and the 1968 events in Jamaica with the Institute of Caribbean Studies, Mona, as well as numerous sponsored speeches and book launches. It is hoped that in a more favourable economic environment the CCT might yet flourish again.

3. For more thorough discussions of Lewis's early life see Anthony Maingot, *The Passionate Advocate: Gordon K. Lewis and Caribbean Studies* (Centre for Caribbean Studies, University of Warwick, 1991) and Anthony Maingot, 'Gordon K. Lewis: The Engaged Scholar as Passionate Advocate' Introduction to *Gordon K. Lewis On Race, Class and Ideology in the Caribbean*, ed. Anthony Maingot (Kingston: Ian Randle Publishers, 2010), xv–xxxix.
4. See Basic Bibliography in Maingot, ed., *Gordon K. Lewis On Race*, 119–21.
5. Gordon Lewis, *Puerto Rico: Freedom and Power in the Caribbean* (New York: Monthly Review Press, 1963).
6. Gordon Lewis, *The Growth of the Modern West Indies* (New York: Monthly Review Press, 1968).
7. Ibid., 415.
8. Gordon Lewis, *Main Currents in Caribbean Thought: The Historical Evolution of Caribbean Society in Its Ideological Aspects, 1492–1900* (Baltimore: Johns Hopkins University Press, 1983).
9. The only work to appear after his passing is the earlier mentioned volume of Lewis's work edited by Anthony Maingot *On Race, Class and Ideology in the Caribbean*, which contains excerpts from what was to have been Lewis's magnum opus, an incomplete, though at the time of his death some 700 pages long manuscript entitled 'The Modern Caribbean: A New Voyage of Discovery.' See David Lewis's Foreword in Anthony Maingot, ed., 2010, vii–xiv.
10. Gordon Lewis, *Grenada: The Jewel Despoiled* (Baltimore: Johns Hopkins University Press, 1987).
11. Ibid., 198.
12. See Paget Henry, *Caliban's Reason: Introducing Afro-Caribbean Philosophy* (London and New York: Routledge, 2000).
13. See Denis Benn, *The Growth and Development of Political Ideas in the Caribbean: 1774–1983* (Mona: Institute of Social and Economic Research, 1987).
14. It is lamentable that more than 20 years after his death so few contemporary scholars of the Caribbean have listened to Lewis's invocation, or followed his example. Two notable exceptions are Nigel Bolland's *The Birth of Caribbean Civilisation: A Century of Ideas about Culture and Identity, Nation and Society* (Kingston: Ian Randle Publishers, 2004) and Aaron Kamugisha's edited double collection *Caribbean Political Thought: Theories of the Post-Colonial State* and *Caribbean Political Thought: The Colonial State to Caribbean Internationalisms* (Kingston: Ian Randle Publishers, 2013).
15. Gordon Lewis, *Gather with the Saints at the River: The Jonestown Guyana Holocaust of 1978* (Rio Piedras, Puerto Rico: Institute of Caribbean Studies, 1979).
16. Gordon Lewis, *Main Currents*, 329.

PART 1
In the Vanguard of Caribbean Thought

1 | Deciphering the Marx-Burke Counterpoint in Gordon K. Lewis's Work

Anthony P. Maingot

In an essay in *Caribbean Contact* in July 1984,[1] Gordon K. Lewis argued that one of the lessons of the tragic events in Grenada on October 19, 1983 was that radical social change and militarization 'are a heady mix, with clear dangers.' He reminded the reader that 'the old European socialist tradition,' of which Marx and Engels were an integral part, was strongly anti-militarist. He then resorted to Edmund Burke's 1796 *Letters on a Regicide Peace* to state the moral objection:

> The blood of man should never be shed but to redeem the blood of man. It is well shed for our family, for our friends, for our God, for our country, for mankind. The rest is vanity; the rest is crime.[2]

Lewis was not in any way rejecting the Grenadian revolution. He applauded it because as he asserted with not a small dose of hyperbole, it 'showed that a small island folk-people could put together a spirited mass movement of protest and resistance unmatched by any other people in the region.'[3] His criticisms were kept well within the bounds of classical Marxism. It was within that tradition that he faulted the New Jewel Movement (NJM) leadership's choice of a Leninist strategy rather than Rosa Luxemburg's strategy of 'spontaneity.' The former was elitist and militaristic, the latter a genuine popular and democratic response of the masses.

In this *Caribbean Contact* essay, as in so much of Lewis's work, one is faced with a theoretical paradox: rather than a consistent and uninterrupted Marxian analysis, he repeatedly leans on Burke and moderate, i.e., Fabian, English socialism to make moral assertions. It appears as if Lewis kept Burke in a parallel theoretical realm, ready to be used when Lewis's Marxian analysis proved inadequate to explain fully his qualms about basic decency and humane behaviour. What we have, thus, is an ideational counterpoint between a grand theory of social change and a set of deeply-held personal convictions about the nature of 'civilized' behaviour.

It was never a case of Lewis using Marxism either opportunistically or, as do so many in the Caribbean, as a unicausal radical critique of the *status quo*. His training in classical and radical theory was too profound for such ideological posturing and radical bravado. Students have to assume that his ideas on social change had to have an internal logic and consistency in the interpretation of historical causality.[4] Lewis had many facts, not many faces. That being the case, new revelations compel us to re-evaluate assertions such as the following made on page 269 of Lewis's 1974 book, *Notes on the Puerto Rican Revolution*:[5] 'There is finally,' he wrote, 'the disillusionment with the old style politics of court action, peaceful demonstration, and political activism; these have now to be replaced with open armed self-defense.' This is so, he argued, because American capitalism was in its aggressive, 'imperialist phase.'[6] The latter, of course, is Lenin's adaptation from Hobson's theory of imperialism and Lewis cites it without presenting the most minimal evidence that significant numbers of Puerto Ricans were responding to any such 'phase.' It was much more a statement of his ideological position than a result of any empirical findings. All this to say that in pursuing the consistency of Lewis's anti-traditionalism even revolutionary inclinations, we have to ask why it is that it is Edmund Burke, whom Lewis calls 'the great figure,' that he cites most frequently. Understand, however, that it was invariably Burke the anti-imperialist and supporter of colonial liberation. This was only logical since in a way, all of Lewis's works are attacks on imperialism and colonialism in all its forms. Anti-imperialism, he once admitted, came 'easy' to him as was the British socialist tradition and English progressive thought which, he noted, was 'influenced as much by Burke as by Marx.'[7] Marx certainly had an impact on key Fabians, especially through the influence of the London School of Economics where Harold Laski and the Marxist Ralph Miliband taught for decades. Laski had great respect for Marx's writings but lamented the 'canons of orthodoxy' which Lenin and then Stalin lay on them. Lenin, said Laski, was an 'intellectual heretic.'[8]

But again the paradox: why was it invariably in Burkean not Marxian terms that Lewis phrased his anti-colonialism? His life-long opposition to the Puerto Rican Estado Libre Asociado, for instance, was more than once phrased with this quote from Burke on colonial bondage:

> This servitude, which makes men subject to a state without being citizens, may be more or less tolerable from many circumstances, but these circumstances, more or less favorable, do not alter the nature of the thing. The mildness by which absolute masters exercise their dominion, leaves them masters still.[9]

Even in a rare visit with the Rastafarian leadership in Jamaica, Lewis indicated that he believed Burke had helped him understand the righteousness of their demands. 'For, as Edmund Burke remarked, every people must have some compensation for its slavery.'[10] Yet, one must again be reminded that Burke believed in traditionalism, in the accumulation and testing of experience over generations, and spoke of the advantages of the 'collected reason of ages' as distinct from the radical rationalism of revolutionaries.[11]

Keep in mind that Burke's vehement opposition to the French Revolution led even such luminaries as Thomas Jefferson and Thomas Paine to consider him a 'reactionary' and Karl Marx to describe him as 'that celebrated sophist and sycophant' who had 'sold-out' to the American rebels.[12] English historian J.H. Plumb was even harsher: 'Most of Burke's political philosophy,' he noted, 'is utter rubbish, and completely unhistorical...meaningless verbiage of political theology'[13] – undeservedly harsh in an extreme since Burke was no ideologue. He could, and did, distinguish between one 'revolution' and another and between different stages or circumstances of a revolutionary process. Even in that great counterrevolutionary tract of 1790, *Reflections on the Revolution in France*, Burke refused to be ideologically fixed and dogmatic asserting that he could not stand forward and give praise or blame to anything which relates to human actions, and human concerns, 'on a simple view of the object.' 'Circumstances,' he maintained, 'give in reality to every political principle its distinguishing colour, and distinguishing effect. The circumstances are what render every civil and political scheme beneficial or noxious to mankind.'[14] That is the basis on which he judged the American Revolution beneficial and thus no threat to Britain, while the French, in their Jacobin stage, were noxious and a clear threat to the British system. As Ruth A. Bevan accurately notes: with Burke, it was 'Man in the concrete, it's with common human life and human actions you are to be concerned.'[15]

Burke's thoughts on Empire and the colonies came most explicitly – and, as was his wont, most passionately – in the cases of the American Revolution and the British rule in India. He argued for the reform of the East India Company based on considerations of humanity and justice. The natural rights of men – all men, regardless of ethnicity or station – he said, were sacred. His concern was 'our distressed fellow citizens in India.'[16] In his 1788 push to have the Governor General of the East India Company, Warren Hastings, impeached, Burke begged the judges of the House of Lords to be impartial 'so that Asia would not think that a European enjoyed rights denied to others.' 'God forbid,' he said, 'it should be bruited from Peking to Paris, that the laws of England are for the rich and the powerful; but to the poor, the miserable, and the defenceless, they offer no recourse at all.' As he said in his opening speech at the impeachment of Warren Hastings:

> The laws of morality are the same everywhere, and...there is no action which would pass for an act of extortion, of peculation, of bribery, and of oppression in England, that is not an act of extortion, of peculation, of bribery and oppression in Europe, Asia Africa, and all the world over.

Notice that in none of this is there any concern, much less consideration, that factors such as race, religion, regionalism, nationalism might in themselves be agents of social change and drivers of a liberation movement.[17]

One has to wonder what Lewis made of the cold – even callous – 'scientific' nature of Marx's analysis in the following footnote in his chapter in *Capital* on the value of labour power. Noting that slave labour should not be considered unpaid labour because 'the property-relation conceals the labour of the slave for himself,' he adds the following footnote:

> The 'Morning Star,' a London free-trade organ, naïf to silliness, protested again and again during the American civil war, with all the moral indignation of which man is capable, that the negro in the 'Confederate States' worked absolutely for nothing. It should

have compared the daily cost of such a negro with that of the free workman in the East end of London.[18]

Is the moral issue of slavery, of human bondage, to be subordinated to the comparative costs of maintaining a slave as distinct from a *free* workman? It can make sense only in a general scheme in which 'superstructural' factors are, if not irrelevant, at least quite secondary. The point being that while Lewis was convinced by the broader Marxian theory of social change, his analysis in and of the Caribbean kept bringing him back to superstructural – especially moral – factors. Again, the differences between Marx and Burke on this score are revealing and, arguably, even explanatory of some of the paradoxes in Lewis's analyses of the region.

Marx and Burke on Ethnic Minorities

Because ethnicity and in particular religion were merely superstructural, Marx spent little time or effort on its import. The one time he dealt directly with it was in his 1843 essay, 'On the Jewish Question.'[19] Although he was of high rabbinical family on both sides, his father had converted to Lutheranism and he himself was an avowed atheist. Because he disdained religion everywhere, he had no use for it in India. Burke, on the other hand, believed religion was a stabilizing force and felt that way about Hinduism in India.[20] But there might have been more to Marx's attitude towards the Jews. It is difficult not to see in Marx's call for 'the emancipation of society from Judaism' a deep-seated anti-Semitism no matter how cleverly made a part of his theory of social change.[21] He equates the despised (and, yet, according to his ontology, historically necessary) economics of commerce with 'Judaism,' which he in turn equates with 'huckstering.' Logically, his wish is to liberate society from both. 'Mammon,' he says of the Jews, 'is his idol which he adores not only with his lips but with the whole force of his body and mind. The social emancipation of the Jew,' he concluded, 'is the emancipation of society from Judaism.'[22]

How different the Burkean approach to ethnic minorities in general and the Jews in particular. He came to the issue of the rights of minorities naturally. He was, he always said, a 'minority' and it is known that even after he had scaled the ladder of British politics, he continued to socialize with the marginalized Irish community in

London. J.H. Plumb, who, as noted above, was no friend of Burke's political philosophy, did recognize that 'as an outsider who never got in, Burke often felt himself drawn to the oppressed, the wronged, the impotents of society.'[23] The following is illustrative. In 1781 British Admiral Rodney conquered the Dutch island of St Eustatius which had been selling armaments to the American rebels. He was especially harsh on the Jewish merchants, confiscating all their personal and commercial property and deporting all the by now destitute Jewish adult males to Antigua and St Kitts.[24] Burke vehemently attacked Rodney in Parliament:

> ...a sentence of general beggary pronounced in one moment upon a whole people. A cruelty unheard of in Europe in many years.... The persecution was begun with the people whom of all others it ought to be the care and the wish of human nations to protect, the Jews....[25]

Burke was concerned with this minority as human beings but also because he understood their critical economic function. They were, he said: '...the links of communication, in the mercantile claim...the conductors by which credit was transmitted through the world....'[26] Predictably, given English anti-Semitism, the British Parliament not only failed to request restitution from Rodney, they elevated him to a peerage as Baron Rodney.

Lewis had to be attracted to Burke's view of the nation composed of groups as a historically engendered cultural complex much more than to Marx's disregard of these groups as he portrayed the nation evolving in predictable economic stages. He had to weigh on his well-developed personal sense of justice, Burke's nationalist sensibilities versus Marx's secular proletarian internationalism. Burke opposed his nation's imperialism. Marx, while abhorring it, conceded it as historically necessary. It is Burke's deep sentiments about the oppressed Irish versus Engels, equally indignant at England's oppression of these same Irish, but who concluded, without an ounce of the milk of human kindness, that that oppression had led to an Irish migration of *lumpen* which, 'as is well known, it is their job to provide England, America, Australia, etc., with whores, casual labourers, pimps, rascals, cheats, beggars and other criminal rabble.'[27]

Even more important than the differences between Burke and Marx and Engels over questions of race and ethnicity, is another major paradox in Lewis's theory of social change. Contrary to Marxian theory which interpreted the colonization by a 'higher' economic order as the necessary precondition to the creation of a working class as the only route to socialism, Lewis's basic theoretical argument is premised on the idea that socialism in Puerto Rico and the Caribbean can be achieved only after political independence, i.e., after a break with American imperialism. 'The cardinal fact to be considered,' he says, 'is the American connection.'[28] No need to belabour the point that in Marxist theory it is precisely that 'connection' which is the necessary historical antecedent to socialism.

How then does one interpret Lewis's declarations of a Marxist orientation, and his paradoxical preference for the type of humanity-centred anti-imperialism professed by Burke? Certainly this is a complex historiographical enquiry but one which calls out for at least a hypothetical answer. Such a hypothesis has to place Lewis in the context of the general climate and attitudes towards Marxist thought (and especially communism) in the England where his philosophy of history was forged.

The Marxian and Burkean in Lewis

One is struck by the fact that despite his professions of Marxist radicalism, Lewis never published anything significant in standard English radical journals such as *The New Reasoner* or the *New Left Review*. His tendency was to seek out standard refereed academic journals such as *The Journal of Politics, The Political Quarterly, Social and Economic Studies,* and *Caribbean Studies*. His first publications in an American New Left journal were in *Studies on the Left*, a largely pro-Cuban Revolution creation of non-Communist radicals such as Saul Landau and William Rouff. Even his search for a publisher for his *Puerto Rico* manuscript started with mainline academic presses. It was finally published by the editors of the journal *Monthly Review*, the socialists Paul Sweezey and Leo Huberman, both also interested in Cuba.

So, in many ways, Lewis's early socialist writings took place in the context of an American New Left's highly romantic vision of the Cuban Revolution as an alternative to the already evident theoretical orthodoxy and ideological dogmatism of existing communist positions.[29] As such, it is best to describe his ideas as Neo-Marxian rather than Marxist. This is evident, first, in his easy relationship (ideologically and personally) with a much more eclectic and flexible strand of Marxism such as that of *Studies on the Left* which promised 'to publish articles by leftists of all shades of conviction and doubt.'[30] This had to appeal to him since he published two of his seminal essays there. Secondly, the emphasis on alienation (from a sovereign state and national identity fundamentally) was very much in the English and American tradition.

Anthony Giddens maintains that one reason why Britain never produced a major radical theorist was 'the absence, in Britain, of a really significant revolutionary socialist movement.'[31] David McLellan makes the same point about the failure of radical Marxism to make inroads in the United States.[32] One can conclude that Lewis arrived in the New World (the US and then Puerto Rico) with a very English, non-doctrinaire approach to Marxism.

What then, to conclude about his basic theoretical approach to Caribbean Studies? The first order of business should be to lay to rest a misconception about his methodology. To repeat, Lewis's approach was radical and Marxian in influence, it was not strictly Marxist either in theory or partisan allegiance. Like Marx, he was concerned with radical social change but, like Burke, he was concerned with what he called 'the larger picture' of societies, with 'the great classical tradition of humanism in the scholarly endeavor.' His constant exhortations that the 'outside' (as he always identified himself) get 'into' the heart and mind of his Caribbean subjects, was closer to neo-Kantianism or neo-idealism than to historical materialism. His review of the work of Puerto Rican José Luís González reflects this fact. 'He writes,' wrote Lewis, 'as a Marxist, but as he puts it, *'marxista sin iglesia'* (Marxist without a church). There is a refreshing absence of what in the churches we call devotional literature. He is an iconoclast. He thinks – as every intellectual must – for himself.'[33]

This is Lewis approving of González's independence of thought. This is also Max Weber explaining why he could not join any socialist party. 'I shall not join these churches,' he once said, because systematic social science cannot answer the question, 'Which of the warring Gods should we serve?'[34]

To Lewis, as to Weber, Durkheim and so many others, Marx was influential as a thinker, not as an oracle or a god. His very British intellectual independence goes a long way in resolving the enigma of his life and the evident Marx-Burke paradox posed at the beginning of this chapter. It is this ideological flexibility which allowed him to understand that in the final analysis both Burke's liberal conservatism and Marx's radical theories had the same polemical foils he had: the abusive and exploitative nature of many economic and political systems of power.

In Conclusion: A Personal Rejoinder

Gordon K. Lewis had been my professor and Master's Thesis advisor at the University of Puerto Rico and later a lifelong colleague and friend. It was from him that I learned that crossing theoretical swords is welcome if it throws more light than heat on a worthy disagreement. I follow his example here.

In his *Grenada: The Jewel Despoiled*, Lewis provides an extended and cutting critique of one of my arguments.[35] I had argued that it was a serious mistake for the NJM elite to abandon their early (1973) manifesto of further developing an active land-owning peasantry producing enough of a surplus to supply state-owned small-island agro-industries.[36] Lewis dismissed such pastoral socialism as utopian and concluded that my idea was that these small islands 'should resign themselves to becoming isolated and charming idyllic spots for the delight of tourists.'[37] Knowing how Lewis's ironic style occasionally crossed the line into mordant sarcasm, I will ignore the reference to my arguments and dwell on his criticism of utopianism. I do so with the firm knowledge that Friedrich Engels would not have been so easily dismissive. In his polemical and very popular 1880 essay, 'Socialism: Utopian and Scientific', Engels dismissed the literary small fry ('Philistines' he called them) who ridiculed the Utopians Saint-Simon Fourier and Robert Owen. There was no such ridicule from Engels, only a great intellectual debt; a 'delight in the stupendously grand thoughts and germs of thoughts',

> ...in Saint-Simon we find a comprehensive breadth of view, by virtue of which almost all the ideas of later Socialists *that are not strictly economic* are found in him in embryo.[38]

Of course the forces unleashed by capitalism would eventually make the ideas of the Utopians less operational. But what if there was no developed or mature capitalist system – as there was none in Grenada. Do the ideas and hopes of the Utopians become irrelevant? Not at all. Theirs were ideas about social injustice, about fair play and decency (as in Owens's successful and profitable experiment with treating his labour decently), indeed, all those ideas which influenced Marx and Engels to seek a 'scientific' approach to social justice. The fatal flaw of the Grenadian Marxists was to dismiss idealism in order to pursue an approach which in the Grenada context was 'scientific' only in theory and on paper. Once social and economic realities showed the stark divergences between theory and reality, only coercion could rescue the grand scheme. And, on this point, Lewis sounds as 'utopian' as I did:

> There is the principle that in a democracy worthy of the name, decisions are arrived at by the process of discussion, and not by the method of coercion.[39]

By including the mass of peasants in the design of the 1973 'Utopian' Manifesto, the NJM leadership was being democratic; by specifically excluding the peasants from the post-1979 'scientific' socialist program, they were being totalitarians.[40] This, and not any Utopian ideas, is what brought the revolution to its tragic end.

Another theme on which Lewis and myself have differed over our long (and to me at least) productive agreement to disagree, has been the value of the Westminster model of government. I have always argued that it was well suited to the nature of West Indian societies. Lewis, as we have seen, was not always so inclined. For this reason, one notes with satisfaction his defence of that system of government in his book on Grenada.[41] No one contemplating the panorama of Caribbean dictatorial *caudillos*, generally, or indeed, specifically an Eric Gairy or the Leninist clique within the NJM, could help but ask, where did such aberrant behaviour originate? It is not my purpose here to put on balance domestic versus external influences on this dictatorial behaviour. Lewis himself raised the issue of the unbounded ambitions among certain NJM leaders. He did not cite Burke on that issue, but he certainly would have welcomed this Burkean admonition:

> Society cannot exist unless a controlling power upon will and appetite be placed somewhere, and the less there is within, the more there must be without. It is ordained in the eternal constitution of things, that men of intemperate minds cannot be free. Their passions forge their fetters.[42]

Lewis, in his more usual Fabian moments as in his book on Grenada, agreed that the best, time-tested, 'controlling power' is a democratic system.

Notes

1. *Caribbean Contact*, July 1984, 7–8.
2. Edmund Burke, *Letters on a Regicide Peace* (1776) cited in Gordon K. Lewis, *Grenada: The Jewel Despoiled* (Baltimore: Johns Hopkins University Press, 1987), 61.
3. *Caribbean Contact*, July 1984, 7.
4. Anthony P. Maingot, *The Passionate Advocate: Gordon K. Lewis and Caribbean Studies* (Coventry: Centre for Caribbean Studies, University of Warwick, 1991).
5. Gordon K. Lewis, *Notes on the Puerto Rican Revolution* (New York: Monthly Review Press, 1974), 269.
6. Ibid., 151.
7. Gordon K. Lewis, 'The Making of a Caribbeanist', (Working paper No.10, Caribbean Institute and Study Center for Latin America, San German, Puerto Rico, 1983), 1.
8. See Harold J. Laski, *The Communist Manifesto: An Introduction* (New York: New American Library, 1982), 63–82.
9. See the citations in Maingot, *The Passionate Advocate*, 10.
10. *The Sunday Gleaner* (Jamaica), March 2, 1958, 10.
11. See the Introduction in Ian Harris, ed., *Edmund Burke: Prerevolutionary Writings* (Cambridge: Cambridge University Press, 1993), xvi–xxxiii.
12. See quotes in Ruth A. Bevan, *Marx and Burke: A Revisionist View* (La Salle, Il: Open Court Publishing Company, 1973), 1–14.
13. See J. H. Plumb, *The Making of An Historian: The Collected Essays of J. H. Plumb* (Athens, GA: The University of Georgia Press, 1988), 28.
14. Cited in Bevan, *Marx and Burke*, 16.
15. Ibid.
16. Edmund Burke. 'Opening Speech at the Impeachment of Warren Hastings' (16 February, 1788), cited in Harris, ed., *Edmund Burke,* 277–97.
17. This is evident in the classical statement on the limits of human agency:
    > Therefore mankind always sets itself only such tasks as it can solve; since, looking at the matter more closely, it will always be found that the task itself arises only when the *material conditions* for its solution already exist or are at least in the process of formation. (**Emphasis added**).
18. Karl Marx, *Capital* (New York: Modern Library, 1906), 591, n. 2.
19. See T. B. Bottomore, ed., *Karl Marx: Early Writings* (New York: McGraw, 1963).

20. On this see Trevor Ling, *Karl Marx and Religion in Europe and India* (London: Macmillan, 1980), 54–58.
21. See 'Karl Marx, On the Jewish Question', in *The Marx-Engels Reader*, ed. Robert C. Tucker (New York: Norton, 1972), 24–51.
22. Note his description of the Jewish Ferdinand Lassalle, Germany's most important Social Democrat (and one who assisted Marx at many turns):

> It is now perfectly clear to me that, as testified also by his cranial formation and hair growth, he is descended from the negroes who joined Moses's exodus from Egypt (unless his paternal mother or grandmother was crossed with a nigger). Well, this combination of Jewish and German stock with the negroid basic substance is bound to yield a strange product. The fellow's importunity is also nigger-like.

(Marx to Engels, London, 30 July, 1862 in *Karl Marx-Friedrich Engels: Selected Letters*, ed. Fritz J. Raddatz (Boston: Little, Brown, 1980), 82.
23. Plumb, *The Making of An Historian*, 28.
24. On this case see the marvellous account by Barbara W. Tuchman, *The First Salute* (New York: Ballentine Books, 1988). Tuchman calls Burke 'the master of outrage' and suggests that he was the first to recommend that the solution to anti-Semitism was to give the Jews a state of their own.
25. Cited in Tuchman, *The First Salute*, 102.
26. Ibid., 103.
27. Letter, Engels to Marx, 23 May, 1856, in *Karl Marx-Friedrich Engels: Selected Letters*, 88.
28. Gordon K. Lewis, *Puerto Rico: Freedom and Power in the Caribbean* (New York: Monthly Review Press, 1963), 510.
29. On this see Kepa Artaraz, *Cuba and Western Intellectuals Since 1959* (New York: Macmillan Palgrave, 2009).
30. Note the similarity of tone with George Bernard Shaw's Preface to his edited book, *Fabian Essays in Socialism* (1889): 'The reader need not fear oppression here, any more than in the socialized State of the future, by the ascendancy of one particular cast of mind.'
31. Anthony Giddens, *Capitalism and Modern Social Theory* (Cambridge: Cambridge University Press, 1971), 185.
32. David McLellan, *Marxism After Marx* (London: The Macmillan Press, 1980), 312–30.
33. Gordon K. Lewis, review of José Luís González's work, *Sunday San Juan Star Magazine* (November 28, 1976): 7–8.
34. Max Weber quoted in Giddens, *Capitalism and Modern Social Theory*, 195.
35. Gordon K. Lewis, *Grenada: The Jewel Despoiled* (Baltimore: Johns Hopkins University Press, 1987), 31–32.
36. Anthony P. Maingot, 'Requiem for a Utopia', *The Miami Herald* October 30, 1983, 10, 60.
37. Lewis, *Grenada*, 32.
38. Friedrich Engels, 'Socialism: Utopian and Scientific', in *The Marx-Engels Reader*, 688.
39. Lewis, *Grenada*, 175.
40. 'One of the most debilitating aspects of the NJM's membership policy was its bar against small farmers joining, on the grounds that they were property owners and the NJM was a worker's party.' Cited in Steve Clark, 'The Second

Assassination of Maurice Bishop', *New International, A Magazine of Marxist Politics and Theory*, no. 6 (1987): 34.
41. Lewis, *Grenada*, 21.
42. Cited in Louis I. Brevold and Ralph G. Ross, eds., *The Philosophy of Edmund Burke* (Ann Arbor, MI: University of Michigan Press, 1961), 31.

2 | Gordon Lewis and the Writing of Afro-Caribbean Political Thought

Paget Henry

The primary focus of this chapter will be some of the significant omissions in Gordon Lewis's writing of Caribbean political thought. Consequently, of Lewis's many books it will be concerned more with *Main Currents in Caribbean Thought*[1] than any of the others. This is a work of great erudition that was meticulously researched and elegantly written. It is a genuine Caribbean classic and a text on which I have drawn extensively on several occasions. The aim of this important work is to trace, over the period from 1492–1900, the historical development of the political ideologies of the various cultural groups that constituted the foundations of the modern Caribbean. Although executed with great skill, I will show that Lewis's account of the beginnings of Caribbean thought in the sixteenth century overlooked the contributions of the African population. Very present are the contributions of the Spanish, French, English, Tainos and Caribs. Puzzlingly absent are the contributions of Africans. As Lewis was such an outspoken critic of the racist practices of Caribbean society and a strong supporter of many of the black leaders who had come to power in the region, this is indeed something of a paradox. I will argue that the key to this paradox was Lewis's rather restricted conception of the creole culture of the region and the identities that it gave to Afro-Caribbeans. However, before taking up this issue directly, we must put *Main Currents in Caribbean Thought* in the context of Lewis's intellectual development and, within the latter, his concept of creole culture.

Lewis, Caribbean Studies, and Creole Theory

Gordon K. Lewis was born in Wales in 1919. After studying at Oxford and Harvard and teaching in the United States for a short while, he arrived in Puerto Rico in 1951 to work on its new constitution. Enamoured with the region, Lewis would soon adopt it and make it his home. In 1955, he started teaching at the University of Puerto Rico at the age of 36. At the time, he was a young scholar of European political thought and history, the craft and scholarly legacy of which he would give to his adopted Caribbean with great passion and commitment. When I think of Lewis's scholarship, I think of textual productions that are truly regional in scope, skilfully researched, interdisciplinary, and of very high imaginative quality. His books are models of archival research that make use of sources old and new and move with admirable ease between history, philosophy, political science, and literature. Lewis's home in Puerto Rico was filled with newspapers from just about all of the territories of the region. He absorbed a lot from these papers in his effort to understand his new adopted home.

Lewis's first major contribution to the field of Caribbean Studies, *Puerto Rico: Freedom and Power in the Caribbean,*[2] was and still is a landmark text. It established very clearly his commitment to the nationalist movements that were sweeping the region and his abilities as a researcher, thinker and writer. The detailed nature of this 600-page book demonstrated the depth and thoroughness with which Lewis had undertaken what, in the opening dedication of the book, he called 'his apprenticeship in the understanding of Puerto Rican life and politics.' The book also introduced many of the basic positions and themes that would become permanent features of Lewis's thought. For example, it made clear his deep commitment to the future not only of Puerto Rico but also of the region as a whole. Further, it established the Fabian socialist framework of his thought, his strong opposition to Western imperialism as well as the internalization of many of its values by Puerto Rican elites. Both imperialism and its local internalization were the sources of devastating consequences for the development and integrity of Puerto Rican society. Finally, this first major work gave us Lewis's initial take on Caribbean creole culture and also the field of Caribbean Studies.

His initial take on this field was closely related to his views on the impact of Western imperialism. He saw much of the literature in the field as being from what he called 'the perspective of absentee scholarship, an evil in its own way as absentee economic and political control.'[3] This grip of absentee scholarship on the field of Caribbean Studies had to be broken. Lewis's discursive strategy for breaking this grip was the writing of texts from what he called 'the perspective of the creole culture.'[4] Thus in one of its first appearances, Lewis formulated his concept of creole theory in opposition to the category of absentee scholarship. In opposition to the latter, it was within this tradition of a Caribbean creole culture that Lewis located his major work on Puerto Rico. Further, he saw it as reinforcing the works of creole Caribbean scholars such as Eric Williams and Manuel Maldonado Denis.[5] In Lewis's view, these works were helping to redress the imbalances created by absentee scholarship.

Five years later, in 1968, Lewis published his second major contribution to Caribbean Studies, *The Growth of the Modern West Indies*.[6] This 500-page meticulously researched work did for the English-speaking Caribbean what his first book had done for Puerto Rico. It covers the period from about 1900 to 1966 – that is, the start of the era of formal political independence. This work also opens with further statements on the themes of imperialism, and Caribbean creole culture that were introduced in Lewis's first book. In *The Growth of the Modern West Indies*, this creole or syncretic culture is developed not in opposition to absentee scholarship but by the examples of Trinidadian carnival and calypso. The continuing importance of the theme of imperialism is taken up via a discussion of the growing Americanization of both carnival and calypso. As a result, Lewis suggested that the Caribbean region is still 'nothing much more than a geographical expression…to the legacy of its colonial history in all of its manifold forms.'[7] In spite of this new layer of Americanization encrusting the creole cultures of the English-speaking Caribbean, Lewis vigorously defended his theoretical reading of them as being fundamentally mixed or syncretic against M.G. Smith's reading of them as fundamentally unmixed, culturally plural systems. Lewis acknowledged the various ethnic groups and the hierarchical relations, both within and between them, to which Smith consistently pointed. However, in Lewis's view, the theory of cultural pluralism just did not account for the observable degrees of mixing and progressive creolization that carnival and calypso indicated. After this theoretical engagement with the concept of creole culture, Lewis then proceeded, as in the case of his study of Puerto Rico, to give an impressively detailed account of the development of national societies in the territories of the English-speaking Caribbean.

These two major works were followed by many others that included: *The Virgin Islands: A Caribbean Lilliput*; *Notes on the Puerto Rican Revolution*; *Main Currents in Caribbean Thought*; and *Grenada: The*

Jewel Despoiled.[8] At the time of his death in 1991, Lewis left behind an unpublished 700-page manuscript entitled, *The Modern Caribbean: A New Voyage of Discovery*, selections from which have been published in the 2010 volume, *Gordon K. Lewis on Race, Class and Ideology in the Caribbean*.[9] Together, these works constitute a very impressive oeuvre that makes it unmistakably clear why Lewis was and still is such an important figure in the field of Caribbean Studies.

But in spite of the very real success that these works brought him as a Caribbean scholar, Lewis retained a nagging sense of himself as an outsider. This sense of himself can be clearly seen in his 1983 essay, 'The Making of a Caribbeanist'. In this essay, he outlined very specifically what an outsider must do in order to become a 'serious Caribbeanist'. The individual must divest himself or herself of such ethnocentrist assumptions (as Eurocentrist prejudice) whether he, or she, is a European socialist or an American liberal, or even just a self-proclaimed 'value-free social scientist.'[10] Further, the outsider must seek to 'identify those values that, shaped by the historical evolution of the Caribbean peoples, can be seen as Caribbean values sui generis; and then, having identified them to attempt to give them some reasonable sympathy.'[11] However, achieving such a sympathetic identification with Caribbean values and aspirations is both a scholarly and an existential journey that the outsider can never really be sure that he or she has completed.

Both intellectually and existentially, Lewis achieved a high degree of sympathy with the basic values of the region and thus overcame the problems of the outsider to a very credible degree. Consequently, there can be no doubt about his status as a 'serious Caribbeanist'. His identification with the fortunes and future of the Caribbean was clear in his strong support for the nationalist aspiration of the region. It was around these nationalist projects and their discursive legitimation that Lewis saw a set of creole Caribbean values. These values sprang from the resistance of Caribbean people to their long history of enslavement and colonization by Europe, and also from the fact that this resistance was expressed and systematically elaborated in the mixed or creole languages and cultural discourses that resulted from the meeting of the different cultures of Africa, Europe and India in the Caribbean region. Thus the 'Caribbean values sui generis' with which Lewis, the

Caribbeanist, identified were very closely connected to his conception of Caribbean creole culture.

Lewis on Caribbean Creole Culture

From the foregoing overview of Lewis's intellectual development and contributions to the field of Caribbean Studies, we can see that his concept of Caribbean creole culture developed over time and that he formulated it in a number of different ways. In all of its varying forms of presentation, it consistently referred to the hybrid or mixed nature of Caribbean culture and also to the equally hybrid or mixed nature of the identities that it gave to its members. Further, in *Main Currents in Caribbean Thought,* Lewis asserts that 'the very essence of popular culture, everywhere, is its intrinsic plasticity, its capacity to incorporate new experiences into its basic values and attitudes.'[12] As we saw earlier, in his first book, Lewis formulated his theory of Caribbean creole culture in opposition to 'the perspective of absentee scholarship.' In his second formulation, it was developed in relation to the art forms of carnival and the calypso. These were for Lewis among the major indicators of the new and original culture of the region rather than the more unmixed inheritances from Europe such as the established churches.

In *Main Currents in Caribbean Thought,* we get yet another formulation of his theory of Caribbean creole culture. Here it is developed more systematically as the hybrid product of the history of European colonialism. According to Lewis, the evolution of Caribbean society has been marked by the emergence of three crucial formations: the growth of colonialism; the instituting of slavery; and the rise and growth of 'a distinctive Creole culture and Creole institutions based on the twin factors of race and class.'[13] These three factors created the 'general mixture of popular religions, rich and inventive languages, island political forms, oral folklore, folkways,' all of which helped to constitute the 'famous *magie antillaise.*'[14] In short, it was colonialism and the resistance to it that produced the moral and cultural earthquakes out of which were forged the new values and hybrid forms that are the key marks of modern Caribbean culture. This third formulation of the concept of Caribbean creole culture also takes in the relations of this culture to practices such as carnival and calypso singing, as Lewis did in *The Growth of the Modern West Indies*. What is new in this analysis of the relations to carnival and calypso is the direct link that Lewis then establishes between creole culture and the legitimating of the new nationalist politics of the period. On this link, Lewis wrote:

> If...any awareness of a Caribbean nationhood has developed in the region – that is to say, a felt differentiation of national identity – it has been, certainly, the end result of Creole values, norms, and modes of self-consciousness carried and defended by those groups, mostly of worker and peasant, that have the most easily identified themselves with their particular island society.[15]

Finally, in this third formulation of his theory of Caribbean creole culture, Lewis links this syncretic tradition to the systems of political and ideological thought that he would outline and examine in the remainder of this book. After introducing this cultural tradition and a number of European figures such as Las Casas and Labat, Lewis writes: 'all this, then, constitutes the historical background to the growth of Caribbean thought.'[16] This turn specifically to thought is very important for Lewis, as he is aware that for the absentee perspective the Caribbean is a region without a tradition of important ideas. Thus one of the primary purposes of *Main Currents in Caribbean Thought* is to put that view to rest. Thus for Lewis,

> It is urgent to insist upon the systems of thought, even more than the collective life-experience out of which they were born. For it has been the general attitude of writers on the region – metropolitan and, in some cases, local – that there is no history of ideas in the region worth speaking about.[17]

The primary example of this attitude that Lewis discusses is Phillip Curtin's text, *Two Jamaica's: The Role of Ideas in a Tropical Colony, 1830–1965*.[18] As a result of the legacy produced by works such as this one, Lewis pointed to an 'anti-Caribbean animus' that had conspired to conceal the deep and rich movements of ideas that have indeed been integral parts of the life of Caribbean society. This movement of ideas, Lewis insists, cannot be separated from the creole culture that has come to define the region.

This in brief was the developmental trajectory of Lewis's theorizing of the concept of creole culture. As we can see, it grew in scope and complexity over time. This third formulation was the one that informed the writing of *Main Currents in Caribbean Thought*. However, in spite of the greater scope and complexity of this third formulation there are some significant areas of underdevelopment. Good examples of such areas are the uneven discursive spaces that the theory gives or allocates to the different cultural groups before and after they have experienced the processes of creolization. Thus the space given to Afro-Caribbeans within the categoric framework of the theory is one that adequately represents them after their creolization, particularly after they had become openly nationalist. However, as formulated in this third attempt, the theory cannot raise and answer questions such as: What were Afro-Caribbeans like before creolization? What were their thoughts, values, political ideologies before crossing the Atlantic and subsequently arriving in the Caribbean? Were these ideas and values important contributors to the beginnings of Caribbean thought? There is too little conceptual space within the categories of the theory for articulating and analysing such issues. In contrast, the conceptual space available for raising and answering these questions in regard to Europeans is large and used very extensively. In the case of Amerindians, there is a definite space, but not as large as the one for Europeans, that permits the asking and answering of these pre-creolization questions. However, in contrast to the case of Afro-Caribbeans and Euro-Caribbeans, the conceptual space for analysing their post-creolization experiences is practically non-existent. These are noticeable imbalances in the categoric structure of Lewis's theory of Caribbean creole culture that would definitely affect the writing of *Main Currents in Caribbean Thought*. Looked at as a group, these imbalances suggest that Lewis had come up against definite limits that arose from his apprenticeship, his archival methodologies, time for data collection, and the overwhelming complexity of cultural life in the Caribbean.

Lewis was probably drawn to creole theory as it reflected and illuminated the inner journey that he had travelled on his way to becoming a 'serious Caribbeanist.' As we saw, this process of apprenticeship involved the isolating of a core set of Caribbean values and making a sympathetic identification with them. However, as one cannot completely divest ones heritage of 32 years, this process of adopting the Caribbean as home and becoming a Caribbeanist must have been for Lewis one of mixing and merging the ideas and values of his Welsh heritage with those that he had acquired during his time in the Caribbean. As such, this inner transformation that Lewis went through could very easily be described as a process of creolization. It was probably through this lens of cultural mixing that Lewis saw the experiences of other cultural groups making up the Caribbean milieu.

This was certainly the lens through which Lewis saw Afro-Caribbeans. They were an already creolized group, and hence had already left behind their African past. Thus even though he makes many references to the Afro-Christian religions of the region, he never really showed any abiding interest in their specifically African inheritances. They were for him already post-African creolized religions. Thus he did not share Melville Herskovits's profound interest in the African heritage of Afro-Caribbean culture and the extent to which it survived in the daily lives of Afro-Caribbean people.[19] On the contrary, Lewis was very critical of Herskovits's theory of African survivals. With regard to these survivals, Lewis wrote in *The Growth of the Modern West Indies*:

> It would perhaps be more valid to say that they reflect, in their mere capacity to survive, the presence of continuing forms of economic and social slavery from which the West Indian common man must find relief and escape. They are a function, that is, of presently felt socio-economic deprivations rather than proof of ethno-historical continuity. The fact is that, all in all, the West Indian person has been deprived of a meaningful kinship with his origins and has sought relief in sheer movement – dance, cricket, carnival, activist religion, migration itself. The outlets, in their turn, have taken on qualities of intimacy and spontaneity arising inevitably from the social traffic of small populations living an open street life in the sun-drenched luminosity of the Caribbean atmosphere.[20]

This is one of Lewis's most revealing statements on Afro-Caribbean culture. Here the mode of existence of African culture in the creole phase can only be indirect, that is, in the form of compensation for repressive socio-economic conditions rather than as authentic cultural presences with genuine existential roots in the Afro-Caribbean subject. This strong resistance to the notion of genuine African survivals was not only consistent with Lewis's ideas on creolization but also helped to keep him focused on the more recent nationalist phase of Afro-Caribbean culture. Further, this resistance to the idea of

African survivals helped to define the limited conceptual space that Lewis assigned to Afro-Caribbeans in his theory of the region's creole culture. As we noted earlier, the theory cannot readily expand this limited conceptual space to include the pre-creole or African phase of Afro-Caribbean culture. This is its major disadvantage in relation to Herskovits's theory as this African phase had to be there, just as it was in the case of Euro-Caribbeans, and also in the case of Lewis himself.

Main Currents and the Writing of Caribbean Political Thought

In chapter two of *Main Currents*, Lewis outlines the sixteenth and seventeenth century beginnings of Caribbean political thought. This outline of its origins would frame the more detailed discussions of the region's proslavery, antislavery, and nationalist ideologies that would be taken up in the three subsequent chapters. In the prefatory chapter, Lewis makes brief introductions of the major figures who would play crucial roles in establishing the Caribbean tradition of political thought. The first of these introductions acquaints us with Renaissance period in Europe and the subsequent age of discovery. Marking this period were the scientific revolution, the Cartesian rationalism upon which it was based, the rise of capitalism and its imperial spirit. In short, we are introduced to the European and his/her rapidly changing home ground. Next, Lewis introduces us to the Euro-Caribbeans, who are presented as the Caribbean counterparts of Euro-Americans, Euro-Brazilians, and others in the Americas. Third on Lewis's introductory list are the Amerindians – the Tainos and the Caribs in particular – as well as the mythical and pristine world in which they lived. Following these three sets, Lewis turned to introducing the contributions of specific European countries – England, France and Spain in particular – as well as some key figures such as Bartolome de Las Casas, Francisco de Vitoria, Juan Gines de Sepulveda, Richard Hakluyt, and Jean-Baptiste Labat. Consequently, when he makes the final introduction – the incipient intellectual class of the region – these are some of the names that figure prominently.

Clearly missing from this introductory list of the dramatis personae of Caribbean political thought, are the voices of the Africans, who will make the great contributions to the region's creole culture, as well as the political world that they were bringing with them. What was happening in Africa while Europe was going through its Renaissance period? What were African sages thinking and speaking? What were African political leaders doing? What kind of states were they making and legitimating? Questions like these and their initial answers are absent from Lewis's introductory exercise. Consequently, Africans are not really present in this introduction to the origins of Caribbean political thought. This puzzling erasure is, I will suggest, connected to the restricted conceptual space that Lewis assigned Afro-Caribbean culture in his creole theory. As noted before, this was a space without a reverse gear. Consequently, it did not permit Lewis to return to the receding African horizons of Caribbean creole culture in the same way that the presence of such a gear allowed him to return to and engage the receding European past. Thus, it is with this particular restriction on the Afro-Caribbean heritage that Lewis will then proceed to analyse in great detail the proslavery, antislavery, and nationalist texts that have defined the Caribbean tradition of political thought.

As these subsequent chapters make clear, Lewis saw the roots of Caribbean political thought in the imperial and discursive exchanges that the planters and their supporters had first with the Amerindians, then the Africans, and finally the Indians from India. Out of these exchanges emerged a series of opposing ideologies that would constitute the foundations of Caribbean political thought. The key issues that would establish these foundations are the opposing responses of various members of these groups to the European projects of colonization and slavery. For Lewis, 'the essence of ideology is perceived self-image, how any societal group sees its function within the general matrix of the social structure, how it sees other groups, and what particular arguments it produces as a means of self-justification.'[21] Given this view, he argued further that 'every ruling class was mainly concerned with power and the uses of power and has only attempted some sort of philosophical rationalization of its position when challenged by hostile forces.'[22]

The planters of the Caribbean region were no exception to this ideological pattern of ruling classes. Consequently, Lewis argued that 'the heart of the Caribbean planter ideology is, it goes without saying, the search for a rationalizing justification of Negro slavery.'[23] He documents the development of this ideology through the works of a number of the settler historians such as William Young in St Vincent,

Thomas Atwood in Dominica, J. Poyer in Barbados, and culminating in the works of Bryan Edwards and Edward Long of Jamaica.

From the perspective of Caribbean political thought, these writings all shared in the project of imagining, instituting and legitimating a colonial plantocratic state. This was a white supremacist construction of the state that would give Caribbean planters the democratic rights of Europeans at home and in other colonies while at the same time protecting and legitimating the practices of Amerindian and African slavery. In other words, the structures of governance that the planters wanted, required a political ideology that would somehow make into a coherent whole, the contradictory demands for white supremacy and planter freedom, and Amerindian and African slavery along with their racial inferiority – hence their availability for planter economic exploitation. In short, a slave-based ideology of racist liberalism that would legitimate the colonial plantocratic state that was in the making.

In opposition to this planter proslavery ideology, Lewis sets an antislavery ideology that he argues is based primarily among the enslaved Afro-Caribbean masses. However, in addition to the contributions of the slaves, Lewis also examines those of Europeans and Euro-Caribbeans who held antislavery views such as James Ramsay, Thomas Clarkson and Victor Schoelcher. As the planter was the indispensable starting point for the description of the proslavery ideology, the slave is Lewis's starting point for his description of the antislavery counter-ideology. However, articulating this counter-ideology will be much more difficult as it 'was denied any real literary expression.'[24] Because of this lack of literary expression, Lewis returns once again to the creole culture of Afro-Caribbeans in his attempts to articulate their ideological responses to the proslavery ideologies of the planters. This examination of Afro-Caribbean creole culture makes up the core of chapter four and is Lewis's most insightful analysis and passionate defence of this cultural tradition against its many detractors.

In his analysis and defence, Lewis surprisingly places his focus on religion rather than on the structures of governance that Afro-Caribbeans were imagining, attempting to institute and legitimate. This in my view would be the more appropriate institutional site for uncovering Afro-Caribbean political thought and its antislavery ideologies. Rather, the political ideology that Lewis would extract from this re-examination of Caribbean creole culture would be 'the ideology of slave religion.'[25] The political elements that Lewis would extract from his analysis of Afro-Caribbean religions are the modes of resistance to slavery that were embedded in or legitimated by Afro-Caribbean religions such as Vodou, Santeria and Myalism. This focus on resistance and religion brings with it an increase in the visibility and importance of continental Africa to the region's creole culture. However, this increased visibility does not make it possible for Lewis's focus on resistance to connect with African traditions of state-making, patterns of legitimating the exercise of power, concepts of citizenship, tradition of warfare and other political practices that would be relevant to the political responses of Afro-Caribbeans. As a result, beyond practices of resistance we really do not get from Lewis a clear articulation of the counter-ideology of Afro-Caribbeans that would be the equivalent of the proslavery racist liberalism of the planters. In short, although we learn a lot about the Afro-Caribbean religious imaginary from Lewis's analysis, we really do not get from it much insight into the political imaginary of Africans and Afro-Caribbeans.

Thus, in spite of the brilliance of Lewis's religious analysis, it fails to provide this crucial chapter with what it really needs: a vision of the post-slavery state and its antislavery African or black nationalist legitimating discourses that would be the politico-ideological equivalent of the colonial plantocratic state and its proslavery legitimating discourses. If, as Lewis suggests, ideology is about power and self-image in relation to others, then limiting his account to the resistance of Afro-Caribbeans clearly cannot give us an adequate picture of their ideological stance. The categories of resistance must be extended to include past conceptions of the state that have been established and the ones that are likely to come as a result of practices of resistance.

Even when Lewis takes up towards the end of the chapter, rather than at the beginning, the ideology of the slave rebellions, he is unable to pull off its rescue. He is unable to rescue this chapter because of his strong religious focus and the restricted vision of political Africa. As a result, he is unable to see a definite line of political thought, state-making and practices of governance running from the small African chieftaincies through the political kingdoms such as Dahomey, Songhay, classical Ghana, and Mali to the political activities of African slaves in the region. This was the line of continuity that Lewis did not establish although it was absolutely necessary for the success of this chapter.

In the next section of this chapter, rather than continue in this critical mode, I think that my goal would be better served by shifting to an expository mode in which I will briefly outline the contours of African/Afro-Caribbean political thought and state-making in which the antislavery ideology of Afro-Caribbeans needs to be located.

The Missing Foundations of Afro-Caribbean Political Thought

The crucial suggestion emerging out of the preceding sections is that it is the political discourses, the processes of state formation, the political writers and actors – in short, the political dimension of Caribbean creole culture – which Lewis really needs in his chapter on proslavery ideologies. As in the case of religion or music, a creole conception of Afro-Caribbean politics must bring together African and European political traditions of thought to produce new political formations that would be the equivalents of Shango or Santeria in religion or calypso, meringue, zouk, or reggae in music. However, in order see these political equivalents it will be necessary for us to make use of an Afro-Caribbean reverse gear so that we can properly introduce the African political heritage that was forced to mix with the European one and produce the hybrid political structures of the region.

The Africans who came to the Caribbean on the slave ships were not members of stateless societies and thus without inhabited political worlds and practical traditions of governance. On the contrary, these Africans came from societies with long traditions of state-making in which political power was organized on the models of chiefdoms and monarchical kingdoms. Thus Africans arrived in the Caribbean with political visions, values and discourses that legitimated these long and diverse lines of states. It was indeed the political traditions, ideas and practices inherited from these exercises in state-making that constituted the African base for the political dimensions of Afro-Caribbean creole culture. Thus it becomes vital that we examine these different state formations, their histories, and the distinct political ideas associated with them. Without these political institutions and their histories, we have no basis for an Afro-Caribbean creole tradition in politics and political thought.

The African Chiefdoms and Kingdoms

What were African chiefdoms and kingdoms like? What kinds of political orders did they establish? What specific set of rights and responsibilities did they confer upon their members? I will begin with the chiefdoms, for expository purposes, in spite of the fact that the literature most available to Lewis tended to focus on the kingdoms. Chiefdoms were among the earliest and most basic creations of the African political imaginary. They date back to at least 10,000 years ago with the settled agriculture of the Neolithic era. These chiefdoms contained all of the key elements of the political orders that would later be compounded to produce the kingdoms. As such, they constituted the elementary forms of African political life and are therefore important links to political identities in pre-colonial Africa.

As an institution, the African chiefdom consisted of seven basic parts. First was the chief, the highest authority figure and executive centre of this political system. In addition to his executive functions, the chief also had important spiritual and ritual functions to perform. Second, there was the queen mother, who symbolized the birth of the state. Third, there were the royal families from which the chief was selected. Fourth, there was the military arm of the state. Fifth, there was the judicial arm which consisted of courts or institutions of conflict resolution. Sixth, there was a council of elders with which the chief was expected to carry out his governing functions. Seventh and finally there were the members of this political community.

Although primarily consultative and advisory in nature, the council of elders had a number of other important functions to perform. First, it was responsible for the selecting and en-stooling of a new chief from the designated royal families. Second, it had the function of representing the voices and interests of the people. The council was supposed to let the chief know the thoughts, desires and responses of the governed to his rule. Third, in extreme cases of misrule the council had the power to unseat or de-stool a chief.

From this brief description, it should be clear that there are several organizing principles competing and working simultaneously to produce and maintain these chiefdoms as ongoing political institutions. Thus spiritual, autocratic, gerontocratic, and proto-democratic principles can all be observed as operative in these African chiefdoms.

Consequently, in the literature on these states, different scholars tend to emphasize one of these principles over the others to produce characterizations of African chiefdoms as proto-democratic, autocratic, or gerontocratic.

Elsewhere, I've characterized West African chiefdoms as 'spiritocratic' in contrast to theocratic, and over the gerontocratic, autocratic, and proto-democratic characterizations.[26] In my view, the spiritocratic reading captures best the original and unique conceptions and organization of power in these pre-colonial African political systems. In these chiefdoms, power is first and foremost the spiritual power of the deities and ancestors and only secondarily, the rule of the chief and the council. In a spiritocratic chiefdom, it is not the power of the people, the elderly, the council or the chief that is supreme, but that of the gods, goddesses, and ancestors. Consequently, the central challenge of such a state is the institutionalizing of the power and rule of the deities as living forces of everyday life in spite of having to do it through the agency of ordinary men and women.

I now turn briefly to the monarchical kingdoms such as Ancient Egypt (3100 BCE – 332 CE), Kush (1100 BCE–670 BCE), Meroe (670 BCE–300 CE), Aksum (300 CE–800 CE), Ethiopia (850 CE–present) in the east; and the kingdoms of ancient Ghana (500 CE–1200), Mali (1235–1450), Songhay (1468–1591), Borno-Kanem (900–1750), the Hausa city states (1100–1790); the kingdoms of Ife (1100–present), Benin (1100–), Oyo (1300–1790), and Asante (1670–) all in the West.[27] In these kingdoms, as well as those in the north and south, we can observe indigenous processes of larger scale and more complex forms of political organization that can be described as monarchical. This reorganization of power along monarchical lines was driven largely by conquest, and by the imposing of a surplus-extracting or tribute-paying mode of production in the place of simpler family-based communal modes. In other words, chiefdoms were transformed into kingdoms by military conquests, the taxing of the conquered, and the capturing of lucrative trade routes that were also taxed, or the trade itself taken over. With the surpluses generated in this manner, political elites would expand their armies and increase the size of their kingdoms. The chiefs of conquered territories would either be replaced or made to swear oaths of loyalty to the rising king, pay him tribute, and make their armies available to the king when they were not defending the chief's territory.

This pattern of political reorganization, of monarchical state-making can be seen in the cases of all the kingdoms listed above. From this list it should be clear that this movement from chiefdoms to kingdoms had been taking place over millennia. In the case of Egypt, monarchical transformation began as early as 3100 BCE and lasted until 332 CE, making it the longest lasting of the monarchical civilizations. In contrast to those of the east, we have the Dahomean and Asante kingdoms beginning their rise in the mid-1600s, and building their trading foundations on the new Atlantic slave trade organized by Europe, as opposed to the gold, salt, ivory, cereals and Arabic slave trades that had supported the earlier West African kingdoms. Between these extremes of Egypt and Dahomey or Asante, we have the monarchical formations of classical Ghana of the Soninke (not to be confused with today's Ghana, which includes the Asante), Ethiopia and the Hausa city states. In short, this movement between chiefdoms and kingdoms via the political economy of a tribute paying mode of production had been the basic pattern of state formation in Africa right up to and after the start of the Atlantic slave trade. This pattern of political formation was interrupted and suspended by the imposition of European colonial states on these African chiefdoms and kingdoms as these imperial powers incorporated African economies and trade routes into their expanding world economy. This world economy radically transformed global patterns of trading and also the nature of the state formation required for its protection.

The above pattern of larger kingdoms emerging out of smaller chiefdoms can be clearly seen in the case of the Asante kingdom. The history of the political formations and deformations that eventually resulted in the rise of the Asante kingdom date back to 800 CE, when the smaller Aguan and Dja kingdoms combined. This merger lasted 200 years until it was destroyed by the Azawad kingdom. Out of the defeated Aguan/Dja kingdom came several others. One of these was the Kumba kingdom of over 20 confederated chiefdoms, which lasted approximately 400 years until it was defeated by the mighty kingdom of Songhay. Another important kingdom that emerged from the collapse of the Aguan/Dja kingdom was the Bona kingdom. It lasted for about 400 years until it was conquered in 1595 by the kingdom of Quattara/Diula. After this defeat, three Bona princesses left the kingdom to found new ones. Osei Tutu, the founder of the Asante kingdom in 1695 is reputed to be the great-great-grandson of one of these princesses. In the 1620s, the most powerful kingdom in the region was the Denkyira. It was after defeating the Denkyira that Osei Tutu was able to establish the hegemony of the Asante kingdom, and the dynasty of the Asantehenes that survives into the present.[28]

In spite of the strong militaristic features of the African kingdoms, they retained many of the spiritual practices that were rooted in the chiefdoms. For example, in the case of the Asante the identity of the state reflected very much their spiritual conception of the human being. Among this group, the human being was seen as consisting of three basic parts: the honan or body, the sunsum or ego, and the Okra or soul. For the Asante, it was the Okra or the spiritual part of the person that was most important. The Okra was the carrier of one's destiny and the centre that connected the individual to the gods and the ancestors. It was from this spiritual conception of the individual that the Asante kingdom acquired its spiritocratic principles and mode of organization.

Thus in addition to being the military leader of the Asante, the king or Omanhene was also the earthly representative of the sun god, Nyankopon, and was believed to receive special energies from this deity that it was his responsibility to pass on to his nation. Thus the Omanhene's stool had to be a golden one. Similarly, the queen mother or Ohemmaa was the earthly representative of the moon goddess and her stool had to be silver. In short, both Omanhene and Ohemmaa had to be media or channels through which the deities could exercise their rule over the nation.

Even more revealing of the correlation between the spiritual identity of the state and that of the individual was the fact that among the Asante the golden stool of the Omanhene was considered to be the Okra or the spiritual foundation of the nation, and thus the carrier of its destiny. It was the Okra of the Omanhene that received the special energies from the sun god. Consequently, a very important ritual that the Omanhene had to perform was the regular washing of his Okra to assure the public of his spiritual purity and thus his ability to receive the special energies from Nyankopon. In short, although a highly militarized monarchical kingdom, the Asante state still displayed many of the spiritocratic principles that it inherited from its origins in the smaller chiefdoms.

Finally in this overview of pre-colonial African political formations, we need to mention those solidarity oriented formations that don't fit neatly into either of the categories of chiefdoms or kingdoms. These formations have sometimes been mistakenly labelled acephalous. Some of the Igbo political systems illustrate this type of political organization that is based on kinship models of solidarity. In these systems, the chief rules with heads of kinship or lineage groups. Lineage groups are institutions that metaphorically extend the bonds of solidarity and sameness found in immediate families to larger groups in the society. The production of these ever widening circles of brotherhood and sisterhood is the primary goal of these institutions. When they become the basis of a political community, as in the case of some Igbo groups, then solidarity, inclusiveness, decision by consensus, recognizing the voices of the ancestors who are heads of these groups and the voices of the deities become the primary values and codes orienting political life. In institutional terms, they result in decentralized forms of government, conflict avoidance and great emphasis on cooperation and strengthening bonds of solidarity. Consequently, in the words of A.E Afigbo, we get political communities that see themselves as unions 'of living blood relatives, the dead relatives, and the gods of the community – a sort of spiritual commonwealth.'[29]

African Chiefdoms and Kingdoms in the Caribbean

In my view, it was political imaginaries capable of such achievements and practices in state-making and governance that the Africans arriving on the slave ships brought with them to the Caribbean. In other words, left to themselves, these would have been the kinds of political orders they would have imagined and attempted to re-create. However, as we know very well, they were not left alone but subjected to the imperatives of the colonial plantocratic states of the region and their white supremacist justifications for the practices of Amerindian and African slavery. In contrast to the system of indirect colonial rule that Europeans imposed on the chiefdoms and kingdoms of continental Africa, the Caribbean was incorporated into the European world economy through systems of direct colonial rule. In this system of colonial rule, Amerindian and African chiefs were not incorporated into the lower rungs of the colonial state, but were completely removed from all systems and processes of governance. If, as Rex Nettleford has suggested, patterns of creolization are determined by a not so hidden battle for institutional space,[30] then the unique conditions of political creolization in the region become immediately obvious, especially when compared to the conditions of religious or musical creolization. These conditions were clearly ones that were marked by an extremely high degree of exclusion of African political formations, with all available institutional space and legitimate authority going to the European political formations. Only in the case of philosophy have we found another area of African self-expression that experienced correspondingly high levels of institutional and discursive exclusion. Under these hierarchical and difficult conditions of mixing, we would expect the production of hybrid formations that don't mix very well and therefore do not constitute viable or genuine creole political structures.

Given these extremely hostile conditions for political creolization, there were only two factors supporting the survival of African political traditions. First was the embedding of these traditions in the memories and linguistic categories of Africans – particularly the griots, whose job it was to memorize the dynasties and the orikis or praise songs of the chiefs and kings. The second was the already noted practice of slave owners relying on new supplies of labour from Africa rather than new births among the already enslaved. It was primarily on account of these two factors that we are able to talk about African chiefdoms and kingdoms in the Caribbean and their subsequent mixing and hybridizing with European political structures and discourses.

The building of African chiefdoms and kingdoms in the Caribbean and the Americas occurred first in those early instances of marronage in which the African regained significant measures of sovereignty from the European world economy and its colonial practices. Among these cases were the seventeenth century maroon societies of the Caribbean and Brazil (the quilombos). Among the better known of these maroon societies were those in the Sierra Maestra forests of eastern Cuba, the Cockpit region of Western Jamaica, the Massifs region of Haiti, the Cordilleras region of the Dominican Republic, and the Saramaka region of Surinam.[31] But by far the most famous of these African maroon communities was Palmares in Brazil.

The political orders of these maroon societies were established on the organizing codes and principles of African chiefdoms and kingdoms. In the view of Richard Price, early maroon societies were organized as centralized states, loose and shifting federations, or as isolated bands.[32] He also notes that 'before 1700, the great majority of maroon leaders on whom we have data were African born.'[33] After the eighteenth century, he continues, 'a striking number of leaders during this period were Creoles,' who called themselves 'captains, governors, or colonels rather than kings.'[34] Consequently, this first phase in the politico-ideological history of Afro-Caribbeans could very accurately be designated as one of African nationalism. As such, it represented a clear alternative to the colonial state and other formations arising out of the European political tradition.

In the figures of Cudjoe in Jamaica and Boni in Surinam, we can see reconstructions of middle sized African chiefdoms. Among the Saramakans, Price's accounts of the military, diplomatic and political statesmanship of the Chiefs – Ayako, Abini, and Etja – are excellent studies in African political leadership in the Caribbean.[35] Further, his account of the gaamaship or, 'chief-over-all of Saramaka,' of the well-known Alab, further illustrates these early reconstructions of African chiefdoms and kingdoms in the Caribbean. In the case of Palmares in Brazil, which was led by its famous king Ganga-Zumba, R.K. Kent referred to it as 'an African state in Brazil.'[36] He also noted that the 'significance of Palmares to African history is that an African political system could be transferred to a different continent...and that it could endure for almost a full century against two European powers, Holland and Portugal.'[37] In short, however we characterize them, the structures, practices and ideas of governance in these early maroon societies should have been the first phase in Lewis's account of the politico-ideological formation of the Afro-Caribbean.

Also very much a part of this African nationalist response were the slave uprisings, such as the 1736 aborted insurrection in Antigua, in which the goal was to take complete control and replace the colonial state with an African kingdom. From the court documents on the planned uprising in Antigua, historian David Barry Gaspar has shown that a king was crowned in the Akan tradition, an alternative government was formed, an army of hundreds recruited, and a comprehensive strategy for taking complete control of the island was outlined.[38] What was especially ingenious about this planned uprising was the manner in which King Court was crowned (en-stooled). He was en-stooled during the day on Market St. in the heart of St Johns and in full view of the public. However, it was done in the form of a classic Akan Ikem play, which many whites stopped to observe on their way into or out of town. To the Afro-Antiguans, it was not just a play but also a real en-stooling. Court was en-stooled with his Queen mother and afterwards became the undisputed leader among the Afro-Antiguans. Unfortunately, the governor's ball, which was the already extensively dynamited site for the start of the uprising, was postponed for 19 days and the conspiracy was uncovered. Had this planned uprising succeeded, Gaspar suggests that it would have 'catapulted Antigua onto the stage of world history as the first territory in the slave heartland of the Caribbean in which slaves seized full control.'[39]

The Repatriational Political Order

At the same time that political leaders like Cudjoe, Nanny, Papa Legba, Boni and King Court were forming maroon communities, attempting complete takeovers, and creating African nationalist political orders, the hundreds of thousands who were still enslaved were faithfully crafting political orders that were quite different from the nationalist ones. One of the first of these alternatives to the nationalist orders was one that the Jamaican political scientist, Clinton Hutton, has called 'the repatriational' political order.[40] Gone from the core of this political order were the active pursuits of African chiefdoms and kingdoms, their orikis and legitimating discourses. These political practices were replaced by a re-imagining of the concept of freedom that Hutton has termed repatriational freedom. This was a concept of freedom that was fashioned by enslaved Africans out of their memories of Africa and their dreams of returning home. As the harsh reality of the permanence of slavery in the Caribbean sank in, these dreams and memories of the African homeland ironically sought the aid of death in order to keep themselves alive. Modifying the spiritual meaning of death in African religious thinking, it now became the doorway not just to ancestorhood, but also to the desired return to Africa. Indeed as Hutton notes, the belief that death meant freedom from slavery was widely held and celebrated as such in funeral rites across the African diaspora.[41] Hutton continues:

The deceased, aided by various rituals of transition and repatriation, which the community of the living was expected to perform at the dead yard, the burial ground and perhaps at other designated sacred spots, was transported back into the ancestral homeland into a state of happiness, freedom, sovereignty and belonging among the ancestors.[42]

In short, this was a political vision in which death became the door to freedom and to returning to Africa.

The Political Impact of Lodges and Friendly Societies

Making a significant contribution the creolization of politics in the Caribbean was the rise of European styled lodges and friendly societies in the early decades of the eighteenth century. In particular, the rise of these institutions, such as the Freemasons, introduced a number of European democratic practices into the political culture of many Afro-Caribbeans. The African American scholar, Corey Walker, has shown that Freemason lodges were established in the region as early as 1738 in Jamaica and 1739 in Antigua.[43] Further, he linked the appeal of these lodges to their striking similarities to African secret societies in terms of their rituals, organizations, and social goals. Thus in the transition from African secret societies to Afro-Caribbean lodges, Walker sees a creole move that parallels the transition from Twi or Yoruba to Afro-Caribbean languages. In these lodges, traditions of African monarchism were forced to mix with those of European democracy, giving rise to some of the earliest expressions of creole political culture. In these organizations, there were written constitutions, elections, rules of communicative order and other democratic practices that had to conform to those of the lodges in England of which they were branches. Out of this mixing came the political culture of these lodges, their traditions of public speaking, public service, and conceptions of strong leaders. In many of the territories of the region, several of these lodge leaders were important precursors to later generations of political party leaders.

The First Political Theorists

In addition to forming maroon communities, planning political takeovers, imagining new orders of freedom, and organizing lodges,

Africans in the Caribbean were also running away to write antislavery texts. Many of these writers would become founders of the Africana tradition of political thought. Particularly important for the Caribbean were the figures of Ottobah Cugoano (1757–?) and Francis Williams (poet) of Jamaica (1702–?). They were a part of a larger group of eighteenth century African Christians who had been able to escape enslavement in various parts of the world colonized by Europe, and to write their life stories or their verses. Thus in addition to Cugoano, we had Anton Amo (1703–59), Lemuel Haynes (1753–1833), Olaudah Equiano (1745–97), Ignatius Sancho (1729–80), John Marrant (1755–91), James Gronniosaw (1705–?), Prince Hall 173?–1807), and many others. These writers were important sources of inspiration for each other. Thus Cugoano acknowledges John Marrant and Albert Gronniosaw as his predecessors, and Lemuel Haynes, the founder of the African American tradition of political thought, makes reference to the work of Cugoano.

Born in Ghana around 1757, Cugoano was kidnapped, sold into slavery, and shipped to Grenada at the tender age of about 13. For nine months he lived the horrors of plantation slavery in the region. In 1772 he was taken to England by his master, Alexander Campbell, where he was able to escape and gain his freedom as a result of the Somerset case that a few months before his arrival had effectively ended slavery in Britain. While working in the household of the well-known artists Richard and Maria Cosway, Cugoano filled his spare time with reading and writing. In 1787, he published his classic, *Thoughts and Sentiments on the Evil of Slavery*.[44]

In this work, Cugoano speaks to us through three distinct voices. First, that of an Afro-Christian prophet, a black Jeremiah, who condemns and warns the West of the moral debts that it was accruing on account of its practice of slavery. Second, Cugoano speaks to us as an African who had been racialized and negrified in the Caribbean. Third, as Anthony Bogues has pointed out, Cugoano also speaks to us as a natural rights political theorist.[45]

In his African voice, Cugoano takes on, among others, British philosopher, David Hume and Nevisian planter, James Tobin, two proslavery or anti-black writers mentioned by Gordon Lewis. In response to Hume's claim that Africans think it no crime to sell one another, Cugoano responds: 'This specious pretense is without any shadow of justice or of truth, and, if the argument was even true, it could afford no just and warrantable matter for any society of men to hold slaves.'[46] He then goes on to describe social and political life in West Africa (Guinea) as he recalls it:

> Those people annually brought away from Guinea, are born as free, and are brought up with as great a predilection for their own country, freedom, and liberty, as the sons and daughters of fair Britain. Their free subjects are trained up to a kind of military service, not so much by the desire of the Chief, as by their own voluntary inclination. It is looked upon as the greatest respect that they can show to their King, to stand up for his and their own defense in time of need. Their different chieftains, which bear a reliance on the great Chief or King, exercise a kind of government something like the feudal institution which prevailed some time in Scotland.[47]

Cugoano's direct engagement with proslavery ideologues such as Tobin and white supremacist philosophers such as Hume establishes him as one of the founders of the tradition of Afro-Caribbean political thought. The many references to his life as a slave in Grenada indicate the profound impact of his Caribbean experiences on his thought. Thus it is indeed surprising that Lewis did not introduce him when he was making references to Hume and Tobin. Lewis mentions Equiano but does not really engage his antislavery arguments, or the broader providential features of his thought.[48]

The Presidential Monarchist Political Order

Adding to these creolizing trends of the eighteenth century and in growing contrast to the African nationalist and repatriational political orders, is a new one, which African political scientist, Ali Mazrui, will much later call presidential monarchism.[49] Like the order of the lodges, this new political order can be seen in the written constitutions upon which these regimes were founded. The first of these presidential monarchist regimes to emerge was clearly the one in Haiti during and after the revolution of 1791. The early Haitian constitutions are strikingly mixed or hybrid formations of African monarchism and French republicanism. James's description of the ideology of the revolution as black Jacobinism is very much on point

– suggesting the mixing of a Haitian black political discourse with the radical republicanism of the French Jacobins.[50] The merging of these two political traditions was reflected in the early Haitian constitutions, which are classic expressions of the creolization of African political traditions in the Caribbean region.

In the Haitian constitution of 1805, the preamble, in a very democratic spirit, declares the document to be written 'in our name and in that of the people of Haiti, who have constituted us legally as faithful organs and interpreters of their will.'[51] Article One of Section Two establishes the formal status of the new nation as the 'Empire of Haiti,' while Article 20 makes the head of state an 'Emperor,' who is to be addressed as 'His Majesty' and also will rule for life. Here we see clearly the opposing tendencies of democracy and monarchy that are embodied in this document. Article 2 very directly states: 'Slavery is abolished forever.'[52] Reinforcing Article 2 in a black discourse of racial solidarity, Article 12 declares: 'No white person, of whatever nationality, shall set foot on this territory with the title of master or proprietor nor, in the future, acquire property here.'[53]

Outlining the basic structure of the Haitian empire/nation, Articles 15, 16, and 17 declare:

> The Empire of Haiti is one and indivisible; its territory is composed of six military divisions. Each military division shall be ruled by a divisional general. Each of these divisional generals shall be independent of the others and shall respond directly to the Emperor or the General in Chief designated by His Majesty.[54]

Here we can see traces of the constitutive codes of the African political kingdoms. Describing further the nature of the Haitian government, Article 23 declared: 'The Crown is elective and non-hereditary.'[55] Yet Article 26 states very directly: 'The Emperor designates his successor, and in a manner he sees most appropriate, either before his death or after.'[56] In a more democratic vein, Articles 50 and 51 declare: 'The law does not recognize a dominant religion,' and that 'Liberty of worship is tolerated.'[57]

These selections should be enough to indicate the hybrid nature of the political formation that was the early postcolonial Haitian state. It was a cross between an African monarchical kingdom and a European democratic republic. In his classic account of the Haitian Revolution,

C.L.R. James described this new state as 'the absolute monarchy in its progressive days.'[58] In the years that followed, these hybrid and contradictory features of the Haitian state only became more marked. The broader or Africana significance of these transitional features become even clearer when we take note of the similar ones that emerged in postcolonial Africa, which led Mazrui to coin the term 'presidential monarchism.'

The Independent Peasantist Order

This eighteenth-century phase in the formation of the Afro-Caribbean political imaginary is rooted in alternative visions of freedom produced by the slave insurrections that occurred after the plantation systems had been firmly established in regional economies with sizeable militias to defend it. The second of these alternative visions of political order to fully emerge, occurred during the course of the Haitian Revolution of 1791, and developed inside the presidential monarchist order just described. This peasantist order, a creation of the Haitian masses, was in strong opposition to the restoration of the plantation system that was an integral part of Toussaint L'Ouverture's presidential monarchism. In contrast to this economic base for the postcolonial political order, the Haitian masses instinctively projected a concept of freedom that was rooted in their ownership of sufficient land to make a decent living form the soil. Haiti and not Africa was now home. Thus they imagined freedom in a postcolonial Haiti as a black state of independent peasants rather than of rural or urban proletarians working for large plantations or corporations. This model of freedom would emerge from many subsequent post-slavery insurrections against the plantation system across the region. It thus constitutes a very persistent and important stratum in the formation of the Afro-Caribbean political imaginary.

Indeed, closely related to this independent peasantist and also to the repatriational political order is the Rastafarian conception of political order that emerged in Jamaica in the 1930s. This distinct conception of political order could be seen as a combination of elements from the two just mentioned. Rastafarian communities are decentralized formations. They are organized around 'yards' or groups of families similar to the Igbo groups we looked at briefly. They rejected all allegiance to the colonial state and swore loyalty to the Emperor of the Kingdom of Ethiopia. The loyalty to the Emperor of Ethiopia gave expression to the repatriational desires, while the decentralized mode of socio-economic organization gave expression to the desire to be free of the plantation system and to work for oneself.

As Lewis ended his account of Caribbean political thought in 1900, the last phases in the development of this tradition of thought that I will note here are the beginnings of its Pan Africanist and Marxist phases. These phases were of course followed by the nationalist/independence phase with leaders such as Norman Manley, Eric Williams, Grantley Adams, Robert Bradshaw, and V.C. Bird, who opened the way for our current set of leaders.

The birth of these new developments cannot be separated from the growing Caribbean diasporic communities in the metropolitan cities of New York, London and Paris. In spite of racism, the greater freedom spaces of these metropolitan communities allowed for modes of political organizing that would not be tolerated in the colonies. In the US, the rise of Pan Africanism and black Marxism cannot be separated from the critiques occasioned by the growing dissatisfaction with Booker T. Washington's leadership of Black America. Washington rose to prominence after the end of the Reconstruction period (1860–80) which had seen African Americans who had been elected to public offices join a governing coalition with northern whites to subdue and attempt to transform a proslavery plantation South.[59] With reconciliation between Northern and Southern whites after 1877, African Americans were rapidly disenfranchised and expelled from American structures of governance. Booker T. Washington was the black leader who worked out an accommodation with this new white political order that demanded the sacrificing of African American political rights.

Migrating to America in the last decades of the nineteenth century, the soon to be Caribbean political theorists, Edward Blyden, W.A. Domingo, Hubert Harrison, and Richard Moore would join African American political theorists such as W.E.B. Du Bois, Monroe Trotter, and A. Phillip Randolph in critiquing the accomodationist political order that was established by Washington. They very quickly took these critiques in the direction of Pan Africanist and socialist alternatives to Washington's position of compromise and accommodation. After moving to Liberia, Blyden became the celebrated voice of Pan

Africanism and its emigrationist alternative to Washington. After the turn of the century, it was Marcus Garvey who became the voice of Pan Africanism. As Blyden and Garvey became the major voices of Pan Africanism, Hubert Harrison in New York and George Padmore in London became the Caribbean voices of black Marxism. A little later, C.L.R. James would join Padmore in this articulating of a black Marxism.

In both London and Paris, it was not the problems of Washington's accommodationist position, but primarily the gathering of students, professionals and workers from all over the African diaspora, that provided the stimulus to resist metropolitan racism and to fight colonialism. The works of Theophilus Scholes, H. Sylvester Williams, the first Pan Africanist conference of 1900,[60] and Garvey's travels to London in his formative years, were all indicators of the ferment that was taking place in these metropolitan capitals. Out of the ferment in Paris, we have the important 1885 treatise, *The Equality of the Human Races*, by the Haitian scholar, Antenor Firmin.[61] As Cugoano took on Hume, Firmin took on Arthur de Gobineau, replying directly to the latter's *Essay on the Inequality of the Human Races*.[62] Firmin would later go on to hold important positions in the Haitian government. With this brief account of the birth of the Pan Africanist and Marxist phases of Afro-Caribbean political thought, I will bring this sketch of the larger tradition of Afro-Caribbean thought to a close and draw some conclusions.

Conclusions

As I read *Main Currents*, and particularly chapter four, the above were some of the political actors, writers, structures of governance, and legitimating arguments that I was expecting to find. Consequently, something like this political profile of the Afro-Caribbean subject is what I think is missing from Lewis's account of 'the historical evolution of Caribbean society in its ideological aspects.' Only such a treatment would match Lewis's skilfully executed account of the European and Euro-Caribbean contributions to the larger field of Caribbean political thought. It was the absence of this comparable treatment that motivated the writing of this essay. However, at the same time that this essay is a critique of Lewis, it is also an attempt to continue and expand the great work that Lewis had undertaken in this important text.

Having responded to these absences in *Main Currents*, three concluding points appear to me to be important, and thus worthwhile making. The first is in regard to the phases and formations that I made the substantive stages in the development of the Afro-Caribbean political tradition. The key point about these phases and formations is that the arrival of a new formation or phase does not necessarily mean the disappearance of earlier ones. Rather, the evidence suggests that these earlier structures of governance, or their constituting codes, tend to persist and sometimes get incorporated into the political orders of later phases. Thus the influences of the marronage tradition on the Haitian Revolution and on the Rastafarian tradition are quite obvious. Also, I presented these phases and formations without criticism, as my primary goal was their articulation and location in the politico-ideological history of our region. Their criticism must certainly be a vital part of this tradition of political thought.

My second concluding point concerns the concept of creole culture and in particular the variations in the levels of domination under which patterns of hybridization or mixing occurred in the Caribbean region. From the work of creole theorists such as Rex Nettleford it seems reasonable to assume that the hierarchical relations of superiority and necessary exclusion established by the project of cultural colonization varied significantly across key fields such as dance, music, literature, scientific and philosophical thought. These variations in hierarchical relations were such that the sense of racial superiority and necessary exclusion were significantly greater in the more rational areas of cultural expression such as science and philosophy. Thus European cultural colonization never denied the existence of African or Afro-Caribbean dance or music, rather it denied their equality with European dance or music. In the case of African or Afro-Caribbean capacities for philosophy, theory or other forms of rational thought, the position was indeed a different and more extreme one. It shifted from the claim of superiority to the more extreme position of denying the existence of African creativity in these areas of cultural expression. Consequently, the battles for institutional space, legitimacy, and public recognition were more difficult ones in the case of African practices of philosophy and theory. It seems to me that the whole field of Afro-Caribbean political philosophy and theory fell within this convention of racial denial, and was further reinforced by the direct challenges to the colonial order that its recognition and cultivation would present. For these reasons, I think that the Afro-Caribbean tradition of political thought was subjected to maximum pressures of erasure, which are necessary for understanding its patterns of creolization and levels of visibility.

Third, and finally, it seems to me that these differences in levels of domination experienced by different areas of cultural and intellectual endeavour have greatly influenced the observable variations in the rates of postcolonial recovery and patterns of creole formation that exist between fields such as history, literature, religion, dance, music and philosophy. The ones in which the hierarchical battles for institutional space and recognition were less extreme have recovered faster and have produced more genuine creole formation in the postcolonial period. Thus, if we take the Caribbean novel or the calypso as examples of successful creole formations, then in the fields of politics, political philosophy and more broadly theory, we are still very much in the early stages of recovery. The hybrid formations we have produced so far still carry within them levels of racial polarization that are too high for the constituent parts from the different cultural traditions to fit smoothly together. Although they are now in the same political system, they are still operating as mutually exclusive binaries. It is my hope that as we continue the work of political reconstruction in the region that we will get past these obstacles and arrive at political forms that will enable us to institute socially the freedom that lives subjectively in us.

Notes

1. Gordon Lewis, *Main Currents in Caribbean Thought: The Historical Evolution of Caribbean Society in its Ideological Aspects, 1492–1990* (Baltimore: Johns Hopkins University Press, 1983).
2. Gordon Lewis, *Puerto Rico: Freedom and Power in the Caribbean* (New York: Harper & Row, 1968).
3. Ibid., vii.
4. Ibid.
5. Ibid., viii.
6. Gordon Lewis, *The Growth of the Modern West Indies* (New York: Monthly Review Press, 1968).
7. Ibid., 18.
8. Gordon Lewis, *The Virgin Islands: A Caribbean Lilliput* (Evanston: Northwestern University Press, 1972); *Notes on the Puerto Rican Revolution* (New York: Monthly Review Press, 1974); *Grenada: The Jewel Despoiled* (Baltimore: Johns Hopkins University Press, 1987).

9. Anthony Maingot, ed., *Gordon K. Lewis On Race, Class and Ideology in the Caribbean* (Kingston: Ian Randle Publishers, 2010).
10. Ibid., 109.
11. Ibid.
12. Lewis, *Main Currents*, 22.
13. Ibid., 10.
14. Ibid.
15. Ibid., 21.
16. Ibid., 24.
17. Ibid.
18. Phillip Curtin, *Two Jamaicas: The Role of Ideas in a Tropical Colony, 1830–1965* (New York: Greenwood Press, 1970).
19. Lewis, *Growth*, 28.
20. Lewis, *Growth*, 29–30.
21. Gordon Lewis, *Main Currents*, 108.
22. Ibid.
23. Ibid., 99.
24. Ibid., 175.
25. Ibid., 88.
26. Paget Henry, 'Africana Political Philosophy and the Crisis of the Postcolony', *Socialism and Democracy*, 21, no.3 (2007): 38.
27. See Basil Davidson, *Africa in History* (New York: Collier Books, 1974); Kevin Shillington, *History of Africa* (New York: Palgrave Macmillan, 2005).
28. Eva Meyerowitz, *The Sacred State of the Akan* (London: Faber & Faber, 1951), 21–26.
29. Quoted in U.D. Anyanwu, 'Erima: Towards A Theory of Igbo Political Tradition' in U.D. Anyanwu and J.C.U. Aguwa 'The Igbo And The Tradition of Politics' (Uturu, Nigeria: Center for Igbo Studies, 1993), 34.
30. Rex Nettleford, *Inward Stretch, Outward Reach: A Voice from the Caribbean* (London: Macmillan Press, 1993), 80.
31. Richard Price, ed., *Maroon Societies* (Baltimore: Johns Hopkins University Press, 1979), 5–10.
32. Ibid., 16.
33. Ibid., 20.
34. Ibid.
35. Richard Price, *Alabi's World* (Baltimore: Johns Hopkins University Press, 1990), 3–101.
36. R.K. Kent, 'Palmares: An African State in Brazil', in *Maroon Societies*, ed. Richard Price (Baltimore: Johns Hopkins University Press, 1979), 170.
37. Ibid., 188.
38. David Barry Gaspar, *Bondmen & Rebels* (Baltimore: Johns Hopkins University Press, 1985).
39. Ibid., 24.
40. Clinton Hutton, *The Logic and Historical Significance of the Haitian Revolution* (Kingston: Arawak Publications, 2005), 59.
41. Ibid., 63.
42. Ibid., 63–64.
43. Corey Walker, *A Noble Fight* (Urbana: University of Illinois Press, 2008), 57.

44. Ottobah Cugoano, *Thoughts and Sentiments on the Evil of Slavery* (New York: Penguin Books, 1999).
45. Anthony Bogues, *Black Heretics, Black Prophets* (New York: Routledge, 2003), 33.
46. Ottobah Cuguano, *Thoughts and Sentiments*, 23.
47. Ibid., 27.
48. Paget Henry, 'Between Hume and Cugoano: Race, Ethnicity and Philosophical Entrapment', *The Journal of Speculative Philosophy*, 18, no.2, (2004): 129–48.
49. Ali Mazrui and Michael Tidy, *Nationalism and New States in Africa* (London: Heinemann, 1987), 191.
50. See C.L.R. James, *The Black Jacobins* (New York: Vintage Books, 1989).
51. Sibylle Fischer, *Modernity Disavowed* (Mona: University of the West Indies Press, 2004), 275.
52. Ibid.
53. Ibid., 276.
54. Ibid.
55. Ibid.
56. Ibid., 277.
57. Ibid., 279.
58. James, *The Black Jacobins*, 247.
59. W.E.B. Du Bois, *Black Reconstruction in America* (New York: Free Press, 1998), 182–91.
60. Theophilus Scholes, *Glimpses of the Ages*, 2 vols (London: John Long, 1905 and 1907); James R. Hooker, *Henry Sylvester Williams: Imperial Pan-Africanist* (London: Rex Collings, 1975).
61. Antenor Firmin, *The Equality of the Human Races* (New York: Garland Publishing, 2000).
62. Joseph Arthur de Gobineau, *Essai sur l'Inegalite des Races Humaines*, 4 vols (Paris: 1853–55).

3 | 'An Extended Debate with Europe?': G.K. Lewis, Denis Benn, Paget Henry, and the Epistemological Challenge in the Writing of Caribbean Political Thought

Tennyson S.D. Joseph

Introduction

Euro-Hegemony and the Epistemological Challenge of Caribbean Thought

One of the enduring contributions of Gordon K. Lewis to Caribbean political development has been his pioneering effort to track the historical evolution of Caribbean political thought. Indeed, Lewis's seminal text, *Main Currents in Caribbean Thought*[1] represents the first conscious and deliberate attempt at compiling, analysing and categorizing the existing body of ideas which, in his view constituted a self-conscious and distinct Caribbean body of political ideas. This task, in itself, was a historically and sociologically significant achievement. Lewis himself identified the work as 'a descriptive and critical analysis of the total complex of ideas, sentiments, outlooks, attitudes, and values that, in the fullest sense of the word, constitute the ideology of the groups that have figured in the Caribbean story.'[2] Lewis's task therefore was to provide a corrective to the prevailing habit of the outside world of failing to 'see the region in...serious terms,'[3] insofar as its creation of thought and ideology was concerned. It is beyond question that Lewis's goal was not only masterfully achieved, but has served as the platform for all subsequent research into the nature of Caribbean political thought.

However, whilst *Main Currents* has been important for making a case for the existence of Caribbean political thought in its own right, there are significant weaknesses in the ways in which Caribbean thought has been characterized by G.K. Lewis and subsequent followers. The fundamental weakness lies in the widely held view that it can best be explained and justified as an intellectual project which derives its legitimacy from its ability to destroy European hegemonic projects. All of the major attempts at writing the history of Caribbean thought, namely Lewis (1983), Benn (1987; 2004) and Henry (2000)[4] have identified this as the essential feature of Caribbean thought. This tendency has been most explicitly advanced by Henry, who argued that,

> ...many of the original features of our philosophical and other discursive practices have been shaped by the colonial problematics and contours of our cultural history. Within this imperial framework, the original contents of Caribbean philosophy emerged as a series of extended debates over projects of colonial domination between four major social groups: Euro-Caribbeans, Amerindians, Indo-Caribbeans and Afro-Caribbeans. The discursive productions of the first group were contributions to the creating of hegemonic situations through the legitimating of colonial projects. The productions of the other three groups were attempts at destroying Euro-Caribbean hegemony through the delegitimating of their colonial projects.[5]

Whilst this self-conscious concern with overcoming European hegemonic projects is of tremendous value in capturing the role of Caribbean thought, its fundamental weakness is that it freezes Caribbean thought as a permanent child of European thought. It pre-supposes a dependent relationship between Caribbean thought in its relation to European thought, with the former as the reactionary junior partner. Thus, Europe proposes and the Caribbean disposes. Whilst such a categorisation might have been useful in establishing what Caribbean thought *might have been* particularly in the initial phase of its first conscious categorisation, it is counterproductive to suggest this as a permanent normative feature of Caribbean thought.

It is this dependent relationship between European thought and Caribbean thought which was criticized by George Belle where he provided a panoramic sweep of Caribbean intellectual productions from the Haitian revolution to Marxist-Socialist thought up to the mid-1980s.[6] His central argument was that whilst Caribbean intellectual productions seek to overcome European hegemonic ambitions, the evidence on close examination, shows these ideas as being far less thoroughly counter-hegemonic than their adherents assumed them to be. In Belle's words,

> ...it can be asserted that to whatever extent a specific Caribbean identity can be associated with a body of ideas and theories of the Caribbean, we in the Caribbean even in our post-colonial conditions are particularly with respect to political philosophy and theory compartmentalised within the intellectual hegemony of Europe. Being compartmentalised within the European civilisation and epistemology any delineation of Caribbean ontology of philosophy and theory does not in fact therefore carry us apparently beyond the hegemony of European culture and indeed still to a large extent, we glory in this reality.[7]

Aims of the Study

The main aim of this work is to move beyond diagnosis and to identify a way out of the current entrapment within this European epistemological hegemonic framework. It utilizes the Afrocentric perspectives of Marimba Ani in *Yurugu*[8] to identify a normative orientation for Caribbean Political thought, away from its current location within a European defined epistemological space. In *Yurugu*, Ani presents a deeply insightful and path-breaking critique of 'European thought and Behaviour.' Of specific relevance is her identification of the conscious act by the Greek philosopher Plato in selectively weeding out aspects of Ancient Egyptian philosophy in his attempt at creating an epistemology more suited to the European consciousness. Significantly, for the concern of this analysis is *how* Plato sets about to achieve his aim. Specifically, therefore, the insights presented by Ani on Plato's creative re-formulation of Ancient Egyptian thought are presented as a method which can be utilised within the Caribbean intellectual tradition to transcend its current entrapment within the intellectual hegemony of Europe.

In order to achieve this, I will first demonstrate the recognition by Gordon Lewis, Denis Benn and Paget Henry of the failure of Caribbean thought to successfully overcome the European epistemological hegemony. The chapter will show how each of these writers, though recognizing the epistemological subservience of Caribbean thought to the European world view, was far more concerned with defending the validity of Caribbean thought, rather than with engaging meaningfully the process of overcoming the weakness. To advance the argument, the study will show how critical reflections on the writing of Caribbean Political thought undertaken by Rupert Lewis and George Belle[9] also suffer from an identical weakness. The central argument is that these writers do not move from diagnosis to prescription, and as such, though their efforts are laudable, they present the weaknesses in Caribbean thought as being insurmountable. Much of this failure is due to their inability to understand the cultural foundations of European thought. As a consequence, these writers fail to appreciate the true requirements of overcoming European epistemological hegemony. This failure is seen, particularly in the case of G.K. Lewis, in his misplaced confidence in the capacity of 'creolization' to effect the required transcendence of European thought.

G.K. Lewis, Denis Benn, Paget Henry and Others, and the Epistemological Challenge of Caribbean Thought

G.K. Lewis and the Problem of European Epistemological Hegemony

In writing *Main Currents in Caribbean Thought*, Gordon Lewis was concerned above all else to respond to the racist view that the Caribbean region was devoid of a tradition of intellectual thought. Thus he saw his task as challenging the 'anti-Caribbean animus' which has held that 'there is no history of ideas in the region worth speaking about'[10] and that the 'West Indies has never created anything' by way of thought and philosophy.[11] In response to this widely held view, Lewis's goal was to make it clear that

> from the very beginning there grew up a genuine Caribbean historiography, a Caribbean sociology, a Caribbean anthropology; in brief, a movement of ideas at once created by European ideologies concerned with the New world, by European residents in the islands, and, later, by a Caribbean intelligentsia itself.[12]

Despite Lewis's presentation of Caribbean thought as unique and original in its own right, the main factors which he highlights as shaping Caribbean thought, all point to the overwhelming dominance of the European presence. Thus he identifies first, the 'influence...of

European-metropolitan modes of thought and the manner in which that influence was felt by the gradually emerging literary elites of the Caribbean urban centers.' The second was 'that of a subtle creolizing movement, whereby all of those modes of thought were absorbed and assimilated and were then reshaped to fit the special and unique requirements of Caribbean society as they developed from one period to the next.'[13]

Lewis's observations raise critical concerns for the whole question of the epistemological dependence of Caribbean thought on European thought. What emerges from his analysis, despite his glorification of the creole, is the deep impact of European ideas and political developments on the evolution of ideas in the Caribbean. Thus, Lewis notes that the modes of thought impacting upon the Caribbean,

> encompassed the whole of European intellectual history itself, in linear historical order: the late medieval humanism of the Hispanic Mediterranean; the rationalism of the French Enlightenment, filtered through the influence of the American and French Revolutions; English humanitarianism, most notably expressed in the campaigns for the abolition of the slave trade and slavery; nineteenth and twentieth-century Socialist thought.'[14]

It is in response to this overwhelming impact of European modes of thought on the Caribbean that Lewis proposes the process of creolization as creating the basis for the emergence of an authentic body of Caribbean thought. However, Lewis's explanation of the process of creolization does little to authenticate Caribbean thought as having truly transcended its European mode. Thus, in describing the role of the creolization process in shaping Caribbean thought Lewis argues as follows:

> The moral and intellectual baggage of Europe, this is to say, once unloaded, became indubitably Caribbean. The end result cannot simply be seen as, so to speak, a provincial expression on the circumference of civilization of something that can be appreciated only at its centre. It constituted, rather, an effort – often groping and uncertain – after a culture to be regarded as genuinely Caribbean; in the course of which it borrowed, sometimes with almost servile acknowledgement and sometimes with embarrassed shame, from the achievements of the older world...Everything taken or received

from the Old World, became different as it was adapted to its new home. The 'middle passage' of transported African slaves was accompanied by a 'middle passage' of ideologies.[15]

Despite Lewis's defence of creolization, what emerges is the emphasis on the 'groping and uncertain' nature of the creolization process, and the 'servile acknowledgement' and the 'embarrassed shame' involved in the process of 'borrowing' in the fashioning of the ideas which make a claim to uniqueness. In short, Lewis acknowledges, though he seeks to explain it away, a built-in 'inferiority complex' in Caribbean thought. What is significant however, is that it is this very sensitivity to an inferiority complex pervading Caribbean thought, which creates the basis for the emergence of its opposite – the transcendence of Europe – as the *sine qua non* of what constitutes true Caribbean thought. It is on this basis that the analysis of Caribbean thought is presented in *Main Currents*, and indeed, in most of the subsequent analyses of Caribbean thought by later researchers.

Thus, for example, whilst Lewis's work covers what he calls the beginning of Caribbean thought in the sixteenth and seventeenth centuries, to the growth of nationalist thought from the seventeenth century to 1900, it is the ideas which have greater potency in countering European hegemony which are treated as more efficacious by Lewis. This is seen for example where Lewis juxtaposes the nationalist thought of the Trinidadian J.J. Thomas against that of the nationalists from the Hispano-Caribbean in particular Cuba, which he sees as being at the vanguard of the Caribbean nationalist movement.[16] His famous condemnation of J.J. Thomas bears this out:

> Thomas is no revolutionary. He takes the English connection for granted; he is no nationalist like the Cuban and Puerto Rican separatists of his day, seeking West Indian independence. His quarrel with Froude is a matter of degree rather than of kind. Froude exemplifies, as he sees it, the worst of the English tradition, whereas he himself appeals to the best of that tradition. His greatest praise in the colonial life itself is for the 'coloured elements.' He appears to accept Froude's assumption that *obeah*, cannibalism and devil-worship characterize Haitian life, only arguing that Froude is wrong to assume that they will be adopted by blacks in the West Indies. He continues to accept the conventional view, later

destroyed by later scholarship, that slavery emancipation was an act of English beneficence...Nor is he an advocate of popular rule anywhere....[17]

Despite this identification of a more highly evolved nationalist consciousness in Marti, Lewis is fully aware of the dominating impact of European thought on Marti's thought. Lewis sees the 'catholic bent' of Marti's mind as making him receptive to 'all of the various currents of nineteenth-century thought, both European and American' and sees this as 'at once the strength and the weakness of Marti's thought.' In Lewis's view, the weakness lay in the 'inability to weld all of the multitudinous material into a single, coherent viewpoint that can be called his own.'[18]

It is this failure in creating genuinely new and creative original thought, which is the troubling feature of Caribbean thought. This failure, it can be argued, is bound with the limitations of the creole. Despite its limitations, however, it is in the creole that Lewis identifies the nearest source of originality and authenticity in Caribbean thought. It is this half-hearted acceptance of the creole as the highest expression of non-European thought, which is the essential epistemological problem of Caribbean thought. Lewis was fully aware of its limitations, but given his primary aim of making a case for Caribbean thought, he failed to explore its implications against the broad question of its ability to escape the epistemological hegemony of Europe. Nevertheless, inherent in Lewis's work was the normative expectation that Caribbean thought should be creating the basis for overcoming projects of European hegemony. This normative expectation, once established, becomes therefore the basis for the future analysis of Caribbean thought, as seen in the work of Denis Benn.[19]

Denis Benn and the Problem of European Epistemological Hegemony

It is significant that the research for Denis Benn's work on the *Growth and Development of Political Ideas in the Caribbean 1774–1983*, was undertaken in the 1970s, prior to the publication of G.K. Lewis's *Main Currents*. Not surprisingly therefore, the aims of Denis Benn are very similar to those of G.K. Lewis, in that he was responding to the fact that the region's rich intellectual tradition remained 'unstructured and unassimilated.'[20] Similarly, like Lewis, he noted the fact that much of the intellectual productions of Caribbean thought, 'represent, in varying degrees, responses to the colonial condition,' and

> relate to the well-known themes such as the nature and extent of political authority and control, the form of economic organisation and the general socio-cultural setting within a political order fashioned by the unique combination of colonisation, slavery and the plantation which together have historically been associated with the development of Caribbean societies.[21]

In a similar fashion to G.K. Lewis, Benn included in his assimilation of Caribbean thought not only the ideas which sought to overturn colonialism, but those which sought to sustain it as well. Thus, Benn includes in his catalogue of Caribbean thought 'the political ideas of Edward Long and Bryan Edwards, who wrote during the late 18th Century' and their ideas are examined 'in relation to the constitutional evolution of the Old Representative System.'[22] Similarly, for this reason, Benn presents a definition of political ideas which incorporates both hegemonic and counter-hegemonic perspectives. Thus, he defines political ideas as 'any set of ideas, with varying degrees of systematisation or coherence, which deal with matters pertaining to socio-political organisation, and which may or may not have direct or immediate implications for political action and conduct.'[23]

However, despite this broad and all inclusive definition of political ideas, Benn, like G.K. Lewis, adheres to a normative perspective which sees the utility of Caribbean thought as residing in its ability to overcome projects of European hegemony. Thus, where Benn assesses the efficacy of an idea, his focus is on its ability to truly overturn European hegemony. This is seen very clearly, for example, in his treatment of the ideas of Marcus Garvey. Thus, whilst Benn identifies the intellectual contribution of Garvey as the 'reaffirmation of the cultural nationalist position elaborated by Blyden', he was cognizant of the fact that 'Garvey's position on the cultural question was not without ambiguity' since 'there existed in Garvey's philosophy an apparent confusion between race and culture.' Specifically, Benn was critical of the fact that, in spite of his emphasis on African culture and civilization, in seeking to institute alternative cultural forms for the 'New World Negro', he fell back on the principle of race and colour rather than culture, strictly defined. Hence, in the sphere of religion, apart from the reversal of colour symbolism, the African Orthodox Church instituted by him still subscribed to the broad outlines of a Christian orthodoxy based on elements derived from the Episcopalian and Roman Catholic liturgy. *The problem of defining a relevant African cultural identity in part derived from the fact that the African cultural heritage as a concrete historical reality, as distinct from a conceptual entity, was largely unknown to Garvey* (Emphasis added).[24]

This is the crux of the problem which afflicts not only Garvey, but pervades all Caribbean thought. It is this lack of knowledge of African Cultural heritage as a concrete reality which accounts for the inability to fully transcend European epistemological hegemony. It is also a problem rooted in the very nature of the creole itself. Central to the notion of the creole is the remoteness of the concrete African experience as distinct from the forcefully imposed impact of European world views. In such a context, any reliance on an African cultural experience as a way out of European hegemony, is always 'conceptual' and not rooted in concrete historical experience. As will be shown later, both the cradles of civilisation thesis of Cheikh Anta Diop,[25] and Marimba Ani's exploration of Plato's epistemological transcendence of Ancient Egypto-African thought, provide a framework in which the fashioning of a non-European cultural response can be undertaken.

What emerges from the exploration of Benn's work therefore is the continuation of G.K. Lewis's expectation that authentic Caribbean thought *ought to* transcend the modes of European thought. In both Benn and Lewis this expectation is reflected in their identification of instances where various ideas posited by Caribbean thinkers are shown to be less than efficacious in fulfilling their claims as alternatives to European hegemonic perspectives. Despite this failure however, the expectation continues to be the basis for the definition of Caribbean thought. This expectation is taken to its highest point in Paget Henry's *Caliban's Reason*.

Paget Henry and the Problem of European Epistemological Hegemony

Of the three works under review, Henry's *Caliban's Reason* is the most explicit in presenting Caribbean thought through the normative lens of overcoming European hegemony. Further, Henry appears to be most sensitive to the question of the cultural foundations which separate Afro-Caribbean epistemology from that of the European tradition. As a consequence of his normative stance, Henry is less willing to accept the 'embarrassing paradoxes and contradictions' which have been integral in the formation of Caribbean philosophy. Critical among those contradictions are, 'the paradoxes of anti-African biases in an Afro-Caribbean philosophy, its patterns of creolization, and the over-identification with European philosophies in a tradition that is supposed to be critical of the European heritage.'[26]

Significantly, Henry directly identifies the work of G.K. Lewis and Denis Benn, as perpetuating the tendency to restrain Afro-Caribbean philosophy within the hegemonic overlordship of Europe. The bases for these weaknesses are neatly captured by Henry, who argues that,

> One of the primary results of Lewis' analysis is the hegemonic position of European texts and discourses within the tradition. Although critical of this hegemony, Lewis is so caught up in its power that he has a very hard time seeing the intellectual contributions of Afro-Caribbeans...Thus, the picture that emerges is one of radical discursive and communicative inequality between Euro and Afro-Caribbeans. Although not as extreme, much the same pattern emerges from Benn's work. From both authors we can conclude that the colonial cultural system that framed our intellectual tradition established within the tradition a radical inequality between Afro- and Euro-Caribbeans that reflected the politico-economic order of the society.[27]

Henry therefore, identifies squarely, the problem of Caribbean Political thought. The problem lies in its inability to overcome the hegemonic project of Europe. He however, identifies the failure, not as a failure of Caribbean thought in itself, but as the inability of the assimilators of Caribbean thought to overcome the 'invisibility' of Afro-Caribbean thought. In short, Henry appears to blame the messengers. Despite this however, Henry identifies a number of significant internal 'problems of afro-Caribbean philosophy.' Among these is the fact that it is

> marked by deep fissures, wide cleavages, and oppositional constructions of binaries of dualities such as spirit/matter, spirit/history, pre-modern/modern, poeticism/historicism, race/class. Consequently, it is a poorly integrated body of thought that is conscious of itself primarily in part and only rarely as a whole.[28]

Whilst Henry recognises these weaknesses, he offers very little by way of transcending their limitations. What he offers is greater insistence that the Afro-Caribbean perspective should be deliberately enlarged above the European in the analysis and assimilation of Caribbean thought. He also offers a strong hint of the weaknesses of creolization in fulfilling that goal. He does not however, offer an epistemological route out of the inferiority complex of Caribbean thought. In short, Henry does not take Caribbean thought beyond the point to which it had been brought by Benn and Lewis, despite the critical weaknesses which he identifies in their work. A similar tendency is seen in the reflections on the writing of Caribbean thought presented by Rupert Lewis[29] and George Belle.[30]

Rupert Lewis and George Belle and the Problem of European Epistemological Hegemony

In his review of G.K. Lewis's *Main Currents* and Denis Benn's *Growth and Development,* Rupert Lewis complains that in *Main Currents* the 'weight of the analysis bears heavily on European and planter impact in the region and the writings of the Westernised creole intelligentsia.'[31] In acknowledging the impact of Europe on the shaping of Caribbean thought he concedes that the

> ruling class in the region has for most of our history been European or creole white and has been profoundly racist. Africa has been for them barbaric, the people uncivilised, inferior. Their ideas have held sway because of their economic power regionally and their role in the development of the world economy and trade.[32]

Rupert Lewis's diagnosis, like the other works identified here, is therefore sensitive to the dominance of European ideas impacting on the writing of Caribbean thought.

Just like Paget Henry, Rupert Lewis is concerned with the conceptual errors made by G.K. Lewis arising largely out of his exaggerated exposure of pre-eighteenth century European humanists, a tendency which accounted for what Henry has seen as contributing to the invisibility of Afro-Caribbean thought. Thus, for example, where G.K. Lewis asserts that Negrophobia does not appear in the Europeans writings until the eighteenth century, Rupert Lewis disagrees, arguing that to accept this position would be to 'make too many concessions to the so-called European humanist trends which were certainly not dominant either in the Catholic or protestant hierarchy which backed the transatlantic slave trade' and to underestimate the 'genocidal wars against the indigenous peoples of the Americas.'[33]

Even more significant for the concerns with the cultural and technical requirements for overcoming European hegemony is Rupert Lewis's identification of the compelling research of Martin Bernal[34] into the link between the denial of Africa's contribution to Western thought, the consolidation of the slave economic system and European global power, and the emergence of anti-black racism. Thus, in contrast to G.K. Lewis's denial of the presence of Negrophobia in the Caribbean prior to the eighteenth century, Rupert Lewis suggests that,

> it is truer to say that the systematisation of racist ideology really developed in the eighteenth century. This would square with Martin Bernal's findings in his classic work *Black Athena* (1987) where the African roots of ancient Greek civilisation which fed European science, culture, and religion in the modern period was replaced by an Aryan model which denied all of this. Marx had already pointed out that Plato's *Republic* was an idealisation of the Egyptian system of castes. Too many remain ignorant of the African sources of classical Greek thought, of Plato, Aristotle, Pythagoras, and others, thus perpetuating Eurocentrism in the classroom.[35]

This observation by Rupert Lewis, and specifically his identification of the debates surrounding Plato's relationship to Egypto-African political systems and philosophical ideas, shows him to be pointing to the basis upon which an authentic challenge to the intellectual hegemony of Europe can be mounted. However, the full implications of his perspective are not pursued to their logical conclusion. Rupert Lewis instead, is content merely to raise the issue as a way of identifying a conceptual error in G.K. Lewis's treatment of Caribbean thought.

Significantly, the very point at which Rupert Lewis ends is the point at which the perspective of George Belle[36] begins. Belle's analysis of Caribbean political thought is rooted firmly in his understanding of the political philosophy of the ancient Egyptians, and his knowledge of Western Philosophy's tremendous debt to Negro Egypt. Belle's central argument is that whilst Caribbean thought is defined largely as engaged in combating European hegemonic perspectives, its failure to connect with African political philosophy in antiquity has frustrated its purpose. His argument is best illustrated through his treatment of Rastafari. Belle argues that,

> Black nationalism economic and cultural and even religious nationalism a la Rastafari subjected to critical assessment will also fail to escape this ontological compartmentalisation [within the epistemological hegemony of Europe]. In the case of Rastafari a claim to glory is rooted in the Solomonic lineage. But Solomon is a monarch of relatively recent antiquity in the context of African dynastic history; and Solomon is a 'lesser' monarch when compared to Sheba. And Rastafari has touched very little, the source of 'Solomon's wisdom.' Rastafari in fact reverses the historical route of tutelage, by crowning ancient Ethiopia with 'Solomon's crown.' The Ethiopic-Nubian and dynastic Egyptian of the pyramid age is extant 2000 years before in all his glory, and is far more glorious than Solomon at his best. African cosmology is therefore slighted, by this assumption of Judaeo Christian theocratic primacy.[37]

Belle's analysis of the epistemological challenge facing Caribbean thought comes closest to providing a concrete response to the condition. According to the logic of Belle's argument that response can begin

> by re-engaging the full impact of mankind's historical cultural experience; by seeking original essence, by analysing civilizational conflict in broadest perspective; by identifying the European paradigm as child/and infant in human historical space and identifying the birth of the extant cultural hegemon; by the isolating of the overthrow of a universal paradigm sourced in mankind's experiential essence, which had no need to be hegemonic.[38]

Ironically however, whilst Belle identifies the method, he does not apply it. Thus, though in his review he alludes constantly to Caribbean nationalist thought as providing a '*key* that was not completely turned in the lock of the unopened *psychic clasp* of the hegemon,' Belle himself fails to advance onwards to the actual turning of the key.

A Taste of Plato's Medicine: Overcoming European Hegemony:

It is ironic that the method for the actual turning of the key, to free Caribbean thought from its European epistemological moorings, can be best sourced in the so-called father of Western philosophy, the Greek philosopher, Plato. This turn to Plato is not a consequence of Eurocentrism. It is rooted in the historical awareness of Plato's conscious and deliberate overcoming of the African philosophical thought systems upon which embryonic Europe had been dependent, and which he had simultaneously admired and despised. In this sense, Plato's attitude to his Afro-Egyptian parent, was akin to the current attitude of Caribbean political theorists to the inherited European world view imposed by Colonialism. In seeking to overcome European hegemony, therefore, Caribbean political theorists and philosophers concerned with the transcendence of European epistemological hegemony are well placed to give Plato a taste of his own medicine.

In the fulfilment of this task, it is useful to study the work of Marimba Ani,[39] who has gone furthest in uncovering Plato's role in overturning the then dominant African perspective. Ani argues that the African world view, and the world views of other people who are not of European origin, adhere to certain common perspectives. In highlighting the specific features of the African world view, Ani notes that the

> universe to which they relate is sacred in origin, is organic, and is a true 'cosmos'. Human beings are part of the cosmos, and as such, relate intimately with other cosmic beings. Knowledge of the universe comes through relationship with it and through perception of spirit in matter. The universe is one; spheres are joined because of a single unifying force that pervades all being. Meaningful reality issues from this force.[40]

She argues that 'these world views are 'reasonable' but not rationalistic: complex yet 'lived' and 'tend to be expressed through a logic of metaphor and complex symbolism.'[41] In contrast, she argues that the European epistemological mode tends to 'rob the universe of its richness, deny the significance of the symbolic' and to 'simplify phenomena until it becomes mere object.'[42]

Ani therefore sets herself the task of identifying 'what happened with embryonic Europe that was to eventually generate such a radically different world view' and specifically she sought to find out 'what part did Platonic thought play in this process?' In response to these questions, she argues that the underlying basis for this radically different world view was the European need to 'control' and to gain 'mastery' over the environment. This need was therefore served by reducing all phenomena to a knowable quantity.[43] In this task she identifies the role of Plato's thought as being critical in moving away from the established world-views, particularly the dominant African perspectives under whose intellectual influence the Greeks had existed. According to Ani,

> Any discussion of the nature and origin of European epistemology must focus on, if not begin with Plato. This is not to say that he was not influenced by the pre-Socratic African philosophies that preceded him. But what Plato seems to have done is to have laid a rigorously constructed foundation for the repudiation of the symbolic sense – the denial of the cosmic, intuitive knowledge. It is this process that we need to trace...It led to the materialization of the universe as conceived by the European mind – a materialization that complemented and supported the intense psycho-cultural need for control of the self and others.[44]

Ani isolates Plato's work in the Republic as the place where his intent is most vigorously pursued. In that work Plato succeeds in creating the universe as 'object.' Plato achieves this feat through the glorification of the 'thinking being' removed from the universe, thus separating the knower from the known.[45] An important aspect of Plato's feat was achieved through the transcendence of both the pre-Socratic sophists, as well as the Homeric method which had previously held sway. Particularly repugnant to Plato was the fact that the Homeric epics 'evoked emotional response from an audience that felt itself to be personally involved with the subject matter,' and that the poetic mode represented the 'habit of self-identification with the oral traditions.'[46]

Thus, the weakness with the Homeric tradition from the European perspective was that it de-emphasised the distinction between subject and object, knower and known. A similar problem of 'subjectivity' can be identified in the Sophist claim that 'man is the measure of all things' or 'justice is the interest of the stronger.'[47] Both of these positions deny the possibility of objective truth.' Plato's task was therefore to consciously produce an epistemological method which would suit the cultural needs of an emerging European consciousness.

Ani summarises Plato's success in achieving his goal and their implications for thought in the following way:

> A theory of the universe, a theory of the state and a theory of human nature are implied in Plato's epistemology. Justice, or the Good, is achieved when the 'best' controls the 'worst.' The universe is ordered through such control. In the state, the 'highest' control the 'lowest.' The person is constantly at war within himself and is not properly human until his reason controls his emotion, i.e., men were to control women...[T]his new epistemology ('mental habit') can be interpreted as a justification of what was to be manifested as European racism, nationalism, and imperialism.[48]

Further clarification of the differences between the European and non-European epistemological mode have been advanced through the path-breaking 'Cradles of Civilisation' thesis put forward by Senegalese scholar, Cheikh Anta Diop.[49] Diop's thesis rests on strong materialist foundations. He sees the social, cultural and intellectual foundations of the two main distinct groupings of humanity – The African and the Indo-Aryan – as having been shaped by the physical and natural environment in which the original racial clans were formed. Thus, Diop speaks of the 'Southern Cradle' in which black humanity evolved, as being marked by the benevolence of nature, the abundance of the soil, and the relative ease of survival. These material conditions were seen as resulting in certain features of the African consciousness such as matrilineal filial succession, communal ownership, xenophilia, communalism, social security and pacifism, which have critical implications for the ideas and thought systems advanced by the African groups in the Southern Cradle. In contrast, the 'Northern Cradle' out of which the proto-whites emerged, was marked by the harshness of the cold climate, which did not yield easily its fruits. The economic and social systems which evolved in the northern cradle therefore revolved around the mastery and control of the environment, competition for survival, pessimism about the future, individualism, hoarding of private wealth, xenophobia, and other cultural responses conducive to responding to the existing material conditions.[50]

Clearly discernible from the combined perspectives of Ani and Diop are critical issues which hold implications for the differences between European and African thought, philosophy and epistemology. Their perspective provides a key to understanding the specific choices and preferences advanced by Plato in his determination of the preferred features of Western thought. Equally important, is that their perspectives detail in concrete terms, the nature of the task to be undertaken if a true and complete break with the European epistemological mode is to be successfully effected by Caribbean thought. The concluding section therefore seeks to apply the insights of Diop and Ani to the operationalization of Caribbean Political thought, beyond its current entrapment within European epistemological hegemony.

Implications for Caribbean Thought

What has emerged from the preceding analysis is that much of the failure of Caribbean thought in overcoming European intellectual hegemony resides in the fact that Caribbean thought has failed to create a new epistemology rooted in the fundamental cultural differences between the European and non-European consciousness. This is not to suggest that an awareness of the differences between the two epistemological approaches has not previously existed. Indeed, Henry clearly demonstrates such awareness. It is on this basis that he rejects the Western idealist Platonic notion which views philosophy as 'an affirmation of the autonomy of a thinking being' and which 'rises above the determinations of history and everyday life.'[51] In contrast, Henry identifies the distinctiveness of Caribbean philosophy as being its rootedness in the reality of everyday life and everyday existence. He therefore sees Afro-Caribbean philosophy is an 'intertextually embedded discursive practice' which is 'often implicitly referenced or engaged in the production of answers to everyday questions and problems that are being framed in non-philosophical discourses.'[52] In this sense the method of Caribbean thought which he advances can be seen as connected to the African, pre-Socratic acceptance of the complex interconnectedness of phenomena.

A similar awareness of the cultural bases separating European from Afro-Caribbean epistemology is also revealed by Henry[53] in an unrelated assessment of the philosophy of Rastafari. Henry identifies the impact of the social realm as having a critical role to play in the shaping of the religious cosmogony of Rastafari. This he sees as lying in direct contrast to the pattern of symbol formation in Europe where it is the fear or dread of the cosmic realm that provides the spark for religious symbol formation. Thus Henry argues that, 'in colonial societies anxiety in relation to rhythm of social life replaces, or eclipses the anxiety experienced in relation to the rhythm of cosmic life. Hence the shift in the pattern of symbol formation that sustains the construction of world views.[54]

It is this sort of analysis which emerges when an analysis of Caribbean thought is grounded in the material and cultural differences between the European world and the non-European world. Whilst Henry shows an awareness of it, and whilst he has gone further than most in touching upon its implications for understanding Caribbean political thought, he however, does not take this awareness to its logical conclusion by engaging in the construction of a new epistemological mode with the boldness identified in Plato's approach. Thus, Henry's analysis does not go beyond seeing Caribbean thought as involved in an 'extended debate with Europe.' Whilst it identifies Caribbean thought as being in opposition to projects of European hegemony, it does not drill into the deeper psychic and sociocultural bases upon which genuinely new thought, and an original alternative to European ideas can be established. It is upon this weakness that the problem of Caribbean thought continues to hang.

The Problem of Creolization

This exploration of the epistemological bases of the differences between European and non-European thought, brings into sharp relief the problem of creolization. The creole by its very definition and formation implies a 'split personality' in which two competing tendencies – the hegemonic and the counter-hegemonic – both have their legitimate spaces. However, in the Caribbean condition, given the centuries of European imposed cultural practices, formalized through the authoritative power of the state, it is the European mode which continues to enjoy dominance particularly in the formal realm.[55] This may account for the absence of 'boldness' a la Plato, by Caribbean writers in stating definitively what constitutes the new epistemological mode upon which the alternative to Europe ought to be constructed. This lack of boldness is a pervasive feature of Caribbean thought, as seen in Belle's recognition of the failure by Caribbean thought to 'turn the key' to unlock new epistemological possibilities. It is seen in countless instances where intellectual alternatives are frustrated by the 'inherited' or imposed cultural aspects of the society.

Thus, for example, ideas constructed upon cultural bases rooted in community and communalism, clash against the culturally imposed experiences of individualism as seen for example in liberal thought; those which de-emphasise hoarding and private ownership, clash against the predominant economic mode of private capital accumulation; family forms like polygamy rooted in understanding of the absence of loneliness,[56] clash against the European Christian nuclear family forms informed by the need for patriarchal control over females particularly in the context of male control over the distribution of private property to offspring; and matriarchy clashes with patriarchy. The list of cultural and psycho-cultural differences is far longer than this small sampling suggests. However, what is clear is that alternative Caribbean thought can only be constructed on the base of firm knowledge of the cultural foundation that gives European thought its distinct character.

Equally clear, is the fact that creolization, given its failure to resolve those critical cultural questions, has also failed to provide a solution to the epistemological challenge of Caribbean thought. This throws into sharp relief G.K. Lewis's weakness in presenting the process of creolization as an authentic basis upon which Caribbean thought could be legitimately constructed. Whilst Lewis had assumed that the creole represented the basis for the creation of new thought, the implication of the preceding analysis, suggests that a more thorough rejection of European cultural foundations is required for genuinely new and alternative thought to emerge. Writers interested in the assimilation of Caribbean thought therefore need to go beyond G.K. Lewis's comfortable acceptance of creolization as the foundation upon which the validity of Caribbean thought should rest.

It is on this basis that knowledge of Plato's method in transcending the African and 'pre-Socratic' epistemological mode provides a useful template through which Caribbean thought can perform a similar feat. In many ways, Plato was in a similar relation to Egypto-African thought which colonised Greece,[57] as are modern-day Caribbean intellectuals in relation to Europe. However, whilst Caribbean thought has largely defined itself as a reaction to European hegemonic projects, Plato's perspective was established through a redefinition of what constitutes thought and philosophy itself. Whilst Caribbean thought has sought largely to justify itself by 'proving' that it has met the European criteria of 'true' thought, Plato was deliberate in determining a new set of criteria which suited his purposes. Plato was successful in transcending the dominant African epistemology by rejecting it whilst fully cognizant of its strengths and method. Caribbean thought, in contrast, whilst fully aware of the hegemonic status of European thought, has fallen into the trap of paying too much attention to it, and has failed to redefine 'thought' and 'philosophy' outside of the terms laid out by Europe. Its productions, therefore, have tended to be reactive to the hegemonic projects of Europe. Whilst Plato was therefore able to create a framework for European thought to assert itself according to its own independent objectives, Caribbean thought has failed to define similar objectives for itself.

However, the efforts by recent researchers, such as Ani,[58] Diop,[59] Karenga,[60] Obenga[61] and Carruthers[62] to understand the cultural basis of ancient Egyptian and African thought, now mean that creolization can no longer suffice as the highest expression of counter-hegemonic thought. This is further buttressed by the fact that the political philosophy of Ancient Afro-Egypt which existed long before Plato, gave Europe a philosophical consciousness of itself.

In this regard therefore, whilst G.K. Lewis and Denis Benn made useful contributions to Caribbean thought through their early attempts at assimilating Caribbean political writings, further effort is needed to move Caribbean thought beyond the creole anchor to which it had been tied by these writers. Similarly, whilst Paget Henry was correct both in seeing Caribbean thought as being concerned with overcoming projects of European hegemony and in seeing Caribbean philosophy as operating on radically different epistemological foundations than those of Europe, the actual method of transcending European thought, remained unmapped. Belle's key, thus remained unturned in the lock. What is required is for the uncovering of the concrete cultural differences separating the European consciousness from that of its Caribbean challengers. It is only through this process of 'knowing thyself' that Caribbean thought can truly achieve the task of overcoming European epistemological hegemony.

Notes

1. Gordon Lewis, *Main Currents in Caribbean Thought: The Historical Evolution of Caribbean Society in Its Ideological Aspects, 1492–1900*. (Baltimore: Johns Hopkins University Press, 1983).
2. Ibid., ix.
3. Ibid., 28.
4. Lewis, *Main Currents;* Denis Benn, *The Growth and Development of Political Ideas in the Caribbean 1774–1983* (Kingston: Institute of Social and Economic Research, 1987); and *The Caribbean: An Intellectual History, 1774–2003* (Kingston: Ian Randle Publishers, 2004); Paget Henry, *Caliban's Reason: Introducing Afro-Caribbean Philosophy* (New York: Routledge, 2000).
5. Henry, *Caliban's Reason*, 3.
6. George Belle, 'Against Colonialism: Political Theory and Re-Colonisation in the Caribbean' (Unpublished paper presented at the *Conference on Caribbean Culture*, Mona, Jamaica, March 3–5, 1996). Published in *Caribbean Political Thought: Theories of the Post Colonial State*, ed. Aaron Kamugisha (Kingston: Ian Randle Publishers, 2013) 174–85.
7. Ibid., 2.
8. Marimba Ani, *Yurugu: An African-Centered Critique of European Cultural Thought and Behaviour* (New Jersey: Africa World Press, 1994).
9. Rupert Lewis, 'The Writing of Caribbean Political Thought.' Review of *Main Currents in Caribbean Thought: The Historical Evolution of Caribbean Society in its Ideological Aspects, 1492–1900*, by Gordon K. Lewis and *The Growth and Development of Political Ideas in the Caribbean 1774–1983*, by Denis Benn. *Caribbean Quarterly* 36, nos. 1 & 2 (1990)153–65; Belle, 'Against Colonialism', 174–85.
10. Lewis, *Main Currents*, 24.
11. Ibid., 25.
12. Ibid.
13. Ibid., 27.
14. Ibid.
15. Ibid.
16. See Belle, 'Against Colonialism'.
17. Lewis, *Main Currents*, 314.
18. Ibid., 295.
19. See Benn, *Growth and Development*; and *The Caribbean: An Intellectual History*.
20. Benn, *The Caribbean*, ix.

21. Ibid., xi.
22. Ibid., ix.
23. Ibid., xi.
24. Ibid., 237.
25. Cheikh Anta Diop, *Civilization or Barbarism: An Authentic Anthropology* (New York: Lawrence Hill Books, 1991).
26. Henry, *Caliban's Reason*, 8.
27. Ibid., 9.
28. Ibid.,13.
29. Rupert Lewis, 'The Writing of Caribbean Political Thought'.
30. Belle, 'Against Colonialism'.
31. Rupert Lewis, 'The Writing of Caribbean Political Thought', 154.
32. Ibid., 156.
33. Ibid., 156–57.
34. Martin Bernal, *Black Athena: The Afro-Asiatic Roots of Classical Civilisation. Vol. 1 – The Fabrication of Ancient Greece 1785–1985* (New Brunswick, New Jersey: Rutgers University Press, 1987).
35. Rupert Lewis, 'The Writing of Caribbean Political Thought', 157.
36. Belle, 'Against Colonialism'.
37. Ibid., 6.
38. Ibid., 7.
39. Marimba Ani, *Yurugu*.
40. Ibid., 29.
41. Ibid.
42. Ibid.
43. Ibid.
44. Ibid., 30.
45. Ibid.
46. Ibid., 31.
47. Plato, *The Essential Plato*. Edited by Alain De Botton and Translated by Benjamin Jowet (London: The Softback Preview, 1999), 18.
48. Ani, *Yurugu*, 35–36.
49. Diop, *Civilization or Barbarism*.
50. Ibid., 112–13.
51. Henry, *Caliban's Reason*, 1.
52. Ibid., 2.
53. Paget Henry, 'Rastafarianism and the Politics of Dread', in *Existence in Black: An Anthology of Black Existential Philosophy*, ed., Lewis R. Gordon (New York: Routledge, 1997), 157–64.
54. Ibid., 159.
55. See Rex Nettleford, *Inward Stretch Outward Reach: A Voice From the Caribbean* (New York: Caribbean Diaspora Press, 1995), 80–90.
56. See Diop, *Civilization or Barbarism*, 112–13.
57. See Bernal, *Black Athena*, 1987.
58. See Ani, *Yurugu*, 1994.
59. See Diop, *Civilization or Barbarism*.

60. See Maulana Karenga, 'Towards a Sociology of Ma'atian Ethics', in *Egypt Revisited*, ed. Ivan Van Sertima, 352–95 (New Brunswick: Transaction Publishers, 1993).
61. See Theophile Obenga, 'African philosophy of the Pharonic Period', in *Egypt Revisited*, ed. Ivan Van Sertima, 286–324 (New Brunswick: Transaction Publishers, 1993).
62. See Jacob Carruthers, *MDW NTR: Divine Speech – A Historiographical Reflection of African Deep Thought From the Time of the Pharaohs to the Present* (London: Karnak House, 1995).

4 | *A Lens of a Different Colour:*
Gordon K. Lewis, Postmodernity and Cuban Antislavery Narratives

Claudette M. Williams

Reading Cuban antislavery fiction through the optic of Gordon K. Lewis's empirically-grounded *Main Currents in Caribbean Thought* follows the precedent set by Lewis himself when he drew on some fictional texts to inform his analysis of the Caribbean's ideological history. Lewis spent a mere three pages of this work on the contributions that nineteenth-century Cuban novelists made to the antislavery cause. Yet many of his general observations about slavery, and the ideologies that sustained or opposed it, find echoes in the fictional works. Without dislodging existing perspectives on Cuban antislavery narratives, this chapter demonstrates how Lewis's all-inclusive map of Caribbean antislavery ideology may help to expand and deepen our understanding of this literary tradition.

Antislavery narratives have been widely recognized as invaluable sources of historical information on slavery in Cuba. My interest in them, however, is as literary creations that allow the slavery experience to come alive for the reader. Like the entire colonial Caribbean experience, these compositions have been studied almost exhaustively since the 1970s by both local and international reviewers. Commentators have been mainly polarized along two nationalist lines. For the most part the Cuban response has been generous, celebrating the works' revolutionary significance but ignoring some of their counter-productive elements. On the other hand, reviewers of an Afrocentric or Black Nationalist persuasion outside of Cuba view them with suspicion at best, and at worst diminish or deny their pedigree as a form protest against slavery. With this binary division of views the question that arises is whether interpretation should focus on where these narratives fall short or highlight what may be regarded as their constructive achievements. To arrive at an adequate answer one needs to take into account both full-length high-profile novels (such as Cirilo Villaverde's *Cecilia Valdés* (1839 and 1882)[1] and Gertrudis Gómez de

Avellaneda's *Sab* (1841),[2] and those less well known shorter narratives that have been dwarfed by them, such as *Petrona y Rosalía* (1838)[3] and *Romualdo, uno de tantos* (1869).[4] A close reading will serve to illuminate certain blind spots in earlier appraisals of these texts, and to expose other possible meanings that emerge when they are viewed in the light of contemporary thinking about the art of representation.

Evidence from the period indicates that such compositions were viewed as threatening to the political establishment. Strict censorship by the Spanish colonial authorities limited their circulation; after a clandestine first appearance, most remained unpublished until the first half of the twentieth century, and even later in some cases. All were written before abolition, and their authors presented an early and blatant example of the non-literary use of literature which is a common Latin American occurrence. Because I am concerned with works of fiction in this analysis, I have not included the one known Cuban slave autobiography written by Juan Francisco Manzano, although it seems to have provided the novelists with some real-life fodder for their fiction.

These antislavery novelists formed part of a minority group of white Creole liberal intellectuals in Cuba's ruling class, who represented the main opposition to both slavery and the slave trade, and who were thereby pitted against the sugar planters and merchants. These intellectuals were also influenced by and collaborated with the international abolitionist campaign. Mirroring the diversity of views in the antislavery movement itself is the absence of ideological unity within the group. Some members were propelled by political expediency (dissatisfaction with Spanish colonial rule and a desire for independence); others by the imperatives of Christian humanitarianism, and yet others by economic interest, tribal loyalties or Negrophobia. Some were slave owners. All were separated from the enslaved by a social and racial gulf and felt the need to establish the credibility of their undertaking. Presentation of enlightened self-images was integral to their project. Their opposition to slavery ranges from strident to subtle and from reluctant to radical.

Inseparable from the discussion of the early novels is the debate surrounding the modes and conditions of their production. In the first decades of the nineteenth century, literary *tertulias* (gatherings) organized by Domingo del Monte, famous patron of the literary arts, provided the main forum for writers and literary *aficionados* to engage in discussions of slavery and other social issues. Del Monte's writers' club served as incubator for the early antislavery narratives of the period. As leader and mentor, he had great influence over the shape and content of the literary creations of the young and sometimes inexperienced writers in his group, but it is also evident that his influence informed but did not completely control their compositions.

I use the concept of postmodernity to frame my analysis of these narratives, based on ideas and themes that recur in the theoretical discussions. Avoiding the variant term postmodernism with its connotation of a codified theory, I prefer the looser designation postmodernity (or the postmodern age) as an umbrella term that covers a general way of thinking which, though not new or exclusive to the period, has become fashionable in Western artistic and intellectual culture since the 1980s. The postmodern 'mind-set' embraces formerly outlawed events such as dissonance, ambivalence, instability and unresolved tension; it promotes peaceful coexistence of different and even contradictory ways of being, thinking and seeing. The postmodern perspective prefers shades and nuances to polarities and dichotomies, an ethos that is summed up in this statement by Antonio Benítez-Rojo, a Cuban writer who went to the US in 1980 and worked in academia until his death in 2005: 'There cannot be any single truth, but instead there are many practical and momentary ones, truths without beginnings or ends, local truths, displaced truths, provisional and peremptory truths of a pragmatic nature.'[5]

In his 1989 classic *The Repeating Island: The Caribbean and the Postmodern Perspective*, Benítez-Rojo has customized an assortment of postmodern ideas to fit the specifics of a global Caribbean cultural context, helping us in the process to appreciate the limitations of any fundamentalist approach to the region's reality. Although the works I am dealing with precede the age of postmodernity by more than a century, they yield new insights when subjected to postmodern scrutiny.

Lewis is one postcolonial scholar whose vision of the dynamics of Caribbean slavery accords well with general postmodern principles. But he is not alone; he is joined by other scholars like H. Orlando Patterson, Rebecca Scott, Franklin Knight and Barbara Bush. Heterogeneity and complexity are the defining themes of the story of slavery as told by Lewis and scholars of similar vintage. To a remarkable extent, the antislavery views of the colonial novelists support many of the findings of these postcolonial scholars. My operational definition of the term *antislavery* in this context allows it to be applied to any literary gesture, however tenuous or indirect, whose implication or effect is to destabilize or subvert slavery's ideological foundation.

There is a tendency to collapse all the narratives into a single category and to speak about them in the same breath. But all antislavery narratives are not one antislavery narrative. Taken together they reflect the heterogeneous and multifaceted institution that was slavery. Every type of slave and slave owner is featured. And although commentators have referred to them as if they were all stock characters and static stereotypes, the novelists treat them as complex human beings liable to change over time. Hence the cases of the 'negrification' of the mulatto slave by her African-born lover and the proselytizing of the young slave master who converts to the cause of abolition.

Many studies of these narratives also turn the spotlight on the slave characters, and leave the representations of the enslavers mainly in the shadows. But as noted by Patterson, (in reference to another colonial context) 'an examination of the lives of the slaves must begin with an understanding of the socio-economic order of their masters, since within this wider framework the slaves were only one element, albeit the most important, in the total structure and functioning of the slave system.'[6] And for the novelists themselves, the enslavers are of equal and sometimes greater interest than the enslaved.

Rather than the homogeneity often ascribed erroneously to slave owners, the fictional portraits reflect the class-based rivalries, political antagonisms, and xenophobic obsessions by which they were divided historically. Slave owners are also separated by temperament and motivation: the repentant and the recalcitrant, the benevolent and the brutal and the occasional case of the slave owner in whom brutal and benevolent personas coexist. Gender difference is also played out among them with the spark of compassion in a slave master offsetting the intransigent cruelty of his wife, or where the older slave master's discreet sexual exploitation of the enslaved woman (accompanied by a token regard for her humanity), contrasts with his rakish son's vicious sexual aggression. Glimmers of generational difference also manifest where the conservative slave mistress is pitted against her more progressive son. The novels attest repeatedly to pervasive instances of coerced sex. But the incidence of consensual sex (though treated only sporadically) is not completely ignored, and support Lewis's claim that sex 'took the edge off the endemic hatred between white master and black slave.'[7]

Richard Jackson[8] is a noted pioneer in the study of these narratives. He bemoans the fact that the writers devote too much time to the cruelty of the masters. And it is true that some stories dwell *ad nauseam* on slavery's horrors. But accenting their sadistic cruelty is the authors' way of pathologizing the slave owner's personality, as Lewis describes it, thus making a powerful antislavery statement. Jackson's distress can be further alleviated if one is attentive to the psychographic profiles of the enslaver class which are a significant focus of these writers and a collateral aspect of their antislavery agenda. Their approach accords well with the psychological dimension of Lewis's perspective of the slave-owning class. Lewis observes that the vast body of documentary colonial literature enables the student to catch glimpses of the self-image of the plantocracy. 'For the essence of ideology,' he maintains, 'is perceived self-image, how any societal group sees its function within the general matrix of the social structure, how it sees other groups, and what particular arguments it produces as a means of self-justification.'[9] Probing the inner recesses of their minds allows the novelists to undercut the awesome power of slave owners by casting them in the role of slaves themselves, enthralled by their neuroses, paranoia, and insecurity. Their anxious efforts to crush the slightest act of disobedience or insubordination in the enslaved, their fear of granting them even the slightest freedom, appear to be neither whimsical nor simply perverse. Rather, they signal the precariousness of their hold over the slaves.

Depictions of the enslaved also manifest the diversity and complexity of slavery to which Lewis draws attention in *Main Currents*. Jackson is right when he chides the authors for devoting too little time to slave rebellion. At a casual glance, the recurring images of submissive slaves in these narratives seem to justify such a criticism. Most authors avoid the figure of the robust rebel slave, purportedly heeding the call for moderation by their patron Del Monte. But it is also true that sufficient attention has not been paid to the instances of overt and outright slave resistance in their fictional universe. The anxious search for radical expressions of slave resistance has also blinded many a reviewer to the pervasive signs of covert slave defiance in these works. Though the novelists take account of the myriad accommodations that slaves were forced to make, they do not construe the latter's silence as a sign of loyalty to their owners or as complicity in their own victimhood, as some reviewers have argued. Absence of verbal protest is not attributed to lack of an antislavery consciousness. Repeatedly sabotaging the appearance of accommodation, the authors sense in the depths of the slaves' soul the muffled noise of discontent, even where they lacked the ability to express it verbally or the opportunity to translate promise into action. Thus, as an antislavery gesture, the authors put paid to the notion of the slave as a mindless work machine.

While some fictional slaves do not contemplate the option of open rebellion, they use other strategies to express discontent or to influence their fate. Conscious of the meagre legal provisions for improving their condition, some slave characters seek or contemplate a change of owners. Similarly, though not representing the literal acts of *petit marronage* such as self-administered poison and abortion, for which female slaves were famous, a similar self-sacrificial spirit is incarnated in the female slave who *chooses* to surrender to the sexual desires of her master, hoping to save her slave lover's life. The fictional slaves show their understanding of their owners' mentality, and exploit the latter's ego-satisfaction needs by masking their true feelings and feigning subservience. Surrender to their owners' tyranny does not quell their enduring desire for the dignity of freedom. The slave lovers who do not run away are not portrayed as instinctive cowards; they contemplate avenues of escape, and reject them through a process of prudent reasoning. Lewis reminds us of the dilemma of such slaves: 'Those who openly rebelled, after all, were always a minority, if only because the penalties for revolt – being broken on the wheel or literally roasted alive…were in themselves sufficient to deter all but the most intransigent.' And he concludes in his trademark pithy style: 'Not every slave was a Spartacus, or even potentially one.'[10] Nonetheless, Lewis gives primacy to the instances of their psychological resistance and secret defiance of their owners' despotism. His view finds an echo in the antislavery authors for whom the inviolability of the slaves' free will marks the frontiers of their bondage and, equally, the limits of the master's power – a challenge to the Marxist theory of the dominant ideology's stranglehold over the subordinate classes.

The antislavery significance residing in the representation of slave culture is yet another oversight in appraisals of the subversive content of these narratives. Lewis and others, however, include under the antislavery rubric, the ideology immanent in African survivals that fuelled different types of resistance in the minds and actions of the slaves. In this regard, antislavery author Anselmo Suárez y Romero, who wrote his novel *Francisco* in 1838[11] was ahead of his time. His recording of unique African cultural retentions in the everyday life of the field slaves is remarkable, as is his sensitivity to the resilience of their African cultural practices as a metaphorical manifestation of the slaves' defiance of their bondage. Given the anti-African tenor of the dominant proslavery world view at this time in Cuba's history, the absence of any trace of white ethnocentrism in Suárez's comparison of African folk forms to those of Euro-Creole culture is outstanding. The approving tone in this author's language suggests openness to the slaves' cultural difference and a will to understand it in African terms. Suárez's enlightened vision is a far cry from the jaundiced perspective of the Havana sugar planters who in 1790 reported to the Spanish king that their barbaric African dances were the slaves' favourite form of entertainment.[12] Moreover, his implicit comparison of the slaves' distinct and vibrant African-derived counterculture with the cultural void in the Euro-Creole world also amounts to a tacit undermining of the ideological pillars of slavery.

Returning to my initial question of whether interpretation should focus on the shortcomings or the positive achievements of these stories, the postmodern answer is that it must do not one or the other, but both. The counter-productive consequence of anti-black racism in these so-called liberal authors has been a major irritant to some reviewers. Lewis alludes to this paradox when he notes that the emergent Cuban bourgeoisie embraced the liberal philosophies of their European counterparts, adding racist prejudice to their class-based bias. Thus, the narratives are not easily reduced to either unproblematic liberalism or unequivocal conservatism. It is possible to decry the authors' Eurocentric leaning and recalcitrant racism while recognizing the value, however minimal or unwitting, in their critical perspective. In this regard, Antonio Benítez-Rojo's thinking about Caribbean cultural studies is apposite: 'No perspective of human thought – whether premodern, modern or postmodern – can by itself define the Caribbean's complex sociocultural interplay…Every Caribbean person knows that the Caribbean is much more than a system of binary oppositions.'[13]

Neither as a corpus nor as individual works do these compositions satisfy the fundamentalist wish for a master narrative featuring chronically heroic slave rebels and terminally villainous slave owners. The authors were well aware that slavery did not always present the enslaved with opportunities for heroism. In the postmodern age, flawed or modest heroes can find accommodation alongside exemplary ones. If their representations of the enslaved as submissive and weak are regarded as dubious antislavery statements, the authors' unflattering portraits of the enslaver qualify as a more unequivocal measure of antislavery value. The corollary of the powerless slaves' hidden strength is the veiled vulnerability of their enslavers.

We may choose to read only the tragedy of slavery in these narratives, or we may expand the lens we use to view them – not to minimize the tragedy but to show how the authors subtly undermine the foundations of the institution. With its openness to dissonance, a postmodern reading is not compelled to either sanitize the stories or smooth over their contradictions. A postmodern world view is unperturbed by the coexistence of residual prejudice and strong opposition to the practice of slavery in some authors. Neither is one compelled to interpret these literary endeavours as either self-serving or altruistic; instead they may be qualified as both. In a similar spirit, no code of silence need be imposed on the stories of slave passivity or submission; these stories exist side by side with others that tell of the slaves' struggle to maintain a human identity under a system whose aim was to dehumanize them. Acknowledgement of the minor signs of covert rebellion to relieve the bleak picture of slave passivity must be accompanied by recognition of the faint redemptive glimmers of light in the malevolent world of the slave owner.

While it is important to give pride of place to Cuba's two available slave accounts of their experience, one ought not to discount the value of the outsider perspective that the Euro-Creole writers of antislavery fiction provide. Their narratives are testimony to their capacity for empathy and their will to compensate for their limited knowledge by imagining what slavery might have meant to the slave and using these imaginings to fuel their antislavery protest. Locating the stories within their historical context, Lewis notes quite candidly that

> the novelists...managed to compose a morally inspired social analysis critical of the slavery institution. To have asked them to have done more would be to assume on their part a supernatural ability to transcend the limitations of the time and the society in which they had to live and survive.[14]

These Euro-Creole authors had come a long way from the eighteenth-century racist European world view that fed Edward Long's belief that an orang-utan husband would not be a dishonour to a Hottentot woman. They were miles away from the thinking that necessitated the English abolitionist Granville Sharp's search for scientific evidence to prove that the African Negro was a human being and not an animal. By recognizing the slaves' humanity, and in some cases by making this theme into their anthem, Cuban antislavery authors were disrupting the dominant ideology on which slavery was built.

When viewed collectively, the narratives tell a humanized version of Cuba's social and political history. In this regard, one may part company with Lewis, who complains that 'the economic side of slavery is hardly ever looked at' and that 'the plots, invariably, revolve around family domestic situations rather than general social-class or racial-caste situations.'[15] For in judging a literary work one has to distinguish between sociological value and sociological method. Given the symbiotic relationship between family and society, the authors who represented domestic situations were obliquely representing the society. It is precisely their translation of sociological event into lived individual human experience that gives these narratives their special value.

Notes

1. Cirilo Villaverde, *Cecilia Valdés* (1889 and 1832; repr., Havana: Editorial Letras Cubanas, 2002).
2. Gertrudis Gómez de Avellaneda, *Sab* (1841; repr., Havana: Instituto Cubano del Libro, 1973).
3. Felix Tanco y Bosmeniel, *Petrona y Rosalía* (1838; repr., Havana: Editorial Letras Cubanas, 1980).
4. Francisco Calcagno, *Romualdo, uno de tantos.* (1869; repr., in *Noveletas Cubanas,* ed. Imeldo Alvarez, Havana: Editorial de Arte y Literatura, 1977), 279–388.

5. Antonio Benítez-Rojo, *The Repeating Island: The Caribbean and the Postmodern Perspective*. Trans. James E. Maraniss (Durham, NC: Duke University Press, 1996), 151.
6. Orlando Patterson, *The Sociology of Slavery* (London: Granada Publishing Ltd., 1973), 15.
7. Gordon K. Lewis, *Main Currents in Caribbean Thought* (Baltimore: Johns Hopkins University Press, 1983), 141.
8. Richard Jackson, *The Black Image in Latin American Literature* (Albuquerque: University of New Mexico Press, 1976).
9. Lewis, *Main Currents*, 108.
10. Ibid., 176.
11. Anselmo Suárez y Romero, *Francisco,* (1839; repr., Havana: Publicaciones del Ministerio de Educación, Dirección de Cultura, 1947).
12. Gloria Garcia, *La esclavitud desde la esclavitud* (Havana: Instituto Cubano del Libro, 1996), 71.
13. Benítez-Rojo, *The Repeating Island*, 295.
14. Lewis, *Main Currents*, 236.
15. Ibid.

5 | *Opening the Canon:*
The Place of Theology in Caribbean Intellectual Thought

Delroy A. Reid-Salmon

Introduction

Discourses on Caribbean intellectual thought are undertaken without recourse to theology. Given that much study has been done on the role of religion in the making of Caribbean society,[1] theology has not been considered as playing a pivotal role nor viewed as an essential intellectual component. The normative practice is to marginalize, disregard and dismiss theology as unimportant rather than to consider it as having any relevance to intellectual discourse and public life. This practice of exclusion and disengagement is not only evident in the absence of course offerings in theology as a discipline in any department but also in the absence of any teaching faculty in the discipline of theology at the University of the West Indies (UWI), which is considered the premier academic institution in the Caribbean.

Whereas the denominational related institutions are the ones offering the study of this subject, such as the Ecumenical United Theological College of the West Indies; the Roman Catholic St Michael's Seminary; the Evangelical Jamaica Theological Seminary and Caribbean Graduate School of Theology; The Seventh Day Adventist Northern Caribbean University, and others throughout the region, it demonstrates the marginalization of theology in mainstream Caribbean intellectual life. Is it reasonable to conclude that this peripheral status of theology reflects the practice of the separation of church and academy or of religion and reason? This is unlikely to be the case, given, for example, the presence and prominence of religious buildings such as chapels located on the various university campuses, which symbolize the religious life of university constituencies.[2]

The marginalization of theology in Caribbean intellectual thought must be understood within its social and intellectual context. It is, however, beyond the scope of this work to discuss the context of this marginalization. Attention, nonetheless, should be called to the fact that UWI as the foremost institution and standard of intellectual life in the Caribbean,[3] may be accountable for the marginalization of theology as a discipline in Caribbean intellectual tradition. One possible reason for this marginalization could be the period in history when the university was established.[4] It was during the so-called 'postmodern' period when privatization of faith was one of its definitive characteristics and normative practices.[5] Consequently, theology would not have been regarded as an appropriate discipline of study in this new kind of university system.[6]

It is true, of course, with the separation of faith and reason, that from its inception, the UWI sought to be an inclusive institution. Harry Goulbourne points out this definitive intent in the constitution or charter of the university. It states: 'No religious, political or racial test shall be imposed or required of any person in order to entitle him or her to be a student or member of the university or to occupy any position in or on the staff of the University....'[7]

But what is particularly noteworthy, is that despite this clearly defined purpose to be an inclusive institution, the university excludes religion as a discipline of study. Notwithstanding this practice, the university gives academic accreditation to theological institutions such as the Anglican Codrington College in Barbados and the Roman Catholic college St John Vianney, in Trinidad and Tobago and others that have been mentioned already. The precise reasons for this contradictory practice remain to be discovered. Thus, it is reasonable to ask if this is due to the religious nature of theology. Should this be the case, then it is even more important for the inclusion of theology as an academic discipline in UWI, in that religion has played a definitive role as an agent of decolonization[8] in the formation and development of Caribbean society. What this suggests is that while the notion of the separation of faith and reason speaks of the separation of theology from the academy, it does not mean the separation of theology from intellectual life.

As indicated above, the ambiguity surrounding the place of theology in society can be related to the notion of religious practice as a private affair. The belief is that theology deals with matters of private life and not public issues. This belief is not only erroneous but at a much more profound level, raises the issue of privatization of life which threatens the welfare of the common good and civic life[9] by undermining commonly held beliefs, values and convictions that define and nurture civil society.

Calling for theology as a discipline in Caribbean intellectual thought, is not to suggest that theology should occupy any special place or enjoy any special privileges in this tradition. Indeed, it is reasonable to ask why theology and not religious studies, when there are a variety of religions in the Caribbean.[10] Taking this concern into account, this essay is not about religious studies. Yet, it warrants that a distinction be made between religious studies and theology. Religious studies on the one hand, is the study of religious phenomenon.[11] Theology on the other hand, as is discussed later in this chapter, is the study about God's way in relating to humanity in a particular social and historical context.

Precisely for this reason, this work is not about privileging any form of theology over any religion, but providing a theological interpretation of life predicated on the notion that theology exists before all religions and is an inclusive intellectual discipline that originated in antiquity.[12] It calls for commitment to a way of life in solidarity with the poor and oppressed and to working towards the realization of the transformation of society for the good of all humanity and creation.[13]

Certainly, from a theological perspective, religious pluralism does not address the ultimate cause of evil in the world. In this regard, theology is not only radical to point out evil but seeks to reconcile the understanding of God with suffering and evil and demonstrates, as this study argues, the possibility of an alternative form of life in history. It is on this basis theology is not only relevant but must be afforded its proper place in society.

The practice of compartmentalizing and attributing a marginal significance to religion, particularly theology, reflects a deficiency in Caribbean intellectual thought. The time has come for critical reflection on the relationship between theology and other intellectual disciplines. The rapid growth of a globalized world and the relentless advancement of knowledge and insatiable pursuit of learning are indications that theology's engagement with the development of the society's intellectual tradition is long overdue. By this engagement, I do not mean the all-important descriptive[14] and critical interdisciplinary study or mere conversation with other disciplines of learning. Instead, I mean the constructive endeavour in seeking, identifying and asserting the place of theology within Caribbean intellectual thought.

This study, then, demonstrates that although Caribbean intellectual tradition is fully established,[15] the tradition is incomplete without the inclusion of theology. I am contending for the 'opening of the Caribbean intellectual canon' realizing that this is a very daunting task. Nevertheless, I maintain that theology is a constitutive element in Caribbean intellectual thought, and I therefore attempt to explicate this thesis by providing a working definition of the key terms, and an explanatory excursus of the subject. I conclude with a descriptive discussion on the task of theology in Caribbean intellectual thought.

Theology Defined

Theology has various definitions.[16] Theology is the self-conscious study about God that seeks to interpret faith[17] — beliefs and symbols — for contemporary society. Others say that it is critical reflection on the life of the oppressed from the perspective of faith in God.[18] Still, some hold that theology is the intellectual pursuit about the meaning of God and God's relationship with humanity and creation through the prism of one's history, experience and context.[19] The meaning of theology I propose, however, is that which seeks to answer the questions of the meaning of life — Who am I? Why am I here? Where am I going? In other words, theology is an intellectual discipline that addresses the issue of human identity, purpose and destiny.

Towards A Definition of Caribbean Intellectual Thought

By Caribbean intellectual thought, I mean the body of ideas and thought that shape and inform the formation and development of Caribbean society. These ideas are born out of the Caribbean experience and become both the tools and framework for interpreting the nature and meaning of life for Caribbean people.[20]

The current nature of Caribbean intellectual thought, however, as represented in the standard texts or presumably, canonical texts,[21] consists primarily of socio-political ideas but has omitted the theological. Taking into account this observation, I detect, for example, within Gordon Lewis's seminal text, *Main Currents in Caribbean Thought*, theological ideas, which I insist are essential components in Caribbean intellectual thought.

Caribbean Intellectual Thought and Theology

While *Main Currents in Caribbean Thought* is not a text on religion or theology, Lewis's approach to Caribbean intellectual thought acknowledges theology as a constitutive factor in the development of Caribben society. Lewis expresses some theological ideas in the context of his broader argument of anti-slavery ideology but specifically the ideology of enslaved religion. He recognizes the place of theology in Caribbean intellectual thought by arguing that religion plays a role in the making of the Caribbean society. While he did not identify any particular task of theology, Lewis shows that in the making of Caribbean society, the enslaved Africans equally contributed to such creation as did the European enslavers. Lewis states:

> For if the European colonizer built this 'new world,' so did the colonized African. Pre-eminently, that new world – denied expression in either technology or poetical structures – found its classic, architectonic expression in the proliferating secret Negro religious cults [*Black religion*] of Americas....[22]

As Lewis argues, European and African religious ideologies and thought have a conflictual relationship[23] but they both contributed to the making of Caribbean society. Continuing his description of this conflict of world views, Lewis observes that Caribbean society was created as

> European religious ideology, - bibliolatrous, closed, monotheistic, intolerant inquisitorial - was thus faced with the challenge of an Afro-American [*Black*] religious ideology – open, congregationalist, ecumenical, pantheistic, and ultimately democratic – both fighting for the soul and spirit of Caribbean masses.[24]

By this statement, Lewis underscores the pivotal role religion played in building Caribbean society, indirectly identifies the essential element of theology in Caribbean intellectual thought and attests to the theological world view of these makers of Caribbean society.

This world view asserts that liberation is the essence of theology. Liberation is not only from slavery but from the ideology that devises and divides humanity into a hierarchy of masters and slaves, rich and poor. The contents of liberation include the sanctity of the human being and the equality of all persons. Lewis states that these notions 'became slowly, generation after generation, the final corrosive force that challenged the very basic assumptions of the slave-based order.'[25] By this remark, it shows that Lewis is aware that theology can be a tool to deconstruct ideological and cultural hegemony.

Lewis makes another important observation concerning the element of theology in Caribbean intellectual thought. He observes that the antislavery missionaries were not necessarily radicals and revolutionaries. Lewis describes this unawareness convincingly; 'The missionaries themselves may not have realized the ultimate implications of the doctrine of Christian liberty that they preached.'[26] This is a very insightful observation about the nature of theology but it is not the focus of this work. The concern is the place of theology in Caribbean intellectual thought beginning with the task of theology.

The Tasks of Theology

Theology has many tasks but here I discuss three which are essential. Theology as an academic discipline is more than its contents. This dynamic inter-play between form and content is one of the distinctive features of doing theology in the Caribbean context. This approach, as Caribbean theologian Burchell Taylor notes, 'represents a new way of doing theology in contrast with how it had been done in the traditional centres of Europe and North America.'[27] While doing theology is contextual, equally important is the view that theology begins with the self-awareness of God who is both the object and the subject of theology.

Theology does not only concern the being of God but also the meaning of human life and destiny. Theology has something to say about human existence pertaining to but not limited to suffering, poverty, crime, disasters, as well as about equally related public issues like imperialism, slavery, colonialism, capitalism, democracy, and globalization. Taylor offers a concise explanation of this issue. He reveals that 'this means in essence that the theological project is itself an active and dynamic response to contextual realities in terms of the life situation and historical experiences of the people.'[28] Here, Taylor addresses the contradictions between faith and human existence which lead us to consider the first tasks of theology in Caribbean intellectual thought.

Pursuit for Truth

The first task of theology in Caribbean intellectual thought is the commitment to the life of the mind. Theology is not a repetition of beliefs or speculation about knowledge but a relentless pursuit for truth or 'faith seeking understanding.'[29] This perspective presupposes that learning and faith are inseparable. For example, Noel Erskine, writing of the Caribbean theologian Horace Russell as an intellectual, argues that Russell understands the 'intellectual life as a calling from community and church on one's life.'[30] For Erskine, Russell departs from the model of separation of faith from the life of the mind not only in his academic achievements but through his vocation of relating faith to the social existential condition of human beings in order to create the context for emancipation and the fullness of life.[31]

This suggests that theology helps to better understand the human condition. This understanding of the task of theology debunks the myth that it has no place in public life and in intellectual inquiry. This task of theology involves stripping away and exposing pretensions, distortions and falsehoods about life. Interestingly, there is the precedent of a tradition of theology confronting social, structural and systemic issues represented in ground-breaking texts on Caribbean theology in works such as Idris Hamid's *Troubling the Waters*, Noel Erskine's *Decolonizing Theology*[32] and Lewin Williams's *Caribbean Theology*. In light of this tradition, Caribbean thought cannot be regarded as a full-fledged intellectual tradition without the inclusion of theology.

Analytical Tool

The task of theology is more than the pursuit of truth in order to understand how to relate faith to public life. The task is also analytical, critically engaging structures, systems, ideologies, values, policies and practices by asking questions about the causes and reasons for their existence. Against this background, theology is in a prophetic dialogical engagement with any dominant intellectual tradition in deconstructing social, political and religious hegemony as expressed through the oppressive systems and structures of institutions and world powers. Theology asserts that the beliefs, values and practices of these powers are not normative where they define and determine the standards and contents of intellectual discourse. For example, the dominant intellectual tradition in the Caribbean has not seen the need to critique whiteness as a symbol of the ideal good, beauty and privilege.[33] For this reason, it is imperative for theology to deconstruct discourses and re-image intellectual traditions that distort and misrepresent the truth.

This critical engagement is what historian Horace Russell attempts to do in a very important but nascent work on black identity, 'The Emergence of the Christian Black: The Making of a Stereotype.' Russell examines how the Western intellectual tradition created its notion of the black human being. This was done as a symbol of the so-called West Indian and as a paradigm for understanding and developing black humanity. For Russell, the British abolitionists attempted to create a new human image of black identity in order to support their cause by regarding black people not as sinful human beings but as fallen savages.[34]

Russell recognizes the problem of this creation of the new human being. He calls attention to creating the model black human being and accepting such persons as humans. Without discussing this distinction, Russell points out that one can create any model person but cannot force its acceptance by others. What this evinces is that while the intellectual tradition created notions of the model person, it does not necessarily mean that this intellectual tradition accepted these same persons as human beings. This reveals inherent systemic institutional racism within this system and internalized racial superiority, which unfortunately, Russell did not address. Above all, why is the need for the acceptance of white people so central to black identity and existence, as evidenced in the contemporary trend of bleaching or whitening of the skin,[35] and the acceptance of Eurocentric beliefs, cultural values and practices, normative?

In dealing with this phenomenon, Russell is remarkably descriptive but not equally constructive. For example, he identifies the attempt of the Western intellectual tradition as represented by the abolitionists and the British missionaries to engender acceptance of black humanity through the creation of free communities or 'Free Villages.' As he notes, 'The events are remarkable because what occurred was not just the settlement of a people or the acculturation of the African but the creation of a new man [*Human being*].'[36]

Russell acknowledges, however, that 'These happenings were sad because for a long time this new man [human being] took his standards from a Europe which had created him.'[37] While this insight calls attention to the problem, it would be even more helpful if he provided an idea of this new human being outside of the European construct. The ideologies and structures of society that degrade and dehumanize any person or people must be vigorously confronted and challenged. For this reason, theology functions as a prophetic analytical tool as it confronts biases and discerns limitations in terms of myopic vision, insular self-understanding and internationalization of Eurocentric values and cosmology with the aim of creating both a wholesome sense of self[38] and a just society. This now leads me to identify the third task of theology in Caribbean intellectual thought.

Constructive Task

Besides addressing the quest for truth and its function as an analytical tool, theology has a constructive task. Given the nature of society, including the diversity of persons, multiplicity of cultures, numerous needs, changing situations and complexity of issues, we can never settle for the idealization of any particular notion of society or way life. To the extent that this is done, it is nothing more than the empty ideological projection of a politics of progress that influences triumphalist aspirations and mistaken notions of creating a just society.

Certainly, the uncritical acceptance of such a way of life as normative is one instance when and where the constructive task of theology is crucial. In this setting, theology is called upon to rigorously interrogate such notions of life. Its primary task is to expose the makings of this kind of life and to reveal how it is sustained and at whose expense. Essentially, this task of theology is not only to deconstruct but to construct and offer new paradigms for thinking about and envisioning a new and humane social order.

In seeking to create a just society, I am aware of the tendency to disregard theological imagination in favour of the socio-historical on the premise that the latter is empirical, whereas the former is abstract or spiritual. While these two approaches differ, they have their own merit as both provide insights into understanding the complexity of human existence. Rather than being opponents, they are both partners in a common cause, as well as being two distinct dimensions of one reality. Unfortunately, scholars have overlooked or disregarded this aspect of the interdisciplinary character of Caribbean intellectual thought.

This perspective is an indication of the exclusion of theology from Caribbean thought. In this regard, theology is called upon to point to a reality greater than and beyond the existing situation and immediate context. Moreover, this task is rooted in the rich heritage and history of the people representing a communal gathering where the past and the present meet. Theology, therefore, emerges out of a particular historical context with the distinct character of reaching forward to having and living in a just world.[39]

This constructive task of theology, in the terms of Paul Tillich, speaks of matters of 'ultimate concerns'[40] – living, death and hope – but this is only a partial perception and portrayal of the truth. Paul, the Christian writer, attests to this claim. 'We see through a glass darkly' (1 Corinthians 13:12). This statement indicates that human vision of life is blurred and limited. Regardless of this limitation, the constructive task of theology works from the perspective of the life beyond history. Affirming this perspective of the task of theology, theologian James Cone notes:

> There is included in liberation the 'not yet,' the vision of a new heaven and a new earth. This simply means that the oppressed have a future not made with human hands but grounded in the liberating promise of God…God has freed us to fight against social and political structures while not being determined by them.[41]

In Cone's claim, theology calls attention to the ultimate destiny of human beings and attests to what God is doing both in history and beyond history.

As I have been discussing, the constructive task of theology concerns the eschatological dimension of reality. It is this dimension of reality that Caribbean theologian Kortright Davis describes as *'Emancipation Still Comin'.'* Arguing that God liberates, Davis adopts Eric Williams's idea of emancipation from above and from below.[42] Davis, however, goes beyond this description of emancipation in asserting that neither of the two aspects of emancipation is adequate to deal with the struggle for the realization of God's purpose. The alternative option, for Davis, is that emancipation is an ongoing process or activity of God in history.[43] Davis expresses this view by stating, 'Faith lives toward the future…It is an eschatological imperative…that the vision of emancipation must be kept alive and pass on to generations yet to come; for this vision has kept hope alive in the crush of numbing hopelessness.'[44]

Undoubtedly, this constructive task of theology would be greatly flawed if it did not take into account the realization of God's purpose of liberation from oppression, transformation of society and salvation of humanity and all creation. For this reason, Caribbean intellectual tradition must be in the forefront of the mission for the fulfilment of God's purpose that includes the struggle against oppression, injustice and evil, not just as an intellectual but as a theological problem in the fierce combat against the legacies of imperialism, slavery and colonialism. On this account, the place of theology in Caribbean intellectual thought is warranted, as theology invites us to envision a new society and inspires us to work towards making it possible.

Conclusion

This work has called attention to the place of theology in Caribbean intellectual thought by underscoring the various tasks of theology. My intent was not to discuss the essence or content of theology but to suggest that theology matters to human life and society. As such, theology cannot be separated from other disciplines of learning, relegated to the sidelines of society or eliminated from public life. Instead, theology is integral to all public life but especially to intellectual life, as is evident in its task to contribute to the creation of a more humane society and to continue the process of restructuring a world consistent with the well-being of all persons.

Notes

1. The works on this issue include, Edward Kamau Brathwaite, *The Development of Creole Society in Jamaica* (Oxford: Clarendon Press, 1971; Reissued – Kingston: Ian Randle Publishers, 2005); Philip Curtin, *Two Jamaicas: The Role of Ideas in a Tropical Colony* (New York: Atheneum Press, 1970); Mary Turner, *Slaves and Missionaries: The Disintegration of Jamaican Slave Society, 1787–1834* (Urbana: University of Illinois Press, 1982); Robert J. Stewart, *Religion and Society in Post-Emancipation Jamaica* (Tennessee: University of Tennessee Press, 1992).
2. The conducting of funeral services at the university chapel at the Mona Campus of the University of the West Indies, as in the case of the professors Carl Stone and Rex Nettleford, are examples of the constitutive place of religion in Caribbean intellectual life.

3. Alistair Hennessy, ed., *Intellectuals in Twentieth-Century Caribbean Volume I: Spectre of a New Class: The Commonwealth Caribbean* (London: Macmillan Press, 1992).
4. For a study on the history and development of the University of the West Indies, see Bridget Brereton, *From Imperial College of the West Indies A History of the St. Augustine Campus, Trinidad and Tobago* (Kingston: Ian Randle Publishers, 2010); Robert Lancashire and Kenneth Magnus, *The Department of Chemistry UWI, Mona: With Emphasis on the Early Years* (Kingston: Ian Randle Publishers, 2010); Suzanne Francis Brown, *Mona, Past and Present: The History and Heritage of the Mona Campus, University of the West Indies* (Kingston: University of the West Indies Press, 2004); Rex M. Nettleford and Philip Sherlock, *The University of the West Indies* (London: Macmillan Caribbean Press, 1990).
5. See John Locke, 'A Letter Concerning Toleration', in *The Portable Enlightenment Reader*, ed. Isaac Kramnick, 81–90 (New York: Penguin Books, 1995).
6. See Isaac Kramnick, ed., *The Portable Enlightenment Reader*, ix–xxiii; 1–38; 75–180.
7. Quoted in Harry Goulbourne, 'The Institutional Contribution of the University of the West Indies to the Intellectual Life of the Anglophone Caribbean', in *Intellectuals in Twentieth-Century Caribbean Volume I: Spectre of a New Class: the Commonwealth Caribbean,* ed. Alistair Hennessy (London: Macmillan Press, 1992), 31–49.
8. See Armando Lampe, *Christianity in the Caribbean: Essay on Church History* (Kingston: University of the West Indies Press, 2001). See also, Robert Stewart, *Religion and Society in Post-Emancipation Jamaica* (Knoxville: University of Tennessee Press, 1992).
9. See Burchell Taylor, *Free For All – A Question of Morality and Community* (Kingston: Grace Kennedy Foundation, 1983). This volume is a bold attempt by a Caribbean thinker to construct an ethic of the common good for Caribbean society. I am concerned, however, what difference it would make had Taylor taken into account or at least drawn from his African heritage for constructing this notion of morality. See for example, Barry Chevannes, *Betwixt and Between: Explorations in an African-Caribbean Mindscape* (Kingston: Ian Randle Publishers, 2006), 141–95. In the African American context, see Peter Paris, *The Spirituality of African Peoples: The Search for a Common Moral Discourse* (Minnesota: Fortress Press, 1995).
10. The most comprehensive work on Caribbean religious studies is Ennis B. Edmonds and Michelle A. Gonzalez, *Caribbean Religious History: An Introduction* (New York: New York University Press, 2010). For an earlier treatment of this phenomenon, consult Dale Bisnauth, *History of Religions in The Caribbean* (Kingston: LMH Publishing Limited, 1998).
11. Cornel West and Eddie S. Glaude, Jr., eds., *African American Religious Thought: An Anthology* (Louisville: Westminster John Knox Press, 2003), xi–xxvi. For a traditional definition of religious studies, see Gayraud S. Wilmore, *African American Religious Studies* (Durham: Duke University Press, 1989), vii–xxii.
12. Robert Hood, *Must God Remain Greek: Afro Cultures and God Talk* (Minneapolis: Fortress Press, 1990), 121–43. For a classic study on this subject, consult John S. Mibiti, *Concepts of God in Africa* (London: SPCK, 1970). European theology acknowledges this perspective of the origin of theology but it does

not, as expected, attribute it to its African beginning. See for example, Jurgen Moltmann, *Experiences in Theology: Ways and Forms of Christian Theology* (Minneapolis: Fortress Press, 2000), 43–44.
13. Michael N. Jagessar, *Full Life All: The Work and Theology of Philip Potter: A Historical Survey and Systematic of Major Themes* (Zoetermeer: Uitegeverij Boekencentrum, 1997).
14. See for example, Richard S. Hillman and Thomas J. D'Agostino, eds., *Understanding the Contemporary Caribbean* (Kingston: Ian Randle Publishers, 2003), 263–304.
15. See Denis Benn, *The Caribbean: An Intellectual History 1774–2008* (Kingston: Ian Randle Publishers, 2004), 263–77.
16. See Theodore W. Jennings, Jr., ed., *The Vocation of the Theologian* (Philadelphia: Fortress Press, 1985). Consult also the following works for representative study on the nature and task of theology, Gustavo Gutierrez, *A Theology of Liberation*, rev. ed. (New York: Orbis Books, 1988), 3–12; David Tracy, *Analogical Imagination: Christian Theology and the Culture of Pluralism* (New York: Crossroad, 1981), 3–98; James Cone, *Black Theology & Black Power*, 20th Anniversary edition (New York: Harper & Row Publishers, 1989); Lewin Williams, *Caribbean Theology* (New York: Peter Lang Publishing, 1994), 59–121; Jurgen Moltmann, *Experiences in Theology: Ways and Forms of Christian Theology* (Minneapolis: Fortress Press, 2000), xiv–xxiv; 3–27; 43–63; Anthony G. Reddie, *Working Against the Grain: Re-imaging Black Theology in the 21st Century* (London: Equinox Publishing, 2008), 17–31.
17. See Moltmann, *Experiences in Theology*, 43–63.
18. See James Cone, *God of the Oppressed* (New York: Seabury Press, 1975).
19. See Ashley Smith, *Emergence From Innocence: Religion, Theology and Development* (Mandeville: Eureka Press, 1991), 14.
20. See Gordon K. Lewis, *Main Currents in Caribbean Thought: The Historical Evolution of Caribbean Society in Its Ideological Aspects, 1492–1900* (Baltimore: Johns Hopkins University Press, 1983); Bill Schwarz, ed., *West Indian Intellectuals in Britain* (Manchester: Manchester University Press, 2003); Benn, *The Caribbean: An Intellectual History*; Silvio Torres-Saillant, *An Intellectual History of the Caribbean* (New York: Palgrave Macmillan, 2006).
21. See for example, Benn, *The Caribbean: An Intellectual History*. Benn is careful to note that he is focusing primarily on the political dimension of Caribbean thought. For a more comprehensive study but still excluding theological thought, consult Torres-Saillant, *An Intellectual History of the Caribbean*. For a more interdisciplinary work, see Kenneth Hall and Denis Benn, eds., *Contending with Destiny: The Caribbean in the 21st Century* (Kingston: Ian Randle Publishers, 2000). What is rather disappointing about this work as a study claiming to reflect the views of the best minds in the region on the challenges facing the Caribbean for the next century and beyond is that it does not include religion – not even theology. Instead, this study only reinforces my argument of the need to regard theology as a constitutive element in Caribbean intellectual thought.
22. Lewis, *Main Currents*, 188. While Lewis recognizes the conflicting character of Caribbean religions, his reference to these as 'cults' is troubling. This reflects the dominant Euro-American bias against African-derived religions. For a

penetrating study on this issue, see Dianne Stewart, *Three Eyes For the Journey* (New York: Oxford University Press, 2005).
23. This is one perspective of the nature of the relationship between African and European world views in the Caribbean. Alternatively, it could be argued that rather than being conflictual, this relationship could be dialectical. For further exploration, see Delroy A. Reid-Salmon, *Home Away From Home: The Caribbean Diasporan Church in the Black Atlantic Tradition* (London: Equinox Publishing Ltd., 2008), 60–75.
24. Lewis, *Main Currents*, 190. For a discussion on the relationship between African religion and European Christianity in the formation of Caribbean religion, see Winston Lawson, *Religion and Race: African and European Roots in Conflict – A Jamaican Testament* (New York: Peter Lang, 1996). See also, Robert Stewart, *Religion and Society in Post-Emancipation Jamaica* (Tennessee: University of Tennessee Press, 1992).
25. Lewis, *Main Currents*, 204.
26. Idid., 205.
27. Burchell Taylor, 'The Theology of Liberation', *Caribbean Quarterly* 37, no. 1 (1991): 19–34.
28. Ibid., 21.
29. Daniel L. Migliore, *Faith Seeking Understanding*, 2nd ed. (Michigan: William B. Eerdmans, 2004), 1–9.
30. Noel Erskine, 'The Making of a Caribbean Intellectual', in *Ministry Perspectives from the Caribbean,* ed. Eron Henry, 24 (New York: Caribbean Diaspora Baptist Clergy Association, 2010).
31. Erskine, 25.
32. See Idris Hamid, *Troubling of the Waters* (San Fernando: Rahaman Printers Ltd., 1973); Noel Leo Erskine, *Decolonizing Theology: A Caribbean Perspective* (New York: Obis Books, 1981).
33. Anthony G. Reddie, *Is God Color-Blind? Insights From Black Theology for Ministry* (Great Britain: SPCK, 2009), 49–51. For an excellent representative theological discussion on whiteness, see James Perkinson, *White Theology: Outing Supremacy in Modernity* (New York: Palgrave, Macmillan, 2004); *Shamanism, Racism and Hip Hop Culture: Essays on White Supremacy and Black Subversion* (New York: Palgrave Macmillan, 2005); Laurie M. Cassidy and Alex Mikulich, eds., *Interrupting White Privilege: Catholic Theologians Break the Silence* (New York: Orbis Books, 2007).
34. Horace Russell, 'The Emergence of the Christian Black: The Making of a Stereotype,' *Jamaica Journal* 16 no. 2 (1983): 58.
35. Annie Paul, 'No Space for Race? The Bleaching of the Nation in Postcolonial Jamaica', in *The African-Caribbean Worldview and the Making of Caribbean Society* ed. Horace Levy (Kingston: The University of the West Indies Press, 2009), 94–113.
36. Russell, 58.
37. Ibid.
38. Smith, 7–14 .
39. Noel Erskine, *From Garvey to Marley* (Gainsville: University of Florida Press, 2005).

40. Paul Tillich, *Systematic Theology*, Vol. 1. (Chicago: The University of Chicago Press, 1951), 11–15.
41. Cone, *God of the Oppressed*, 157.
42. Kortright Davis, *Emancipation Still Comin': Explorations in Caribbean Emancipatory Theology* (New York: Orbis Books, 1990), 130–39.
43. Davis, 144.
44. Davis, 139–40.

6 | Toward Reconstituting Caribbean Identity Discourse from within the Dutch Caribbean Island of Curaçao

Rose Mary Allen

Introduction

In the course of time the Caribbean has produced influential thinkers who have reflected in innovative ways on developments in their societies and who have become recognized both inside the region and beyond. Gordon K. Lewis (1919–1991) was one of those significant thinkers. His seminal book, *Main Currents in Caribbean Thought*[1] expounded his views and ideas on the intellectual history and ideological evolution of the Caribbean, an area of study that still remains relatively under-explored today.

My work here examines knowledge production in the social sciences in the Dutch Caribbean, specifically the way in which the leading indigenous scholarship on the island of Curaçao has produced and developed a discourse on identity and identity formation. I will discuss the relevant home-based ideas of local authors such as René A. Römer (1927–2003), Frank Martinus Arion (1936–), Alejandro F. 'Jandie' Paula (1937–), Valdemar Marcha (1945–) and René V. Rosalia (1948–), as well as other promising scholars in that field of research. The writers that I have chosen are locally based scholars who have contributed to indigenous scholarship by looking critically at their society. Of course, there are others, both Curaçaoan scholars living outside the island and foreign (including Dutch) scholars, who have done important work on Curaçaoan society. I will briefly discuss one of them, Harmannus 'Harry' Hoetink (1931–2005), who is well-recognized for pioneering the study of ethnic relationships in Curaçao.

Römer and Paula started to publish soon after Gordon Lewis began writing about the Caribbean in the mid-1950s and set up Caribbean studies together with scholars such as Robert Manners, Eric Wolf, Sidney Mintz, Paul Blanchard, Eric Williams, C.L.R. James and Elsa Goveia. The Curaçaoan scholars whom I discuss have become part of the Dutch-Caribbean canon and their scholarship has become recognized in the Netherlands. However, they have not become recognized as contributors to Caribbean thought beyond the Dutch-Caribbean academic sphere. My reason for discussing these local scholars is therefore also to try to expose them to a wider regional and international audience. In addition, I am convinced that these authors have brought forward, from a Dutch-Caribbean perspective, new, useful and important aspects of the diverse and complex Caribbean reality. Questions that I deal with include: how have the ideas of these major Dutch-Caribbean thinkers been grounded within their own society, and what is their real and potential contribution to the study of identity and identity construction within the broader Caribbean?

Where are the 'Dutch' Caribbean Islands in the Caribbean Identity Discourse?

Lewis reminds us in the preface of his above-mentioned book that 'one cannot claim to be a full practitioner in Caribbean studies until one writes on the Caribbean as a whole.' In the Winter 1992 newsletter of the Caribbean Studies Association, issued on the occasion of Lewis's passing, several authors emphasized his pan-Caribbean vision. He was recognized as a true Caribbeanist, as the architect of Caribbean studies, based on his vision regarding the Caribbean as a whole.[2]

However, in the study of the region there is still an enormous lacuna in knowledge regarding the Dutch-Caribbean islands, a lacuna which Lewis, too, did not fill in his book. The Conference, *'Freedom and Power in the Caribbean: The Work of Gordon K. Lewis,'* provided an opportunity to dig deeper into Lewis's views and to challenge the relative invisibility of the Dutch Caribbean within the regional scholarly discourse. Several authors do underscore the fact that the Dutch-Caribbean societies are very much neglected within Caribbean studies. In her article 'Rereading the Caribbean through *Dubbelspel* by Frank Martinus Arion', Doris Hambuch[3] points to the fact that Édouard Glissant, in his *Le discours antillais*,[4] provides a table of the Caribbean Diaspora to illustrate how creolization as well as *antillanité* or Caribbeanness have been dispersed, yet fails to include the Dutch Caribbean subregion.

Ineke Phaf states that to anyone familiar with the cultural tradition and complexity of the Caribbean, it seems inexplicable that Surinam and the so-called Dutch Antilles (the islands) are 'undiscovered spots, not only in women's literature but also in the general panorama of world culture.'[5] Gert Oostindie and Inge Klinkers make a similar observation in their study, *Decolonizing the Caribbean: Dutch Policies in Comparative Perspectives*.[6] They speak of 'erasure' to refer to the act of neglecting, looking past, minimizing, ignoring or rendering invisible an Other.

One wonders then why this particular subregion has been so neglected. One of the possible explanations for the relative 'invisibility' of the Dutch Caribbean within the wider region might be that the Dutch and Papiamentu languages, which are those most often used in publications of the Dutch-Caribbean islands, make the literature of this subregion less accessible. But then, how come the French scholars in the Caribbean have been able to transcend their language barriers? Is it perhaps due to the more esteemed position of French universally?

The relatively small size of the population of the Dutch Caribbean, compared to the rest of the region, may also partially explain the neglect encountered by the Dutch islands. Meanwhile, an exaggerated focus on the Netherlands could be an explanation why very little production on the Dutch Caribbean islands is received by the wider region. While in the Netherlands, Caribbean Studies has been an important area of study since the 1970s, in Curaçao, however, Caribbean Studies were for a long time the lone concern and struggle of scholars such as Römer and Paula. They consistently placed Curaçao in a Caribbean context. For example, Römer's inaugural address in 1982 as Professor of Sociology at the University of the Netherlands Antilles, now the University of Curaçao, was called *Het Caribisch gebied: een terreinverkenning* [The Caribbean: An Exploration].[7] In this lecture he criticized Charles Wagley's prevailing definition of the Caribbean as (solely) a plantation society,[8] which leads to overlooking and neglecting non-plantation economies in the region. Römer and Paula's efforts bore fruit when in the 1990s, the Caribbean region began to receive more structural attention in certain faculties of the University of Curaçao.

The Beginning of Critical Thinking on Identities in Curaçao

Curaçaoan intellectual thinking on themes regarding identities began to unfold in the mid-twentieth century. With the dissertation of Harry Hoetink, a Dutch sociologist, called *Het Patroon van de Oude Curaçaose Samenleving* [The Pattern of the Old Curaçaoan Society],[9] a new dimension in thinking about the social arrangement of the island was pioneered. It was written seven years after the Surinamese sociologist Rudolph van Lier (1914–87) complained in 1951 in his article *De sociale wetenschappen van de Neger in Amerika* [The social sciences of the Negro in America][10] that there was little research on the black population in the Dutch territories of the American continent. He had already stressed this dilemma in his 1949 dissertation *Samenleving in een grensgebied*,[11] of which an English edition appeared in 1971 entitled *Frontier society, a social analysis of the history of Surinam*.[12]

To date, Hoetink's book remains a classic and is regarded as a standard work for social scientists and historians interested in Curaçao. It marked the beginning of a conceptualization of the historical reality of the island in sociological terms. Hoetink went beyond looking solely at the Dutch colonial administrative political history – as Dutch historians had been doing – and examined the complex social structure and social organization of Curaçaoan society before 1863, the year in which slavery was abolished in the Dutch Caribbean. He analysed how colour, race and ethnic origin determined one's position in the social hierarchy and one's power to practice cultural leadership in society. People from different cultural backgrounds had been placed together in a hierarchical social order of slave-masters (people of Protestant or Jewish religion) and forcibly imported enslaved. Hoetink examined how this influenced the ways in which ethnic groups lived independently and interacted. In this way, he laid the foundation for an understanding of a Caribbean society that had just emerged from the institution of slavery but that was not a typical monocrop plantation economy as most societies in the region had been presumed to have been.

René Römer, a Curaçaoan sociologist, continued, in several of his publications, to elaborate upon similar socio-historical issues in Curaçao. His 1977 PhD dissertation *Een Volk op Weg: Un Pueblo na Kaminda* [A People on the Way],[13] was an examination of the social changes on the island over a period of 400 years. He also emphasized that in spite of the fact that Curaçao did not have a 'typical' plantation economy, colour, race and ethnicity were important determinants of social position, both during and after slavery. During slavery, Curaçao was a three-tiered society, with a considerable middle segment of free(d) Afro-descendants, among whom especially the mixed population was able to surpass the prescribed social boundaries. The three-tiered social structure was well defined, with racial/ethnic and class hierarchies largely coinciding. A person's place in society depended primarily on occupation, ethnic heritage and skin colour.

Römer advanced the local scholarship – and perhaps also Caribbean scholarship – by studying the impact of industrialization on a post-Abolition Caribbean society as a consequence of the establishment and subsequent expansion of the oil-refinery in Curaçao in the beginning of the twentieth century. His analysis shows how industrialization altered the society demographically but also in terms of social mobility and social awareness/emancipation. The changes brought about by industrialization raised political awareness, and led to universal suffrage in 1948. But the acquired right to exercise citizenship through general suffrage did not erase the phenomenon of colour demarcation. Ethnicity, colour and race continued to determine many aspects of life, including occupation, social standing and membership of political parties. By the 1960s and 1970s the masses no longer wished to abide by the social contradictions of Curaçaoan society and claimed their rightful place in society through the labour protest and social revolt of May 30, 1969. The social hierarchies and divisions of the old society could thenceforth no longer be kept in place.

Römer's main contribution to the local scholarship was introducing and applying the discourse that was taking place in the wider Caribbean on society, culture and identity, especially the concept of creolization. In this way, he joined the voices of MG Smith of the Anglophone Caribbean and the above mentioned Rudolf Van Lier of Suriname. By critically reflecting upon the colonial development of their respective societies, these three scholars significantly shaped the thinking about the complexity of those societies. Römer's scholarly work spans the period from 1970 till his death in 2003. In Curaçao, Römer is recognized as one of main national thinkers on the themes of identity and identity formation. For his contribution to Curaçaoan scholarship, the national university dedicated to his legacy, an edited volume published in 2006.[14]

Creolization is a major theme in his work. Römer sought to connect identity and culture with the complex inter-ethnic group relationships in Curaçao. For Römer, creolization in Curaçao emerged from the tensions and contradictions arising from the admixture of the white, Protestant, West-European culture of the Dutch, the Iberian culture of the Sephardic Jews, and the various African cultures, which over the course of time developed their own distinctive character. Contrary to those before him, who saw the widely spoken Papiamentu language as a factor hindering development, Römer (1974) claimed that Curaçao's distinct national culture, attained through creolization, manifested itself especially in Papiamentu. For him, Papiamentu was a constituent of Curaçaoan culture that clearly transcended class boundaries. It is the formation of this language that, according to Römer, defines the autochthonous Curaçaoan or what in Papiamentu itself is called the *Yu di Kòrsou* – literally, Child of Curaçao.

Contrary to other creolization writers, such as the Jamaican Edward Brathwaite who makes a distinction between Euro-creole and Afro-creole,[15] Römer did not classify creole varieties in a society. Brathwaite's classifications describe the sharp and irreconcilable characters of the different groups in a plural society. Römer's conceptualization of creolization does not pay sufficient attention to the structural contradictions of power relations or the social conflicts resulting from slavery and colonialism. Unequal power relationships are important to examine as they affect the ways in which people construct and negotiate Self and Others.[16] Linda Rupert's study, *Creolization and Contraband: Curaçao in the Early Modern Atlantic World*,[17] further determines that *creolization* is not solely a cultural phenomenon. She analyses how through contraband a widespread economic practice in seventeenth and eighteenth century Curaçao – people interacted socially across ethnicity and class.

The socially troubled 1960s, with its culmination in the social upheaval of the May 30, 1969, also had its influence in critical Curaçaoan intellectual consciousness. In 1967, Paula, a Curaçaoan sociologist and philosopher, published his book *From Objective to Subjective Social Barriers*,[18] in which he places the matter of identity and identity formation against the historical and psychological background of the internalization by Afro-Curaçaoans of the standards for self-judgment set by the white elites. He looks at the trans-generational effects of slavery and colonization on the psyche of especially the black popular class, whereby for centuries, racism justified the oppression of one group by the other, with the subjugated forced to internalize the stereotypes of the social order. His book has related very closely to the experiences of many in Curaçaoan society and it was reprinted soon after its first publication. Paula's observations about Curaçao also coincide with those of many other scholars in the region such as Gordon Lewis for the case of Puerto Rico.[19] When Paula wrote his book, several countries in the Caribbean were engaged in a process of deconstructing those feelings of inferiority as they moved toward political independence. In Curaçao, Paula's book became part of a process of growing self-awareness of especially the black population in the 1960s and 1970s. Paula, in a sense, continued his reflection in his 2005 autobiography, *The Cry of My Life: Bitterzoete herinneringen aan een levensweg vol kronkels* [The Cry of My Life: Bittersweet Memories of a Life Full of Twists],[20] which shows the enormous struggle that is involved in shaping national belonging in the context of the cultural and ethnic diversity of Curaçao, historically shaped by the mechanisms of colonialism and slavery, and with the three-tiered social structure in which race/ethnicity/colour and class hierarchies largely coincide, even today.

Frank Martinus Arion has also contributed significantly to critical scholarship in Curaçao. Martinus Arion indirectly endorses Römer's vision on creolization. Apart from being a literary writer, he is also a linguistic scholar who has studied the development of Papiamentu as a creole language. Martinus Arion focuses more on the African elements in the process of creolization. In his dissertation, *The Kiss of a Slave: Papiamentu's West-African Connections*,[21] he made a great effort to decipher the now extinct local language called Guene in order to analyse its contribution to Papiamentu. Guene, also called Gené, Géni or Gueni, spoken in different variants among the enslaved in Curaçao was a Portuguese based creole language, which was displaced at a certain moment in history by the other creole language Papiamentu.[22] Unlike Römer, who saw creolization as the 'westernization of the Africans and at the same time a less desired Africanization of the white elite group', Martinus Arion emphasizes the greater contribution of the groups with little economic power to the formation of Papiamentu. According to him, Papiamentu was able to survive and develop within the colonial setting due to the victory of 'the concubines and the nannies.' Both groups formed an intermediary between the white elite and the black marginalized group and helped pass cultural elements from the latter on to the former.²³

Both Römer and Martinus Arion have drawn attention to the relatively strong position that the creole language Papiamentu has been able to carve out for itself in the Curaçaoan society. Language choice today still functions as an indicator of who is and who is not considered an 'authentic' *Yu di Kòrsou*.²⁴ However, both Römer and Martinus Arion have given insufficient thought to the often ambivalent attitudes in this regard. In spite of the importance of Papiamentu as a cultural signifier, language issues have always been controversial. People often prefer the Dutch language for the purpose of career and social advancement. The decades-long discussion on whether and how to use Papiamentu as a language of instruction in the education system continues, and reflects some of the persistent paradoxes and challenges of national identity in Curaçao. In this regard there are similarities between Curaçao and other Caribbean nations where a creole language exists beside a European language.

In addition, the concept of creolization and other approaches to identity as applied by Curaçaoan scholars, in most cases view cultural identity as the largely local, autonomous and well-delineated cultural experience of Curaçaoan society during and after slavery. They have not considered the significant impact of past and present intra-Caribbean migration on Curaçao's cultural diversity and complexity.²⁵ The influx in the twentieth century of large numbers of labour immigrants from South Asia, China, the Middle East, Portugal, Suriname and the English-speaking Caribbean as well as the Netherlands, added new degrees of ethnic diversity and complexity to the existing multicultural fabric of the Curaçaoan society. Scholars tend to ignore these immigrants who arrived after the establishment of the oil-refinery in 1915 and the influence they have had on the (re)construction of Curaçaoan cultural identity. In such a highly culturally pluralistic society, the idea of shared national identity became rather problematic at that time. Natasha Van der Dijs's *The Nature of Ethnic Identity among the People of Curaçao*²⁶ is one attempt to include the contribution of the immigrants who settled on the island in the beginning and middle of the twentieth century and their descendants. Van der Dijs insists that the definition of who is the Curaçaoan today, apparent in the term *Yu di Kòrsou*, should go beyond the ethnic and racial boundaries of

Curaçao's nineteenth-century, pre-industrial society. There is now also an ongoing awareness by both scholars and cultural policymakers that identities should be also understood through studying the presence in society of immigrant groups, including the late twentieth-century arrivants from the neighbouring Caribbean islands.[27]

A New Understanding of Identities and Self in Curaçao; Questions and Current Challenges

In the late twentieth century and the beginning of the twenty-first century, while most Caribbean countries have left their colonial past behind and some have celebrated their fiftieth year of independence, Curaçao and the rest of the Dutch Caribbean islands still struggle with constitutional changes. The issue is not only about independence, but also whether one could get closer or have a direct link with the mother country. Belonging to the Kingdom of the Netherlands has continued to be seen as an important asset. The statistics of the April 2005 referendum in Curaçao show that 95 per cent of the total population wants the island to remain a part of the Kingdom (in some way or other). It confirms the results of opinion polls carried out in 1997–98 as reported upon in *Ki sorto di reino?- What kind of Kingdom?* by Oostindie and Verton.[28] Until now, people continue to point to societies in the Caribbean such as Haiti and in particular the former Dutch colony of Suriname, claiming that their socio-economic, political and development problems are primarily the result of their independence. From this viewpoint, everything local and domestic continues to be seen as backward and incomplete and a sense of dependency upon the colonial motherland is continued.

The theme of an insecure colonized mind has been taken up by Valdemar Marcha together with his Dutch colleague Paul Verweel.[29] They have introduced the term 'culture of fear', which they define as an attitude of burying one's head in the sand and not confronting one's own problems. The culture of fear may manifest itself in a reticence to express contrary views openly because of fear of reprisals, but also in shyness about asserting one's own cultural identity because it has long been considered backward. According to Marcha and Verweel, the culture of fear was initially a way in which the powerless protected themselves against the colonizers. However, it has become a weapon of self-destruction as it seems to work counter-productively for the population itself. In their view, it reflects a process of internalizing inferiority that functions as an instrument of the prevailing power structure; it is integral to the process of socialization that transmits values and beliefs from old to young, generation through generation. The concept of a 'culture of fear' seems to overlook the fact that Curaçao as a non-independent nation, is still dealing with the colonial challenges of cultural identities, intermixed with those posed by an ever-globalizing world in which national identity and culture are believed to be disappearing. There is still this coloniality of power: the persisting contradictory consequences of colonialism on the self-consciousness of people who are still experiencing colonization.

Rosalia, in contrast, emphasizes cultural resistance in the face of domination in order to understand Curaçao's cultural vitality and to refute also the myths of cultural inferiority of the Afro-Curaçaoans in particular. He underscores what Lewis called cultural nationalism, by which Lewis meant that it is important to study the life of the masses and their contribution to national culture. Rosalia's study of the *tambú*[30] meant a paradigmatic shift in how national history was perceived and researched. He continued a research tradition set by the anthropologists Elis Juliana (a Curaçaoan) and Paul Brenneker (a Dutch priest in Curaçao),[31] considered pioneers in the systematic collection and documentation of orally transmitted history of Curaçao.

Tambú is the name of a certain music form and the accompanying drum, dance, and social gathering of the African enslaved and their descendants in Curaçao. Rosalia analyses how *tambú* was persecuted by the state and the Church during slavery times but was nevertheless able to persist because of its significance as a form of resistance for the oppressed.[32] Thus, rather than viewing the masses as mere objects acted upon, Rosalia, like Lewis, saw them as resilient people, rising to and resisting the severe challenges that they faced.

Rosalia upheld the idea that thought should be applied to action as he combined scholarship with activism in his position as the (former) Director of Kas di Kultura (Cultural House), the agency that implements government's cultural policy. His policy plan of 2001 *Rumbo pa independensia mental* (Toward mental independence)[33] is geared toward a process of attaining mental emancipation and delineates the activities that government should exercise with regard to this process in the society. He introduced among others the celebration of an annual *Siman di kultura* (Cultural week) that showcases traditional Curaçaoan culture.

The search for authenticity and the celebration of traditional culture have been central in the study of the anthropologists Leon Weeber[34] and Ieteke Witteveen who looked at those issues in their research on the notion of authentic identities conducted in neighbourhoods of Curaçao in the 1990s. They introduced the concept of '*kultura propio*' (authentic culture) in order to reconsider the important role of culture and authentic values in sustainable economic development. They did action research through ethnography in Banda 'Bou, an area considered by many as one of authentic Curaçaoan culture, and in Brievengat, a neighbourhood where residents were placed together in public housing in the 1960s. For these two authors, authentic Curaçaoan values include, for example, respect in one's attitudes toward others and toward nature and autonomy in one's aspirations toward work. These values are fundamental to the Curaçaoan social psyche. While they manifested themselves in the past, especially during events such as births, funerals and harvests, in the present they come to expression in particular through Carnaval, as people join in working toward a common goal.

Nevertheless, Curaçaoan scholarship needs to analyse and understand the constant refiguring of identities across insular and national boundaries, now more apparent in the current era of globalization. Curaçao presents itself on the one hand as a postcolonial, newly autonomous 'country' in constant search for 'authenticity' by distinguishing its culture from that of the Netherlands (seen as the colonial culture), while on the other hand it also stresses at times its position as a member of the Kingdom of the Netherlands, considered a stepping stone toward global citizenship.[35] The performance of coloniality still manifests itself in celebrations such as the Queen's birthday, soon to be King's birthday[36] as well as the controversial *Sinterklaasfeest* (Saint Nicolaas feast).[37] However at the same time, a large group of people attend the yearly commemoration on August 17 of Curaçao's largest slave revolt in 1795. Also the above mentioned yearly celebrated Cultural week – the *Siman di kultura* – receives broad popular acceptance and has grown in size and significance. During the week, public and private organizations, such as schools, government departments, stores, banks and multinational corporations decorate their buildings and organize activities to reflect what is believed to be local 'authentic' customs. One may conclude that people seem to have no problem shifting their focus back and forth between belonging to Europe, enjoying political autonomy, desiring (future) independence, having a global outlook, and claiming Caribbean and Latin American solidarity.[38]

This portrayal of the Curaçaoan complexity underscores and gives a new dimension to the Cuban scholar Antonio Benítez Rojo's description of the 'complex social interplay' in the Caribbean. 'Caribbeanness', he says, 'is a system full of noise and opacity, a nonlinear and unpredictable system. In short a chaotic system beyond the total reach of any specific kind of knowledge or interpretation of the world.'[39] In similar ways as the rest of the Caribbean, there is in Curaçao a permanent dialogue and struggle between the competing and conflicting demands of (re)constructing identities and self. Factors that seem to make the Curaçaoan experience with these issues interesting and perhaps unique are its particular details and its timing in comparison with the wider Caribbean. This seemingly contradictory or ambivalent attitude about self and identity has warranted closer investigation and a growing group of local social scientists such as Richenel Ansano, Florencia Cornet, Su Girigori, Jeanne Henriquez, Lianne Leonora, Louis Philippe Römer[40] and Guiselle Martha[41] are bringing together some important analyses of this development.

Some Concluding Remarks

Gordon Lewis passed away in 1991 and therefore did not examine the effect of globalization on Caribbean societies. In this era of significant transnational cultural influence through globalization, cultural identity continues to be part of the challenge faced by Caribbean people, in an intensified way. In the revised edition of *Caribbean Cultural Identity: The Case of Jamaica – An Essay in Cultural Dynamics*, Rex Nettleford[42] states that 'cultural identity continued to be a persistent quest by the Jamaican and Caribbean people for place and purpose in a globalised world of continuous change.' One should bear in mind that Nettleford was saying this at a time when Jamaica had already been independent for 40 years. His statement shows that even former colonies continue to experience trials in choosing whether to follow modernization or to self-affirm their local and indigenous culture. It should therefore not be surprising that local/indigenous culture is constantly questioned and contested in Caribbean states like Curaçao that today continue to operate in a (neo)colonial setting.

In this chapter, I have discussed how Curaçaoan scholarship and discourse on cultural identity have changed over time in terms of approach, perspective and emphasis. I have shown that in a certain way there exists overlap with cultural identity issues in the rest of the Caribbean, but that distinctive developments in Curaçao deserve the attention of scholars in the wider Caribbean as they can enrich the discourse on identity in the region as a whole. Curaçaoan scholars, like their Caribbean colleagues, have studied their society to understand the social complexities that have shaped the construction of the self historically, and that influence the (re)construction of contemporary identities.

Curaçaoans may call themselves Caribbean, Latin American, Dutch, European and global people. These identities are situational and flexible rather than fixed, as people may hold on to several identity categories at the same time and move in and out of them in dynamic ways. Like other Caribbean identities, Curaçaoan identities are constantly negotiated, fervently debated, and convincingly claimed in ways and during circumstances that may not always be clear to outsiders, or even to insiders.

Curaçaoans have struggled and continue to struggle with identity questions. The search to (re)define the self (or selves) and the collectivity (or collectivities) persists. One can state that identity issues as they appear on the island show the complexity of managing ethnicity, class and plurality of culture in the Caribbean. These complex phenomena defined in the past still model present social life and embody contradictory elements such as colonization and decolonization, compliance, pragmatism and resistance, and they guide the continuing search for cultural and national identity as well. Contemporary global issues, within the existing colonial setting and its entangled economic and political dimensions, have made matters of identity even more complex and topical, and calls for new analytical studies.

Notes

1. Gordon K. Lewis, *Main Currents in Caribbean Thought: The Historical Evolution of Caribbean Society in its Ideological Aspects, 1492–1900* (Baltimore, London: Johns Hopkins University Press, 1983).
2. Sidney Mintz, 'Gordon K. Lewis 1919–1991', *Caribbean Studies Newsletter,* 19 (1992): 2–24.
3. D. Hambuch, 'Rereading the Caribbean through Dubbelspel by Frank Martinus Arion', *World Literature Today* 72, no. 1, (1998): 55–58.
4. Édouard Glissant, *Le Discours Antillais,* Ed. Du Seuil, 1981.
5. Ineke Phaf, 'Women Writers of the Dutch-Speaking Caribbean: Life Long Poem in the Tradition of Surinamese Granmorgu (New Dawn)', in *Caribbean Women Writers: Essays from the First International Conference,* ed. Selwyn Reginald Cudjoe, 357–64 (Wellesley, MA: Calaloux, 1990).
6. Gert Oostindie and Inge Klinkers, *Decolonizing the Caribbean: Dutch Policies in Comparative Perspectives* (Amsterdam: Amsterdam University Press 2003).
7. René Römer, *Het Caribisch gebied, een Terreinverkenning* (Curaçao: Universiteit van de Nederlandse Antillen, 1982).
8. Charles Wagley, 'Plantation Americas, a Cultural Sphere', in *Caribbean Studies: A Symposium,* ed. Vera Rubin, 3–13 (Institute of Social and Economic Research, University College of the West Indies, 1957).
9. H. Hoetink, *Het patroon van de oude Curaçaose samenleving: Een sociologische studie* (Assen: Van Gorcum, 1958).
10. R.A.J. Van Lier, De sociale wetenschappen van de neger in Amerika. *Bijdragen tot de taal -, land-, en volkenkunde* 107, no. 2 (1951): 279–303.
11. R.A.J. Van Lier *Samenleving in een grensgebied: een sociaal-historische studie van Suriname* (Gravenhage: Nijhoff, 1949).
12. R.A.J. Van Lier, *Frontier Society: A Social Analysis of the History of Surinam.* Translated from the Dutch by M.J.L. van Yperen (The Hague: Martinus Nijhoff, 1971).
13. Rene Römer, *Een volk op weg: Un pueblo na kaminda: Een sociologisch historische studie van de Curaçaose samenleving* (Zutphen: De Walburg Pers,1979).
14. R.M. Allen, 'Cultural Identity in a Curaçaoan Mirror: A Critical View on René Römer's Contribution,' in *René Römer als inspirator: actualisering van zijn gedachtegoed,* eds. R.M. Allen, Jurriaan de Haan and Goretti Narain,16–29 (Willemstad: University of the Netherlands Antilles, 2006).
15. See E. Brathwaite, *The Development of Creole Society in Jamaica, 1770–1820* (Oxford: Clarendon Press, 1971).
16. Allen, 'Cultural Identity'.
17. L.M. Rupert, *Creolization and Contraband: Curaçao in the Early Modern Atlantic World* (Athens, GA: University of Georgia Press, 2012).
18. A. Paula, *From Objective to Subjective Social Barriers: A Historico-Philosophical Analysis of Certain Negative Attitudes Among the Negroid Population of Curaçao* (Willemstad: Curaçao, 1967).
19. Gordon K. Lewis, *Puerto Rico: Freedom and Power in the Caribbean,* rev. ed., with an introduction by Anthony Maingot (Kingston: Ian Randle Publishers, 2004).
20. A. Paula, *The Cry of My Life: Bitterzoete herinneringen aan een levensweg vol kronkel* (Curaçao: Curaçaosche Courant, 2005).

21. F. Martinus, *The Kiss of a Slave: Papiamentu's West-African Connections* (Curaçao: De Curaçaose Courant, 1997).
22. F. Martinus, 'The Guene Kriole of the Netherlands Antilles: Its Theoretical and Practical Consequences for Better Understanding Papiamentu and Other Portuguese Based Creoles', *Annales del Caribe* 4–5 (1984): 335–50; L. Janga, *Géni: Taal van Verzet: Het Nationaal Museum vormen we tezamen* (Curaçao: NAAM, 2011).
23. F. Martinus, 'The Victory of the Concubines and the Nannies', in *Caribbean Creolization: Reflections on the Cultural Dynamics of Language, Literature and Identity*, eds. K. Balutansky and Marie-Agnès Sourieau, 110–17 (Gainesville: University Press of Florida, 1998).
24. See A. Benjamin, *Jews of the Dutch Caribbean: Exploring Ethnic Identity on Curaçao* (London and New York: Routlegde Harwood Anthropology, 2002), 85; O. Eikrem, *Contested Identities: A Study of Ethnicity in Curaçao, the Netherlands Antilles* (PhD Thesis, Norwegian University of Natural Science and Technology [NTNU] 1999); L.M. Rupert, *Inter Imperial Trade and Local Identity: Curaçao in the Colonial Atlantic World* (PhD thesis, Duke University, 2006).
25. R.M. Allen, 'Music in Diasporic Context: The Case of Curaçao and Intra-Caribbean Migration', *Black Music Research Journal* 32, no. 2, (2012a): 51–66.
26. N. Van der Dijs, *The Nature of Ethnic Identity among the People of Curaçao*, (Curaçao: Curaçaosche Courant, 2011).
27. C. Do Rego, *The Portuguese Immigrant in Curaçao: Immigration, Participation and Integration in 20th Century* (Amsterdam: SWP, 2012); R.M. Allen, 'Twentieth Century Migration from the English-speaking Caribbean Discursive Inclusion and Exclusion', in *Researching the Rhizome: Studies of Transcultural Language, Literature, Education, and Society in the ABC-Islands and Beyond*, eds. Nicholas Faraclas, Ronald Severing, Christa Weijer and Elisabeth Echteld, 13–29 (Curaçao: FPI & UNA, 2013).
28. G. Oostindie and Peter Verton, *Ki Sorto di Reino? – What Kind of Kingdom?: Visies en Verwachtingen van Antillianen en Arubanen omtrent het Koninkrijk* (Den Haag: Sdu Uitgevers, 1998). See also the publication by Lammert de Jong, *Being Dutch, More or Less* (Rozenberg Publishers, 2010) in which the author states that for most people in the Dutch Caribbean islands, in our case Curaçao, having the Dutch passport is the most prized possession of Dutch citizenship.
29. V. Marcha and Paul Verveel, *De cultuur van angst: Paradoxale ketenen van angst en zwijgen op Curaçao* (Amsterdam: SWP, 2003).
30. R. Rosalia, *Tambú, de legale en kerkelijke repressie van Afro-Curaçaose volksuitingen*, (Zutphen: Walburg Pers, 1997).
31. Interviews collected by Paul Brenneker and Elis Juliana, 1958–1960, Tapes Zikinzá-collection, stored at the National Archives, Willemstad (NatAr);Tapes Brenneker/Juliana, interviews collected by Paul Brenneker and Elis Juliana, 1963–1989, stored at the Public Library, Willemstad (Biblioteka Nashonal Kòrsou Frank Martinus Arion).
32. In fact, the *tambú* has continued until the present to have its function as an outlet for protest.

33. R. Rosalia, *Rumbo pa independensia mental: 'Konosé bo historia i kultura pa bo konosé bo mes': plan di maneho i akshon di kultura pa Kòrsou* (Willemstad, Curaçao, 2001): [s.n.].
34. I. Witteveen and L. Weeber, *Kultura, Base pa Desaroyo Propio. Nota di Diskushon pa Dia di Estudio*, 20–21 di Mart. *Rapòrt Integral pa Barionan di Kòrsou; Plan di Urgensha i Kontinuidat/Integrale Ontwikkeling van de Curaçaose Buurten: Urgentieplan en voor Continuïteit* (Curaçao: IPK (Inisiativa Partikular Kòrsou)/ Grupo di Trabou/Universiteit van de Nederlandse Antillen, 1993).
35. Since 1986, the Kingdom of the Netherlands has consisted of three autonomous parts, namely the Netherlands, Aruba, and the five-island federation called the Netherlands Antilles. Constitutional reform has been a lingering issue and at the end of the twentieth century, the cry for constitutional transformation in the Netherlands Antilles became more intense. In a referendum held in April 2005, the Curaçaoan electorate voted to sever ties with the other four islands of the Netherlands Antilles and to remain as an autonomous country within the Kingdom.
36. In the Dutch Caribbean islands, the birthday of the Queen of the Netherlands has been celebrated on April 30 as a national holiday. In 2013, the Queen of the Netherlands abdicated in favour of her son and from then his birthday (April 27) is celebrated as the King's birthday.
37. In the Netherlands, the Sinterklaas feest (St Nicolaas feast) is celebrated as one of the main events of the year, whereby on December 5, principally children receive presents, while families, friends, colleagues, etc., exchange gifts. It is a celebration which starts with the arrival in mid-November of Saint Nicolaas by steam-boat accompanied by his *Zwarte Pieten* (Black Peters). These are his helpers with blackened faces and large, painted on red lips and who wear pageboy uniforms and curly wigs. This celebration has also been introduced in their colonies in the Caribbean, where it has become a traditional feast for especially children. Contrary to the present protests in the Netherlands against the racist characterization of Black Peters, in Curaçao, this part has remained unquestioned.
38. R.M. Allen, 'National identities, Belonging and citizenship in Curaçao: the complexity of changing nationhood narratives and performances in a Caribbean small island context,' in *Multiplex Cultures and Citizenships: Multiple Perspectives on Language, Literature, Education, and Society in the ABC-Islands and Beyond*, eds. Nicholas Faraclas, Ronald Severing, Christa Weijer and Elisabeth Echteld, 29–44 (Curaçao: FPI &UNA, 2012).
39. Antonio Benítez Rojo and James E. Maraniss, *The Repeating Island: The Caribbean and the Postmodern Perspective* (Durham, NC: Duke University Press, 1996), 295.
40. Richenel Ansano, 'To Question Identity: Public Discourse and Transpersonal Ethics in Curaçao', in *Multiplex Cultures*, eds. Faraclas, Severing, Weijer and Echteld, 55–68; Su Girigori, 'Pasado, Presente I Future: Curaçao's Cultural Expression Revised', in *Multiplex Cultures*, 77–82; Jeanne Henriquez, 'Embracing National Culture through a Policy of Difference', in *Multiplex Cultures*, 99–106; Lianne Leonora, 'Will the Real Yu di Kòrsou please Stand up: The Double-bind Cultural Identity of the Citizens of Curaçao', in *Multiplex Cultures*, 127–44; Louis Philippe Römer, 'Making Empire Safe

for Consumption: The Politics of the Colonial "Past" in Non-sovereign Curaçao' (paper presented at the AES Spring Conference, New York, 2012), and Florencia Cornet, *Decolonizing Transnational Subaltern Women: The Case of Kurasolenas and New York Dominicanas* (PhD thesis, University of South Carolina, 2012).
41. Guisella Martha, 'The Other Dutch: Representations of Dutch Antillean Cultural Memory in a Globalized World' (PhD diss., University of Nijmegen, forthcoming).
42. Rex Nettleford, *Caribbean Cultural Identity: The Case of Jamaica: An Essay in Cultural Dynamics* (Kingston: Ian Randle Publishers, 2003).

PART 2
Rethinking Caribbean Politics

7 | The 'Slums of Empire' and Gordon K. Lewis:
Reflections on Decolonization and Sovereignty in the Caribbean[1]

Jessica Byron

Introduction

The Caribbean lends itself to reflections on several dimensions of sovereignty. Its territories offer a wide spectrum of constitutional arrangements and a variety of modes of entry into sovereign statehood. These range from Haiti's unprecedented revolution which toppled slave society in St Domingue at the turn of the nineteenth century to Cuba's long War of Independence at the end of the 1800s, to the slow erosion of British imperial rule, labour uprisings and the awakening of British Caribbean nationalism during the first half of the twentieth century. There are still lingering issues of colonial rule and self-determination, most dramatically demonstrated in the constitutional saga of the Turks and Caicos Islands since 2009.[2] There are various non-independent governance formulae that are still evolving in the French and Netherlands Antilles and in the United States Caribbean territories.[3] Gordon K. Lewis's works were prescient in addressing most of these issues, in making observations and drawing conclusions that remain as relevant today as they were 50 years ago.

As Cynthia Barrow-Giles observes, in the immediate pre- and post-independence periods in the Commonwealth Caribbean, sovereignty and self-determination were 'the leading issues for nationalist discourse.'[4] The acquisition of sovereign statehood was seen as the key to power and it held the promise of development for the disenfranchised populations of the region. And over the last half century, there have been passionate as well as more measured invocations of sovereignty in Caribbean political discourse.[5] Yet, sovereignty is a concept more often honoured in the breach than in its effective exercise. Understandings and assessments of sovereignty in the Caribbean have become increasingly complex, nuanced and often pessimistic. Sir Shridath Ramphal remarks that 'in the era of globalization...sovereignty becomes a pale shadow of itself.'[6]

Nonetheless, while there is a general recognition that national sovereignty has been diluted by the structures and activities of a globalized world, Caribbean emotions can still be stirred by perceived new violations or restrictions of sovereignty, generally by external powers or imposed through multilateral conditionalities, and these may arouse strong feelings of nationalism, frustration and outrage. Sovereignty issues also rear their heads in intra-regional relations. This may occur in territorial disputes or when territorial authorities deny or delay access to their sovereign space to their Caribbean neighbours, and refuse to enter into or honour the mutual obligations contained in regional integration agreements. These are often the easiest ways for a Caribbean society to maintain its fragile and bruised sense of national sovereignty.

Sovereignty is also invoked when reflecting on the status of the non-independent US or European Caribbean territories. They are indisputably better off in some material aspects than most of their independent neighbours who comfort themselves with the argument that such territories still lack control of their sovereign destinies, economic circumstances notwithstanding. These territories in turn, oscillate between the quest for greater integration into their regional environment and collusion with their own metropolitan authorities in restricting access to their space by other Caribbean people, fearing that they will be overwhelmed by migrants from neighbouring islands. Their populations demonstrate ambivalence on the question of national independence, generally rejecting this option at the polls on the grounds that there are economic and security reasons for maintaining their links with the metropolitan power to which they are affiliated. They continue to experiment with more limited and ambiguous forms of self-determination.[7]

So what does sovereignty mean in the current Caribbean context? Clearly it is always contested. Sovereignty issues have manifested themselves in tensions over territorial space and natural resources,[8] political representation and mutual commitments that transcend the national level. Over the last three decades, some of the most cogent regional reflections on sovereignty have been triggered by security relations with hegemonic powers particularly the United States, and by external interventions, externally imposed obligations and the challenges posed by the structures and processes of globalization.

Recent literature has labelled Caribbean political elites' understanding of sovereignty as narrow and state-centric, suggesting that it is an impediment to strengthening regional integration and to effectively addressing contemporary governance challenges.[9] Yet, despite the contention that state sovereignty may be an outmoded concept in a globalized world, it is clear that it is still a crucial normative principle throughout the international community. Given its ongoing significance and its prominence as a theme in the works of G.K. Lewis, this work explores Lewis's thoughts on the subject and examines how Caribbean perspectives on sovereignty have evolved since 1987 when he published his work on Grenada.

The study first surveys classical definitions of sovereignty, looking at the domestic as well as the international dimensions of the concept. It juxtaposes these with contemporary Western academic reinterpretations of sovereignty which have been developed in the context of globalization and unequal levels of power across a very diverse set of international actors. This sets the stage for surveying four major works of G.K. Lewis in which he discusses the value of and prospects for sovereignty and self-determination in Caribbean nascent societies.

The last part of the study interrogates the experiences and understanding of sovereignty in the Caribbean particularly since the Grenadian debacle in 1983, the point at which Lewis's reflections conclude. It evaluates the validity of the Western academic and policy discourse on sovereignty for the Caribbean context. It argues that debates surrounding sovereignty have erupted around the following flashpoints: security policy which is usually linked to transnational criminal networks and to the security interests of the United States; external interventions in crises of political governance in specific states, most notably in Haiti in 2004 and 2010; national reactions to neoliberal economic reform programmes imposed by the international community; and national and regional attempts to implement the CARICOM Single Market and Economy (CSME). It tries to distil Caribbean thinking on these issues from the statements of political leaders, the analyses of Caribbean academics and press commentary about catalytic events. It concludes that more effective Caribbean sovereignty must be rooted in the domestic context, in more transparent and accountable government, in people's participation in the political and policymaking process and in greater levels of personal and community security. Only then will Caribbean populations enjoy a better quality of national sovereignty and also be prepared to give greater support to the concept of pooled sovereignty, the sharing of space and resources and the cession of some power to regional centres of authority.

Classical and Contemporary Definitions and Reinterpretations of Sovereignty

The concept of sovereignty has gone through various permutations of meaning since it first came to prominence in the sixteenth century. At its most basic, it can be defined as having legitimate control and authority over a given territory and population. Andrew Heywood[10] makes a distinction between legal sovereignty which is the 'unchallengeable right to demand compliance as defined by law' and political sovereignty which is 'the ability to command obedience which is typically ensured by a monopoly of coercive force.' One of the earliest definitions of sovereignty was written by Jean Bodin in 1576.[11] Bodin lived in an age when European societies were evolving out of medieval forms of rule towards nation statehood and were often rocked by civil war. His writings, directed at French kings, emphasized the divine right of the sovereign monarch to establish absolute control over national territory and not to be answerable to external sources of authority. His theme was further developed by Thomas Hobbes in *Leviathan*[12] who argued that organized state power was essential to prevent anarchy in society. Hobbes observed that order could either be imposed by force or accepted by consensus. In either case, the sovereign should have a monopoly over the use of force and virtually absolute power in order to maintain peace and security.[13]

Jean Jacques Rousseau in a revolutionary age (1762), modified the concept of sovereignty further from an elite absolute right to rule to the notion of popular sovereignty, based on wider consultation where the exercise of power would be legitimized by the popular will.[14]

An important distinction in the textbook discussions of sovereignty is between internal and external sovereignty. Bodin and Hobbes were concerned primarily with the consolidation of authority within the state – internal sovereignty. But a further dimension of sovereignty is the doctrine of state sovereignty vis-à-vis the international environment.

One of the cornerstone myths of Westphalian international society has been the idea that there is no authority above the state, the state is central in the international sphere and autonomous as an actor, and there should be no interference in its domestic affairs. Internal and external sovereignty are intrinsically linked since the attributes necessary for state recognition, or the external acknowledgement of the state's sovereignty by the international community, are partly contingent upon the demonstration of internal sovereignty — some measure of legitimacy, control of the territory, the presence of a stable population, the institutional machinery of a state and control over the use of force and the collection of revenue. These were felt to be the prerequisites that would ensure that a state was capable of meeting its international obligations. As the crumbling of empires began towards the end of the nineteenth century in Europe, and large-scale decolonization took place in the mid-twentieth century, attention became focused on the external dimensions of sovereignty. In the current context however, in which the domestic merges with the global in so many ways, accompanying the focus on external threats to sovereignty is an acknowledgement of the challenges from within due to low levels of legitimacy and weak state institutions, transnational security threats and various constraints imposed by the wider international community. The writings of Bodin and Hobbes on reinforcing internal sovereignty assume a new meaning.

Understandings and interpretations of sovereignty have evolved fairly rapidly during the past 30 years, driven in large measure by globalization and its encroachment on the traditional functions and powers of the state. As early as 1977, Hedley Bull pointed out the state's eroding authority and the rise of competing centres of authority and control both internally and externally. He invoked the prospect of eventual 'neomedievalism.'[15] John Rapley, building on this theme, pointed out the growing evidence of such tendencies in developing societies in the Caribbean and elsewhere.[16] Many other writers have questioned the relevance today of the traditional meanings of sovereignty.

Stephen Krasner, in particular, has engaged in prolonged rethinking of sovereignty as a fundamental theoretical construct and normative principle in International Relations. Krasner lists four contemporary meanings of and benchmarks for sovereignty. These are domestic sovereignty which relates to the state's control of the actors and activities within its territory; interdependence sovereignty, which concerns its degree of regulation of the transnational activities across its borders – an area where all states have lost control to varying degrees; 'Vattelian' or Westphalian sovereignty which holds that the state is autonomous, not accountable to external authorities; and international legal sovereignty which means that there is mutual recognition of states as legal entities by other states in the international system. Krasner argues that these four meanings of sovereignty are not integrally connected and a state can be recognized as sovereign in some respects while showing a marked lack of sovereignty in other aspects. He suggests that international legal sovereignty is the most common and most superficial dimension while effective sovereignty in the other areas is far less evident for many states.[17]

He describes the entire sovereign state system as a system of 'organized hypocrisy' where the principles regularly diverge from the practices. Violations of sovereignty occur not only through coercion but may also involve collusion by the state concerned since it has voluntarily entered into international agreements which impinge on its autonomy. He focuses in particular on the spheres of international human rights agreements, international financial and commercial arrangements, and regional integration as three areas where sovereignty encroachments are most visible and he elaborates upon several historical and contemporary examples in international conventions and contracts that illustrate how sovereignty may be compromised.[18] He argues that organized hypocrisy, that is, undercutting or circumventing the principle of sovereignty in various ways, occurs in international affairs because there are asymmetrical levels of power among the actors, they have different domestic norms and institutions and there are sometimes no clear, agreed rules and procedures to handle specific situations.[19] Krasner breaks down sovereignty into a number of components, examines practices across these dimensions and ultimately concludes that violations of the norm of sovereignty have *always* occurred because of the intrinsic nature of a system of organized hypocrisy. In later work, he makes the disturbing proposition that 'shared sovereignty' and 'de facto protectorates' should be considered and adopted as policy tools by powerful state actors and international institutions for addressing the problems of 'collapsed and failing states.'[20] Krasner's proposition is critiqued by Fenton (among others) who points out its dangerous policy implications specifically for Haiti when in 2009, calls were being made for such an arrangement to be formally instituted. Fenton argues that shared sovereignty is really just another type of trusteeship system but it is presented as a consensual partnership between the major powers, the international institutions and the state concerned.[21]

Thomas Biersteker[22] develops a slightly different argument to Krasner's. Biersteker, in Constructivist mode, argues that the sovereignty norm has never been static or absolute but is in a state of perpetual, gradual change. He focuses on the evolution of international legal sovereignty from the nineteenth to the twenty-first century, suggesting that there has been continuous evolution driven by state practices and that this has been particularly evident in the norms and procedures for state recognition. He argues that gradually the criteria for recognition came to include not just territory and the capacity to fulfil international obligations but some demonstration of popular legitimacy (1800s), ideological compatibility with dominant actors in the state system (1920s–1970s) and by the 1990s, territoriality had lost some of its significance while adherence to the rule of law, democratic principles and human rights norms had gained greater importance. Biersteker concludes that:

> The international community has become increasingly more obtrusive into what was once assumed to be the domain of the domestic affairs of states…there is some evidence of a progression in recognition criteria over time…by the end of the twentieth century, sovereignty increasingly appeared to be 'conditioned' sovereignty…there has been a general…ratcheting up of intrusion into the domestic affairs of states. [23]

These are the voices of Western academics looking at sovereignty largely from the perspectives of their own societies. Although they acknowledge that much of the reconfiguration of sovereignty has affected 'weaker states' (in Krasner's words) and 'third world states' (Biersteker's words) more than the powerful actors, they do not devote much time to contemplating the sovereignty predicaments of the former. Eroded or ephemeral sovereignty is presented as a fact of life and their work has had a considerable impact not only on international political theory but also on the evolution of international policy. Yet, despite their dismissal of its significance today, the norm of sovereignty remains a compelling popular ideal, including within Western societies.[24] We will now examine in greater detail the sovereignty discourse in the Caribbean, starting with the thoughts of Gordon K. Lewis.

Sovereignty in the works of G.K. Lewis

Lewis has made a tremendous contribution to scholarship on the Caribbean, leaving an invaluable legacy for the generations of scholars who have followed him. His work combines historical narrative and socio-political analysis with encyclopaedic literary references, philosophical discussions and every so often, flashes of satirical, malicious humour and Caribbean *'ole talk.'* It is peppered with choice quotations from Caribbean writers and statesmen of different eras. Above all, he takes a holistic approach to Caribbean history and political development, spanning all the colonial, cultural and linguistic barriers of the region. His work exemplifies the assertion of a more recent scholar that 'any serious study of the Caribbean's history, while acknowledging its diversity, must...pay close attention to the parallel experiences of the different communities inhabiting the region.'[25] Four of his works written between 1968 and 1987 are drawn on in this chapter.[26] One cannot over-emphasize their value as authoritative sources on Caribbean political development and as teaching tools.

The themes of decolonization and self-determination, independence and sovereignty are central to Lewis's work. He was convinced of the need for independence and self-rule in the Caribbean in order for the fragmented, distorted colonial societies to gradually construct national identities and transform themselves into autonomous, viable and confident communities. Independence for Lewis was a rite of passage which would entail assuming responsibility for the fate of one's society and leaving behind the isolation and small-mindedness of colonial existence. Lewis was strident about the social malaise that is left by colonialism and he was critical of governance arrangements in Puerto Rico and in the French Caribbean that had not led to full autonomy.

In the preface to his book on Puerto Rico,[27] Lewis describes it as 'an essay on Puerto Rico as a continuing neocolonial society and on the character of the United States as a neocolonial power in the Caribbean.' Although Puerto Rico is the main focus of enquiry, it therefore also scrutinizes the US track record as governing power in the territory in the Americas where it has maintained its longest colonial/neocolonial presence. He traces all the phases of Puerto Rico's evolution from being a military outpost, a crumbling last remnant of Spain's empire in the Americas to its social, economic and political development as a protectorate of the United States after 1898. He portrays Puerto Rico as possessing broad similarities with the rest of the Caribbean but also as having a very distinctive history of its own. Anthony Maingot, in an introduction to the 2004 edition, reminds us that Lewis was based in Puerto Rico in the 1950s when the island was experiencing major political and socio-economic change. Under Governor Muñoz Marín, it was experimenting economically with Operation Bootstrap and politically with the status of being an *estado libre asociado* or *Commonwealth Territory* linked to the United States. It offered a possible development model for the rest of the Caribbean and Lewis scrutinized it carefully from his perspective as a British political scientist and scholar of Caribbean history.

Lewis looks critically at Puerto Rico's educational system, the industrialization and investment programme and the administration of federal development assistance. He examines at length the institutions and processes of government and the constitutional status of Free Associated Statehood. Although he highlights many positive aspects of economic policy and internal administration, he concludes that:

> The formal title of the territory has changed but it remains nonetheless a territory. Congress continues to hold its *pleins pouvoirs*...All the available evidence about Congressional intent thus points to the conclusion that, in passing the legislation of 1950 to 1952, Congress meant no more than to grant the island the right, within limits, to frame its own constitution....[28]

Puerto Rico remained subordinate to federal authority and heavily dependent economically on the US. Lewis argues that this status offered, at best, a type of second-class citizenship for Puerto Ricans in the United States and severely limited the possibilities for the island's integration into the Caribbean and Latin America. He is also critical of the basis on which plebiscites had been organized to consult with the population on the question of self-determination. He concludes that only full independence would provide a solution for Puerto Rico's obsessive concern with political status and with issues of national and cultural identity.

Lewis's exploration of the Puerto Rican quest for self-determination and development was followed in 1968 by *The Growth of the Modern West Indies,* where he traces the emergence of the British Caribbean colonies from slave societies in the 1830s to the collapse of the West Indies Federation in 1962 and the start of individual sovereign statehood. Lewis is quite critical of British colonial rule and he paints a depressing picture of the social paralysis and lack of opportunity in early twentieth century Caribbean colonial societies. He highlights many damaging social effects which cannot be addressed merely by a political change of status.

The book provides much insight into the crucial phase of Commonwealth Caribbean political development between the 1940s and 1960s. Lewis argues that although British rule left a legacy of constitutional order and respect for the rule of law, it may also have sowed the seeds of benevolent despotism and encouraged elitist proto-democracies. He attributes some bad habits embedded in Caribbean political culture to it, such as opposing for opposition's sake and using 'divide and rule' tactics. Although independence was achieved without violent wars of liberation, he questions the extent to which the Colonial Office was genuinely committed to the concept of self-rule, pointing to the use of delaying tactics and the granting of incremental reform measures after long periods of time.[29] In his chapter on the Leeward and Windward Islands, Lewis gives astute insights into the political atmosphere in the Eastern Caribbean after the demise of the Federation, observing that 'Discussions since 1962 of East Caribbean Federation have exhibited small island insularity and reluctance to give up tiny sovereign worlds with costly, top-heavy administrative structures to a strong, central, more rational government.'[30]

He remarks that only a minimalist federal model would be acceptable to the territories. This statement was later endorsed by Vaughan Lewis when he recommended that a viable sovereignty formula for the Leewards and Windwards must cater to 'the consciousness for island self-rule' and should build an accommodating form of regionalism.[31] One can assess the accuracy of those judgements today, looking at the perpetuation of those 'tiny sovereign worlds,' the progress of the OECS itself, and the intermittent integration talks with

Barbados and Trinidad that have led nowhere. Although the Treaty of Eastern Caribbean Union, aimed at deeper integration among the Leewards and Windwards themselves, was adopted in June 2010, it contains no provisions that will enforce the compliance of its signatories with the commitments. Nonetheless, it must also be acknowledged that the OECS territories have advanced the furthest in the Caribbean in various aspects of functional integration – a shared judiciary, a shared currency and central bank, collective security arrangements, among other institutions – driven by the imperatives of administrative effectiveness and cost management.

Although Lewis applauds the coming of independence, he makes insightful observations about the challenges that would lie ahead for the new states, recommending the following:-

- Civil service reforms that would concentrate on developing initiative, decision-making and implementation skills rather than just 'paper-passing' bureaucrats;[32]
- Indigenization and democratization of the education system;
- The building of partnerships between citizens and state; and
- Breaking down class barriers and elitism and moving towards more equal societies.

Lewis calls for less emphasis on the symbols and rituals of nationalism, and more focus on the development and governance challenges that would lie ahead for the Commonwealth Caribbean countries. He ends with some reflections on sovereignty which he defines as having both political and economic components. Although independence brings formal legal and political sovereignty, Lewis suggests that economic sovereignty is far more elusive and is often controlled by foreign powers. He advocates regional integration and greater integration into Latin America as a means of forging a collective sovereignty that may serve as a defence against the many external risks facing small, new, Commonwealth Caribbean states.

Almost 20 years later in 1983, G.K. Lewis again takes up the theme of sovereignty in *Main Currents of Caribbean Thought*. One section of this text explores sovereignty and the emergence of concepts of citizenship and nationhood in Haiti, the Dominican Republic and Cuba in the ninteenth century. Lewis argues that Haiti's unique status as the only politically sovereign Caribbean country in the early part of that century logically caused its thinkers to take the lead in developing and presenting a Caribbean concept of nationhood. This included ideas of citizenship and economic nationalism. Haitian proponents of the Revolution emphasized its rejection of racial subordination and lauded the principle of making Haitian citizenship accessible to all applicants of African ancestry. Likewise, Lewis points to Haitian writers' espousal of the principle of state-led economic growth strategies for the republic.

He later juxtaposes Haitian and Dominicano nineteenth century ideologies of citizenship. He argues that independence was the catalyst for both countries to address the question of national identity in the form of nationality laws. In early Haitian constitutional law, a citizen was defined as black, citizenship was denied to Caucasians and foreign ownership of property was forbidden. In the Dominican Republic, there were quite different approaches to determining citizenship but there was a similar concern for safeguarding autonomy and national patrimony. His conclusion reiterates some of his own ideas on the nature of sovereignty:

> Whatever the differences, both republics constructed their ideas of nationality and citizenship upon...the conviction that nationality and citizenship can only properly be determined by leaders, constituent assemblies and parliaments composed only of Haitians and Dominicans and responsible only to Haitian and Dominican citizen bodies.[33]

Lewis ends that section of the work with Cuba's 1868 declaration that popular sovereignty and Cuban nationhood must rest on universal suffrage and on bringing an end to slavery. He refers to another major Cuban contribution to conceptualizing sovereignty and freedom, the writings of Jose Marti and his call for independent Latin American political thought and institutions. In effect, he advocated sovereignty of thought, 'for the problem of independence is more than the question of changing constitutional forms: it is a question of changing the basic spirit of things.'[34]

Lewis's ultimate thoughts on Caribbean sovereignty came in 1987 with the publication of *Grenada: The Jewel Despoiled*, written a few years after the demise of the Grenadian Revolution. At this point, Lewis seems to have come full circle and he is both emotional and pessimistic about the future of the English-speaking Caribbean. He downplays the region's record of constitutional stability looking instead at its potential for violent conflict based on inequalities and ethnic and class divisions. He berates the middle classes and political elites for having a neocolonial mentality which leads them to identify their interests with those of the United States. Lewis returns to a theme in his earlier works, the link between economic and political dependence and he argues that weak and vulnerable Caribbean states are extremely prone to becoming embroiled in patron-client relations with more powerful external actors.

Lewis concludes with depressing questions about the viability of very small Caribbean states and the relevance of traditional models of national self-determination and sovereignty. He discusses the problems of insular nationalism and the inadequacy of CARICOM's regional institutions. Nonetheless, he advocates a strengthened and expanded form of regional integration as the only way to address the perils of vulnerability and dependence. He seems to suggest that regional cooperation will either take this form or a more hegemonic brand of regionalism will be imposed by the United States upon Caribbean territories.

We can conclude that sovereignty in the Caribbean context is one of Lewis's major preoccupations in these works. He examines critically the various options for postcolonial governance that have been tried. He emphasizes the constraints of economic dependence, structural and institutional weaknesses and the psychological legacies of colonization for the new societies. Lewis seems to identify at an early stage the hegemonic presence of the United States as potentially the greatest challenge to sovereignty that small Caribbean states would encounter. He also suggests in all his studies that this threat may be partially countered by collective arrangements, regional cooperation and greater integration into the Latin American environment.

Contemporary Discourse on Sovereignty in the Caribbean

Krasner was rather dismissive of the existence or utility value of sovereignty in particular for many developing states. Most other analysts would agree that globalization has fundamentally altered the operational environment for all states and societies, blurring irrevocably the demarcations between internal and external, domestic and international and leading to a loss of control over the domestic sphere for all states and especially for weaker ones. We argue below that there has been recognition of the changing currency of sovereignty in Caribbean discourse. Nonetheless, the concept continues to hold much symbolic and some practical value for Caribbean populations and political elites.

The ideal of sovereignty has a very personal significance for the individual in societies where most of the population holds a recent historical memory of slavery and profound exploitation. Although this memory may be subconscious, it is certainly there. Sovereignty is understood, first and foremost, in the domestic sense. It is linked to the most fundamental sense of personal freedom, to exercising control over one's physical person, to controlling one's domestic space, building a family and a community, to the acquisition and exercise of property rights, to experiencing various rights of citizenship.[35] During the colonial era in the Caribbean, the quest for freedom and personhood led first to the carving out of Maroon communities in some territories and later on to the founding of free villages. Sovereignty at the national level was largely unattainable, so control of one's destiny could only be envisaged at the community level. Likewise, the state machinery was often viewed with deep suspicion by people who experienced its power as predatory and oppressive rather than liberating. Therefore there remains across the region a strong attachment to sub-state territorial spaces and identities. These may be insular spaces or other types of geographical zones within countries. As populations' sense of security and control over their destiny vis-à-vis the state and the global sphere weakens, their attempts to exercise sovereignty over local spaces intensify. In the contemporary period, segments of the local population may get caught between contending domestic expressions of sovereignty: the attempts of the state to assert its jurisdiction over national territory and the resistance by a local faction seeking to maintain its control over a circumscribed space. These can be compounded by the activities of transnational networks, notably by the activities of criminal gangs. So, just as Bodin and Hobbes argued so long ago, national sovereignty still entails the need to establish the state's legitimacy and then its control over the totality of national territory.

On the other hand, Ralph Premdas argues that traditional conceptions of state sovereignty have lost relevance in the contemporary context insofar as they relate to territoriality, identity and citizenship. Caribbean populations exhibit a pragmatic understanding of the deficiencies of their national environments and the compensatory options opened up by globalization, and they migrate in large numbers in search of better opportunities. Premdas points out that Caribbean people show dexterity in manipulating multiple identities and citizenship rights but that they retain a sense of Caribbean identity. Caribbean states should therefore creatively adjust their policies and practices to facilitate the affiliation needs of their migratory citizens and to construct mutually beneficial relationships with their large diasporas. He advocates

> a new international relations of the Caribbean…less territory-based and more people-based, so that inadequacy of state boundaries and exclusivity in claims of sovereign control can be more closely aligned to the multiple identities of the transnationalised and hybridized people of the region.[36]

The scope of sovereignty is a function of levels of power, both in individual and community terms and more globally in the relationship between the Caribbean state and the external environment. In the ensuing discussion, I try to explore how it is visualized by political elites and also the wider societies' understanding and consciousness of the concept of sovereignty. Bishop and Payne [37] in a discussion of the shortfalls of Caribbean regionalism, argued that

> the esteem in which Caribbean states and their leaders seem to hold their sovereignty cannot be underestimated. Whether it is understood analytically, practically or rhetorically, sovereignty has grown into a highly sensitive and emotive issue with politicians typically placing a 'high premium' upon it…regional elites have doggedly attached themselves to a somewhat reductionist notion of sovereignty, characterized by a narrow, state-centric and largely 'zero-sum' understanding of the term.

Although there is some validity to this statement, the following discussion attempts a more nuanced exploration of Caribbean perceptions of sovereignty in order to throw further light on the issue.

The early statements of Caribbean political elites revealed a multifaceted understanding of sovereignty. Unlike their populations, they were primarily concerned with its external aspects. Even while they celebrated the possibilities for self-determination, they emphasized that political sovereignty could be infringed by more powerful external actors and that economic independence was a vital part of the equation. Michael Manley remarked that 'one by one, the great figures of the liberation process of the 1940s and 1950s were coming to realize that political freedom could become a sham...if it did not rest upon the capacity to determine the course of economic development within the boundaries of the new nations'.[38] In similar vein, Eric Williams's Chaguaramas Declaration in 1970 asserts that

> too much dependence on metropolitan governments and metropolitan firms is incompatible with the economic sovereignty of the peoples of the Caribbean...Economic independence means that the major decision-making on economic matters becomes internal to the country. (*However*) It does not mean an end to contact with the outside world.[39]

The spectre of external domination via their economic transactions loomed large even in the most defiant declarations in 1976 and 1979 by Michael Manley or Maurice Bishop. In fact, Bishop gave a sober acknowledgement of the vulnerabilities of micro-statehood in his inaugural speech to the United Nations General Assembly in October 1979:

> I want now to raise the issue of small states in the international community. Notwithstanding our basic position that all states are equal, sovereign, independent entities...there are significant physical, demographic and economic differences among us...As sovereign governments we are separately responsible for our own programmes of economic transformation but our international solidarity and cooperation are critical for the meeting of our goals.[40]

Bishop's statement reveals the inherent ambiguity of the relationship with the international community for the political elites of Caribbean small states. There is strong support for the Westphalian norm of every state's right to sovereignty, self-determination and non-interference in domestic affairs, while the international community is perceived as an ally in protecting this norm. Ronald Sanders points out the symbiotic association, 'the possession of sovereignty is of great importance to small states...it is their status as 'sovereign' states...that gives them access to the international system.'⁴¹ He lists the leverage and visibility that come from having a vote in international bodies, a voice in international fora and the authority to enter into development assistance agreements as advantages of sovereign status. He goes further and claims that the very survival of some small states may rest on the international community's endorsement of the principle of their sovereignty. His statements and those of Maurice Bishop, cited above, underline the dilemma of small Caribbean states. On the one hand, there is chronic dependence on the international community for recognition, protection and socio-economic assistance. On the other hand, the international community ultimately imposes conditionalities on their sovereignty in exchange for this support. This confirms Krasner's claim that states collude with the international community in accepting restrictions on their sovereignty in exchange for various types of benefits.⁴² Certainly, in the case of small, weak states, they may see themselves as having no alternative.

Sovereignty and Economic Issues

We now turn to three dimensions of Caribbean relations with the international community which illustrate their experience and understanding of the nature and limits of their sovereignty. The first concerns states' dealings with the international financial institutions (IFIs) during the debt crises and structural adjustment programmes between the 1970s and the present day. Significantly, even in the 1970s, elite statements about their negotiations with the International Monetary Fund (IMF) tended towards pragmatism rather than inflammatory rhetoric. One example is President Forbes Burnham of Guyana, speaking in 1978:

> We have had to come to arrangements with the IMF not because we were desirous of doing so but because there was little alternative... We all know the IMF is a capitalist organization but in the final analysis we have to live with realities and that is a reality which we must face.⁴³

Such a 'reality check' was also conveyed in Jamaican Prime Minister Michael Manley's two contrasting statements just three months apart. In January 1977, he proclaimed that 'this government...will not accept anybody anywhere in the world telling us what to do in our country. We are the master in our house',[44] but in April 1977, he argued that he 'had no choice'[45] going on to state later on that 'having once been committed to it, I did everything in my power to mobilize the country to have the programme work. What else could I do?'[46]

During the negotiations held by Jamaica and Guyana with the IMF in the 1970s and 1980s, the fiercest resistance to IMF conditionalities came sometimes from factions within ruling parties, but more generally from the political opposition and from the wider population which suffered considerable economic hardships as a result of the austerity programmes.[47] Nonetheless, although IMF programmes continued to be regarded as unpleasant medicine, the initial levels of hostility towards the IFI policies and programmes in the 1970s were gradually diluted by the late 1980s towards greater acceptance of neoliberal economic principles. In the OECS countries, there was accommodation of some degree of IMF oversight of macroeconomic policy via advisory services to the Eastern Caribbean Central Bank from the late 1980s onwards. In Barbados, in the economic downturn in 1991, the government pre-empted an IMF structural adjustment programme by imposing its own, accompanied by a strong mechanism of social partnership and dialogue, thereby retaining greater leverage and policy space in its negotiations with the international agencies.

Academic analyses of Caribbean states' earlier involvement with the IMF concluded that governments could retain greater leverage in the relationship if they 'began the negotiations before the economic crisis becomes unmanageable;'[48] that some countries' economic programmes failed in part due to poor management and a lack of clear objectives;[49] and that economic crisis was generally exacerbated by political crisis and poor political decision-making on the part of the elites.[50] C.Y. Thomas,[51] giving a retrospective look at the Jamaican experience of the 1970s, concluded that radical socio-economic reform projects are by and large incompatible with the adoption of neoliberal economic adjustment programmes, that small Caribbean economies are inherently subject to tremendous domestic constraints and that, finally, the only chance of success for a social justice agenda coupled with IMF-type economic reforms would require a very strong commitment by the government to the marginalized masses and far more democratic participation in crucial political and economic decision-making from the outset. All concur that the IMF programmes resulted in deteriorating standards of living for the middle and lower income groups in the countries concerned and in escalating rates of emigration as people chose to vote with their feet and join the diaspora.

A new round of IMF supervised structural adjustment programmes has taken place in the twenty-first century, starting with Dominica in 2003–2006 and featuring a spate of agreements since the global economic recession began in 2008. In this new dispensation, the IMF has striven to present a sovereignty-friendly image, stressing that the adjustment programmes are more flexible, that they are developed and driven by national authorities and that they include strong measures for social protection.[52] There has been an interesting range of reactions and commentaries from Caribbean actors. Possibly the best case analysis would be that of Dominica which successfully completed a stringent IMF programme between 2003 and 2006. Popular consultation and poverty alleviation measures appear to have been important elements of the programme.[53] Media commentary at the beginning of the programme included not only criticisms and concerns but also the view that IMF surveillance was one of the conditions of membership of that organization, and that the country did not in any case enjoy complete monetary sovereignty since it was already a member of the Eastern Caribbean Currency Union and was constrained by the policies of that grouping.[54]

In most of the current batch of IMF agreements, political leaders continue to affirm the 'no alternative' position and the contemporary changes in IMF policies.[55] Critical commentary in some regional media questions the extent to which IMF programmes are shaped by governmental priorities and choices and expresses scepticism about the degree of transformation in the relationship between the agency and its small developing country clients.[56] Certain analysts partly attribute the financial crises to long term poor economic management by their countries' political elites and suggest that better governance is only possible via international intervention. Such sentiments are captured in the statement, 'What should we fear most? The regular annual deficits and the mounting national debt or the hope of change via the IMF since change does not seem possible with the present electoral system?'[57] And finally, the issues of sovereignty and property rights, power asymmetries and government impotence, the lack of transparency and democratic consultation emerge starkly as micro-states like St Kitts-Nevis contemplate debt restructuring, and the proposed sale of land to international creditors to reduce phenomenally high debt to GDP ratios. One editorial comments on 'the underlying anxiety that we are again becoming a landless people... this tsunami of emotions we are now experiencing is as a result of the earthquake of revelations from the IMF and Prime Minister's press conference of Friday 10th June 2011.'[58]

The present discussion does not allow for a full analysis of Caribbean dealings with another major institution of the global political economy, the World Trade Organization (WTO). Suffice it to say that many scholars and policymakers are also rather pessimistic in their assessment of the limited domestic policy space or gains made in states' attempts to negotiate advantageous international arrangements.[59] Overall, there is consensus that the establishment of the WTO with a strong disputes settlement system has led to a loss of domestic room for manoeuvre. While Caribbean states have grown more sophisticated in their understanding of international trade rules and structures and more technically competent in pursuing their interests in these fora, they still suffer from enormous power asymmetries and their sovereignty is constrained in the domestic organization of production and trade.[60]

Sovereignty and Security

G.K. Lewis and various Caribbean writers mention US hegemonic power and security interests as a major challenge to Caribbean sovereignty. The conclusion of the Shiprider Agreements between 1995 and 1997 between the United States and several Caribbean states became a catalyst for the discussion of sovereignty and security in the era of transnational criminal networks.[61] Patricia Hall, US State Department official, defended her government's position in 1996 when she stated 'All nations in and bordering on the Caribbean... must recognize that global problems require global solutions...If we are to succeed against a threat that transcends national borders, we will have to adopt common strategies that go beyond the traditional limits of national sovereignty.'[62] Notwithstanding this rhetoric of global partnership and cooperation, the US authorities introduced the Shiprider regimes on a bilateral basis, negotiating with each individual

Caribbean state rather than engaging in multilateral discussions. Multilateral engagement only began to emerge in May 1997 with a US-CARICOM Summit on security and other forms of cooperation in Barbados. For their own part, the policies and statements of Caribbean governments demonstrated wide divergences on how to reconcile their sovereignty and security objectives.

Between 1995 and 1996, Trinidad and Tobago and the OECS states signed the original version of the Shiprider Treaty, neither questioning its terms nor proposing a regional approach to negotiating with the United States. Trinidad's Attorney General, Ramesh Maharaj justified the agreement as a means of 'protecting his country's sovereignty against drug barons,'[63] identifying the state's main sovereignty challenge as transnational criminals rather than the relationship with the hegemonic power. The prime minister of Antigua and Barbuda argued that the countries concerned had not surrendered their sovereignty since their governments had made deliberate decisions to protect the national interest through signing the Shiprider, but then went on to state that 'the reality is that a small state by itself cannot expect to maintain its individual sovereignty against larger and more powerful states....'[64] There is little evidence of extensive national consultations on the agreements before they were signed by the respective governments.

The governments of Jamaica and Barbados, on the other hand, interpreted some of the terms of the prototype Shiprider Agreement as infringing national sovereignty[65] and they sought to negotiate more favourable terms. This was done against the backdrop of considerable pressure exerted by the United States authorities in the form of threatened decertification and other sanctions. Their concerns focused on the lack of reciprocity provisions in the agreement; the degrees of partnership with the United States; consultation and authorization procedures in the policing of their marine territory and airspace; and US legal liability and procedures for redress in the case of abuses in the operation of the agreement. Ultimately, they succeeded in negotiating modified Shiprider Agreements which reflected these concerns.[66] In 2004 however, after the Shiprider had been in operation for some six years, Jamaica went on to sign a protocol that extended US powers of action in its waters.[67]

Regional academics and the media played a major role in informing and educating the public about the details of the agreements and the national and international legal principles involved.[68] In general, the issue was framed in terms of a debate on national and regional sovereignties and the relationship with the hegemonic power, with varied perspectives being put forward. Ivelaw Griffith, analysing the issue some years later, adopted a pragmatic, operational approach, making a distinction between 'formal-legal sovereignty' and 'positive sovereignty (*which*) includes having the economic, technical, military and other capabilities to declare, implement and enforce public policy.'[69] He advocates for flexibility on the part of policymakers and a focus on achieving positive sovereignty, particularly in the wake of September 2001 and the launching of the Global War on Terror.

Hilbourne Watson points out that in the rapidly changing global social relations of production, security, like many other issue areas, has been shifting from the national to the global level of decision-making. While this process would affect all state actors, the crisis of the nation-state would logically be felt more keenly in weaker states. The US was restructuring its hegemonic relations in order to retain and reinforce its global position. The Shiprider agreements, together with a number of other recently proposed cooperative security agreements, would facilitate the US in legally exercising extra-territorial jurisdiction over the Caribbean area.[70] Watson examines the Caribbean discourse on preserving the principle of national sovereignty and on adopting a regional approach to negotiations with the US but concludes that it misses the point – 'like capital, sovereignty is becoming increasingly unglued from its traditional moorings in national states.'[71] He calls for a paradigm shift in Caribbean thought away from outdated notions of the nation state and sovereignty without, however, suggesting a concrete alternative.

In the era of the United States' Global War on Terror and the growth of transnational security threats in the twenty-first century, the grasp on national sovereign control in this domain has become increasingly tenuous. CARICOM governments in 2001 identified the transnational drugs trade and rising levels of crime and violence as major threats to their societies and embarked on a regional security cooperation initiative even as their institutionalized cooperation with the US and other external partners deepened.[72] While external support for capacity-building in performing vital security functions has proven indispensable, there are periodic tensions between the security priorities of the Caribbean states and those of their more powerful partners. National and regional sovereignty challenges are posed in the installation of sensitive security infrastructure and cooperation procedures. Moreover, the fight against transnational crime and terrorism may involve adopting controversial surveillance methods or civilian policing techniques that bring into question civil liberties and privacy rights. Just as one commentator stated in 1996 that 'Shiprider is a populist issue that reaches to the heart of what government and representative democracy are all about,'[73] the same is true of anti-gang and counter-terrorism measures today. Arguably, despite Griffith's case for pursuing 'positive sovereignty' and effective public policy capabilities, the adoption of such measures requires much more democratic consultation with parliaments and with entire societies than presently exists. These consultations should encompass questions about the acceptable scope of security measures, should clearly define which national officials have the authority to enter into agreements with external partners and the issues which require cabinet and/or parliamentary approval. Only in this way can the state's legitimacy be strengthened and increasingly controversial areas of collaboration with external partners be rendered more acceptable.[74]

CARICOM Perspectives on External Intervention in Haiti 2004–2010

Haiti simultaneously symbolizes for its neighbours an inspiring historical example of the fight for freedom and sovereignty and unhappy cycles of repression, state decline and international occupation. The observations here are confined to examining CARICOM responses to two Haitian crises – the ousting of President Jean-Bertrand Aristide in February 2004 and the massive earthquake disaster in January 2010 and its aftermath. In both cases, CARICOM's focus, no doubt aimed at countering the international 'failed state' narrative, was the bolstering of Haitian sovereignty and governance capabilities.

In February 2004, CARICOM's protracted mediation efforts towards a power-sharing arrangement between the Haitian government and opposition forces were abruptly terminated by an armed takeover and President Aristide's transport to the Central African Republic with the involvement of the United States and France. These catalytic events provoked outrage from CARICOM's political elites and populations alike. Stating that 'the circumstances under which President Aristide demitted office set a dangerous precedent for democratically elected governments everywhere and promote the unconstitutional removal of duly elected persons from office,'[75] they refused to recognize the interim administration of Gerard Latortue and called for an investigation first by the United Nations Security Council and then by the OAS, of the circumstances under which President Aristide left office. This official position received widespread support from the people of the region although there were mixed responses in Haiti itself. [76] The Jamaican government went further, providing political refuge for President Aristide and his family until he received long-term asylum in South Africa.[77] Despite some ensuing tension with the United States, relations between the Haitian government and the regional grouping were not normalized until an elected government had been installed in 2006. CARICOM actors perceived themselves as standing up for the principles of sovereignty and democratic processes. While some assistance was provided to Haitian asylum seekers during that period, they refrained from participating in the international community's operations in Haiti until the organization of the elections.

After the devastating 2010 earthquake, CARICOM again focused not only on providing relief but defined an additional role for itself of trying to shore up Haiti's battered sovereignty vis-à-vis the rest of the international community. This can be noted in several statements by CARICOM representatives during 2010: 'Haitians must be at the centre of their country's development and reconstruction;'[78] 'CARICOM will serve as a leading advocate on its (Haiti's) behalf in their interfacing with the international community.'[79] As CARICOM's Special Representative to Haiti, Fomer Jamaican Prime Minister P.J. Patterson 'further underscored the critical importance of respecting the sovereignty of Haiti.'[80] Yet another expression of sovereignty concerns came from Prime Minister Roosevelt Skerritt of Dominica, who 'told the media that there were several NGOs doing their own thing in Haiti, oblivious to the vision, strategic direction and wishes of the Haitian government...he urged donors to give more budgetary support to the government of Haiti.'[81] CARICOM's partnership with the OAS in the observation of the 2011 presidential election in Haiti can also be seen as supporting the goal of sovereignty and democratic governance.

Conclusion

G.K. Lewis's reflections on sovereignty and statehood were mostly written before the onslaught of globalization. They expressed his belief in the value of sovereignty and, for the most part, they accurately predicted the principal threats and challenges that Caribbean small states would face after independence. Throughout his career, he emphasized that regional integration could provide a partial shield against vulnerability and hegemonic pressures, even in his work on Grenada which conveyed disillusionment with CARICOM's performance. Nonetheless, more recent chapters of regional integration offer contradictory images which do not entirely support this latter view of Lewis.

As Bishop and Payne contend, regional integration has been viewed mainly as a means of reinforcing national sovereignty. On the one hand, CARICOM governments have experimented timidly with pooling sovereignty and resources in areas of glaring national incapacities and they have registered modest success in certain fields. Likewise, as the case of Haiti demonstrates, governments have on occasion sought to use the regional platform to defend fragile sovereign states. But there are many instances where national sovereignty concerns have worked against effective regional governance. Since the 1990s, national sovereignty has been seen to be progressively under siege. Consequently, national populations and political elites, faced with the discomfort of IMF austerity programmes, the declining global competitiveness of their major economic sectors and rising domestic unemployment, have shown much greater resistance to notions of regional citizenship, resource pooling and the shift from national to regional sovereignty. While they may not be able to defend their space against all the incursions of the international community, they assert their claims vigorously against neighbouring actors with similar capability levels to their own.

It is also the case that, while sovereignty has been defended viscerally upon occasion, our survey of the views of several political leaders, academics and journalists suggests that Caribbean societies carry a very nuanced and complex understanding of sovereignty.

History has certainly predisposed them to place a high value on the sovereignty ideal. However, their actions and utterances indicate a pragmatic acceptance of the limits imposed by power asymmetries and international structures. Caribbean political elites enter into many international partnerships and arrangements, conscious of the sovereignty compromises but having made cost-benefit calculations about the probable outcomes.

Hobbes and Rousseau both linked sovereignty to the state's legitimacy. Rousseau democratized the concept with his idea of 'popular sovereignty.' Contemporary economic and security governance in the Caribbean requires making difficult choices which must be underpinned by far-reaching public consultation and involvement in order to gain legitimacy and support. This constitutes the exercise of popular sovereignty. It is increasingly evident that it can only be achieved with considerable rethinking and restructuring of our democratic institutions. This encompasses strengthening the mechanisms for transparent public information, far more inclusive consultative structures, more effective parliamentary deliberation and oversight of the executive arm of government, stronger regulatory bodies and well-functioning justice systems. Moreover, as Premdas pointed out, the migratory lives and multiple identities of Caribbean people require us to rethink the state and to develop avenues for the diasporic population to exercise transnational citizenship rights, an issue which has not yet been fully explored in most Caribbean polities.

In conclusion, therefore, it is only when Caribbean populations feel more secure in their exercise of citizenship rights and more satisfied with the processes of democratic consultation and deliberation within their own societies that they may perceive their sovereignty as being enhanced. Such a process must underpin the state's regional and international commitments.

Notes

1. The term 'Slums of Empire' was used by British Prime Minister Lloyd George in the 1930s in reference to the Caribbean. See R. Cox Alomar, *Revisiting the Transatlantic Triangle: The Constitutional Decolonization of the Eastern Caribbean* (Kingston: Ian Randle Publishers, 2009), xix and 11.
2. See *Statement on the Situation in the Turks and Caicos Islands, an Associate Member of the Community,* CARICOM (2009a) Press Release 96/2009 24/03/2009, http://www.caricom.org/jsp/pressreleases/2009. Accessed 29/9/2011; *Statement on the Situation in the Turks and Caicos Islands issued at the Conclusion of the 30th Regular Meeting of the Conference of Heads of Government of CARICOM 2−5 July 2009 Georgetown Guyana,* CARICOM (2009b), Press Release 270/2009 4/07/2009, www.caricom.org/jsp/pressreleases/2009. Accessed 29/9/2011; Galmo Williams, *Statement by the Hon. Galmo Williams, Premier of the Turks and Caicos Islands,* CRS/2009/CRP.12, United Nations Caribbean Regional Seminar on the Implementation of the Second International Decade for the Eradication of Colonialism, Frigate Bay St Kitts, 12–14 May 2009, www.un.org/en/decolonization/pdf/crp_2009_08_williams.pdf . Accessed 2/10/2011; P. Clegg and E. Pantojas-García, eds., *Governance in the Non-Independent Caribbean: Challenges and Opportunities in the Twenty-First Century* (Kingston: Ian Randle Publishers, 2009).
3. See C. Corbin, 'Constitutional Reform and Political Identity in the Non-Independent Caribbean,' *Overseas Territories Review* 31/01/2010, http://overseasreview.blogspot.com/2010/01/constitutional-reform-and-political.html Accessed 2/10/2011; Clegg and Pantojas-García, eds., *Governance in the Non-Independent Caribbean.*
4. C. Barrow-Giles, *Regional Trends in Constitutional Developments in the Commonwealth Caribbean* (Briefing Paper, SSRC Conflict Prevention and Peace Forum January 2010), 7.
5. Examples of the former include Jamaica's Prime Minister Michael Manley's speech in 1977, 'We are not for sale. And tell them any time they are willing to deal with an honourable Jamaica built on principle, sovereignty, pride and dignity, then we will talk the investment of the money. But if we are to return to our knees they can keep the money'; Grenada's Prime Minister Maurice Bishop in 1979, 'Grenada is a sovereign and independent country tho' a tiny speck on the world map…No country has the right to tell us what to do or how to run our country or who to be friendly with. We are not in anybody's backyard and we are definitely not for sale'. More measured reflections on sovereignty include Barbados's Prime Minister Errol Barrow's statement to the United Nations General Assembly in 1966 that Barbados would be 'friend of all, satellite of none'.
6. Cited in Clegg and Pantojas-García, eds., *Governance in the Non-Independent Caribbean,* xiv.
7. See P. Wearne, 'Guadeloupe – History', 482 and 'Martinique – History', 594–95 in *Europa Regional Surveys of the World: South America, Central America and the Caribbean 2009,* 17th ed. (London: Routledge 2008).
8. For example, the maritime delimitation disputes between Barbados and Trinidad 1999–2007, the maritime and terrestrial border delimitation

disputes between Guyana and Suriname and of course, the very longstanding territorial claims facing Guyana in relation to Venezuela and Belize in relation to Guatemala.
9. A. Payne and M. Bishop, 'Caribbean Regional Governance and the Sovereignty/Statehood Problem', *Caribbean Paper No. 8*, Centre for International Governance Innovation, (2010) www.cigionline.org Accessed 1/9/2010, 3.
10. A. Heywood, *Key Concepts in Politics* (London: Macmillan Press, 2000), 37.
11. 'Sovereignty is the absolute and perpetual power of commanding in a state...the power of giving laws to all the people in general...the right of declaring war and of making peace, the right of being the court of last resort...the right of instituting and removing even the most important officers and ministers, the right of imposing charges and subsidies on subjects...the right of increasing or depreciating the value of money, the right of requiring an oath of allegiance from all subjects and liegemen without exception....' Bodin, 1576, *Six Books of the Republic*, quoted in W.T. Jones, ed., *Masters of Political Thought Volume Two: Machiavelli to Bentham* (London: Harrap, 1980), 57–59.
12. Thomas Hobbes, *Leviathan (1651)*, cited in Jones, *Masters of Political Thought*, Vol. 2.
13. Ibid., 116–26.
14. 'Let us agree that might never makes right, and that we have a duty to obey only legitimate powers...Since no man has a natural authority over other men, and since might never makes right, it follows that agreements are the basis for all legitimate authority among men....' Rousseau (1762) *Contrat Social*, cited in Jones, *Masters of Political Thought* Vol. 2., 261, 262.
15. H. Bull, *The Anarchical Society: A Study of Order in World Politics* (London: Macmillan Press, 1977), 254.
16. J. Rapley, 'The New Middle Ages', *Foreign Affairs*, May–June (2006): 95.
17. S. Krasner 'Rethinking the Sovereign State Model', *Review of International Studies*, no. 27 (2001): 17–48.
18. Ibid.
19. Ibid.
20. S. Krasner, 'Sharing Sovereignty: New Institutions for Collapsed and Failing States', *International Security* 29, no. 2 (2004): 85–120.
21. A. Fenton, 'Haiti and the Dangers of Responsibility to Protect', January 3, 2009. www.haitianalysis.com/2009/1/3/haiti-and-the-dangers-of-responsibility-to-protect Accessed July 12 2011.
22. T. Biersteker, 'State, Sovereignty and Territory', in *Handbook of International Relations*, eds. W. Carlsnaes, T. Risse and B. Simmons, 161–64 (London: Sage Publications, 2005).
23. Ibid., 163.
24. There were allusions to sovereignty by the Irish and Greek populations and sometimes by their government officials in 2010–2011 as they reacted to the imposition of harsh austerity programmes by the European Union and the International Monetary Fund (IMF) as a condition for financial bail-outs of their economies. Likewise, the various transformations of the European Union from the Treaty of Maastricht (1994) through to the Treaty of Lisbon (2009) have been accompanied by much debate on the theme of sovereignty.
25. Cox Alomar, *Revisiting the Transatlantic Triangle*, 4.

26. G.K. Lewis, *Puerto Rico: Freedom and Power in the Caribbean* (Kingston: Ian Randle Publishers, 2004) first published by Monthly Review Press, 1963; *The Growth of the Modern West Indies* (New York: Monthly Review Press, 1968); *Main Currents in Caribbean Thought: The Historical Evolution of Caribbean Society in its Ideological Aspects 1492–1900* (Baltimore: Johns Hopkins University Press, 1983); *Grenada: The Jewel Despoiled* (Baltimore: Johns Hopkins University Press, 1987).
27. G.K. Lewis, *Puerto Rico*, ix.
28. Ibid., 436, 441.
29. This seems very similar to more recent negotiations on constitutional change between the Overseas Territories of Anguilla, Bermuda, the Cayman Islands, the Turks and Caicos Islands and Montserrat and the British Government, ongoing since the early 1990s.
30. G.K. Lewis, *Growth*, 132–33.
31. V. Lewis, 'Small States in the International Society with Special Reference to the Associated States', *Caribbean Quarterly* 18 no. 2 (1972): 44–45.
32. Lewis, *Growth*, 391.
33. Lewis, *Main Currents*, 286.
34. Ibid., 301.
35. Similar thoughts are expressed by Holger Henke. He describes this as the Caribbean epistemology. H. Henke, 'Drugs in the Caribbean: The Shiprider Controversy and the Question of Sovereignty', *European Review of Latin American and Caribbean Studies* 64 (1998): 29.
36. R. Premdas, 'Self-Determination and Sovereignty in the Caribbean: Migration, Transnational Identities and Deterritorialisation of the State', in *Caribbean Survival and the Global Challenge*, ed. R. Ramsaran, 52 (Kingston: Ian Randle Publishers, 2002).
37. A. Payne and M. Bishop 'Caribbean Regional Governance and the Sovereignty/Statehood Problem', *Caribbean Paper No. 8*, (2010). Centre for International Governance Innovation. www.cigionline.org Accessed 1/9/2010. 3.
38. M. Manley, *Jamaica: Struggle in the Periphery* (London: Third World Media Ltd., 1982), 6.
39. S. Cudjoe, ed., *Eric Williams Speaks* (Wellesley, MA: Calaloux Publishers, 1993), 302.
40. Maurice Bishop, address to 34th Session of the United Nations General Assembly, New York, October 10 1979, www.assatashakur.org Accessed 13/07/2011.
41. R. Sanders, *Crumbled Small: The Commonwealth Caribbean in World Politics* (London: Hansib Publications, 2005), 76.
42. S. Krasner, 'Rethinking the Sovereign State Model', *Review of International Studies* 27 (2001): 23–26.
43. See T. Ferguson, *To Survive Sensibly or to Court Heroic Death: Management of Guyana's Political Economy 1965–1985* (Georgetown: Public Affairs Consulting Enterprise, 1999), 238.
44. See A. Payne and P. Sutton, *Charting Caribbean Development* (London: Macmillan Press, 2001), 77.
45. Ibid., 78.
46. H. Bartilow, *The Debt Dilemma: IMF Negotiations in Jamaica, Grenada and Guyana* (London: Macmillan Press, 1997), 26.

47. C.Y. Thomas, *The Poor and the Powerless: Economic Policy and Change in the Caribbean* (London: Latin American Bureau, 1988); Bartilow, *The Debt Dilemma*; Ferguson, *To Survive Sensibly*.
48. Bartilow, *The Debt Dilemma*, 139.
49. Ferguson, *To Survive Sensibly*; Thomas, *The Poor and the Powerless*.
50. Ferguson, *To Survive Sensibly;* Thomas, *The Poor and the Powerless;* Bartilow, *The Debt Dilemma*.
51. Thomas, *The Poor and the Powerless*.
52. See for example, in the Sept. 2011 IMF Country Report No. 11/270 SKN 2011 Article IV Consultation and Staff Report for St Kitts and Nevis, 4 'It was important for the authorities to demonstrate that they could implement the recommendations of the 2010 Article IV Consultation prior to the start on a program discussion to show ownership. Demonstrating ownership was important to overcome the still very strong stigma in the society concerning Fund adjustment programs.' Similarly, in the press conference following the agreement on a Stand By Arrangement in June 2011, the Head of the IMF delegation states 'the good news is that there are not really conditions...the government of St Kitts and Nevis has set itself targets and what we would do with the government jointly is to review the targets on a regular basis.' www.thestkittsnevisobserver.com/2011/06/10/national-debt.html. Accessed Sept. 1, 2011.
53. See for example, Prime Minister Skerritt's statement in 2006 that any extension of the programme would require wider consultations with the Dominican people. Dominica was also able to use its relations with other multilateral and bilateral donors to construct social protection and poverty alleviation mechanisms.
54. T. Fontaine, 'Dominica and the IMF', www.thedominican.net 1, no. 42, May 7, 2003. Accessed July 20, 2011.
55. One example is Jamaica's Finance Minister Audley Shaw in July 2009 in Parliament, 'Jamaica has no real option at this time but to return to a borrowing relation with the IMF.' See 'No option – Jamaica returning to IMF – Shaw – No immediate effect on public sector' *Jamaica Gleaner* 22/7/2009, http://jamaicagleaner.com/gleaner/20090722/lead/lead1.html Accessed 11/9/2011.
56. See for example, a critical editorial in the *Jamaica Observer* 21/08/2011, 'The IMF cannot escape its responsibility' http://www.jamaicaobserver.com/editorial/IMF-cannot-escape-its-responsibility_948660 Accessed 11/9/2011. See also L. Callender, 'IMF: Friend or Foe, Partner or Prison Warder?' www.sknvibes.com/news/newsdetails.cfm/28667 posted 6/6/2011 Accessed 20/9/2011.
57. Callender, 'IMF: Friend or Foe', 6/6/2011, www.sknvibes.com Accessed 20/9/2011).
58. L. Callender, 'What happens when we become 'Asset Poor' and are still indebted?' 18/6/2011, www.kittivisianlife.com.articles/06-2011/ Accessed 20/9/2011.
59. See R. Grynberg, ed., *WTO at the Margins: Small States and the Multilateral Trading System* (Cambridge: Cambridge University Press, 2006); C. Deere-Birkbeck, E. Jones, N. Woods, *Manoeuvring at the Margins: Constraints Faced by Small States in International Trade Negotiations* (London: Commonwealth Secretariat, 2010).

60. P. Clegg, 'The Commonwealth Caribbean and the Challenges of Institutional Exclusion', *The Round Table* 97, no. 395 (2008): 227–41.
61. The Shiprider Agreements are also known as the Agreements on Maritime Counter-Drug Operations. Between 1995 and 1997, the United States approached all of the independent CARICOM island states to sign such bilateral agreements which would involve joint surveillance of states' maritime and airspace and US naval vessels and personnel being given the legal authority to stop, search and arrest vessels suspected of being engaged in drug smuggling activity. See E. Abrams 'The Shiprider Solution: Policing the Caribbean', *The National Interest*, Spring issue (1996): 86–92, and K. A. Brown (1997), 'The Shiprider Model: An Analysis of the US Proposed Agreement Concerning Maritime Counter-Drug Operations in its Wider Legal Context', *Contemporary Caribbean Legal Issues* no. 1, Faculty of Law, 1997, UWI Cave Hill, Barbados, 80. These initial agreements have since been reinforced and extended by a series of agreements with other Caribbean Basin territories and a multilateral *Agreement concerning Cooperation in Suppressing Illicit Maritime and Air Trafficking in Narcotics and Psychotropic Substances into the Caribbean Area* opened for signature at San Jose, Costa Rica in 2003.
62. *Jamaica Gleaner*, 'JA/US High-level Maritime Talks Open', October 17, 1996.
63. *Jamaica Gleaner*, 'T&T, UK Sign Crime Treaty', May 16, 1997.
64. *Jamaica Gleaner*, 'Bird Defends Countries Which Signed Shiprider Agreement', March 6, 1997.
65. Barbadian Prime Minister Owen Arthur argued that sovereignty was 'not divisible and could not be circumscribed' (cited in H. Watson, 'The "Shiprider Solution" and Post-Cold War Imperialism: Beyond Ontologies of State Sovereignty in the Caribbean', in *Living on the Borderlines: Issues in Caribbean Sovereignty and Development*, eds. C. Barrow-Giles and D. Marshall, 236 (Kingston: Ian Randle Publishers, 2003), while Jamaica's Prime Minister Patterson insisted on Jamaica's right to exclusive criminal jurisdiction in its territorial waters, even while it was willing to cooperate with the United States in narcotics interdiction (Jamaica Gleaner, 'JA/US High-level Maritime Talks Open', October 17, 1996.
66. S. Vasciannie 'Ship Rider Sails Home', *The Gleaner* 19/5/97; *Jamaica Gleaner*, 'Barbados yields to Shiprider', June 24, 1997.
67. *Jamaica Observer*, 'US, Jamaica to sign new Shiprider Agreement', February 5, 2004, www.jamaicaobserver.com/news/55324_US-Jamaica-to-sign-new-Shiprider-Agreement Accessed October 10 2011.
68. S. Vasciannie 'No Longer at Sea', *The Gleaner* 28/10/1996; S. Vasciannie, 'Shiprider Sails Home'; K.A. Brown, 'The Shiprider Model'; R. Singh, 'Frank Talking at Drugs Summit', *Jamaica Gleaner*, December 23, 1996.
69. I. Griffith, 'Security and Sovereignty in the Contemporary Caribbean: Probing Elements of the Local-Global Nexus', in *Living at the Borderlines: Issues in Caribbean Sovereignty and Development*, eds. C. Barrow-Giles and D. Marshall, 221 (Kingston: Ian Randle Publishers, 2003).
70. Watson, 'The "Shiprider Solution"', 230.
71. Ibid., 265.
72. Starting with appointing a Regional Task Force on Crime and Security in July 2001, CARICOM expanded regional security infrastructure notably with the

Council of Ministers responsible for National Security and Law Enforcement (2005), the establishment of the Implementation Agency for Crime and Security IMPACS (2006) and the entry into force of the Treaty on Security Assistance among CARICOM Member States (July 2006). See J. Byron, 'The Caribbean Community's "Fourth Pillar": The Evolution of Regional Security Governance', in *The Security Governance of Regional Organizations*, eds. E. Kirchner and R. Dominguez (New York: Routledge, 2011).

73. D. Jessop, 1996, cited in H. Henke, 'Drugs in the Caribbean: The Shiprider Controversy and the Question of Sovereignty', *European Review of Latin American and Caribbean Studies*, 64 (1998): 33.

74. One prominent example which demonstrated many of the democracy and security policy dilemmas facing Caribbean states was the Jamaican government's delayed response to the US request for the extradition of Christopher Coke which culminated in a military operation in sections of West Kingston in May 2010, the deaths of over 70 persons and the imposition of a geographically limited state of emergency for approximately two months. The uproar in Trinidad in 2010 over the discovery of the Security Intelligence Agency's wire-tapping activities constitutes another example. See R. Ramoutar, 'The Dark Side of Security Intelligence', *Trinidad and Tobago Guardian* December 12, 2010, http://test.guardian.co.tt/index.php?q=commentary/editorial/2010/12/12/dark-side-security-intelligence Accessed 17/10/2011.

75. *Jamaica Gleaner*, 'This Sets a Dangerous Precedent', March 1, 2004 http://jamaica-gleaner.com/gleaner/20040301/lead/lead1/html Accessed October 17, 2011.

76. See C. Granderson, 'The CARICOM Initiative towards Haiti: A Case of Small State Diplomacy', *Focal Point* 3 no. 6 (2004): 1–4; M. Smith, 'An Island among Islands: Haiti's Strange Relationship with the Caribbean Community', *Social and Economic Studies*, 54, no. 3 (2005): 176–95.

77. D. Jackson-Miller, 'Jamaica Welcomes Aristide, New Haiti Government Protests.' www.albionmonitor.com/0403a/copyright/(2004) Accessed October 17 2011.

78. CARICOM (2010d), 'Haitians Must be at the Centre of Their Development', press release 101/2010 11/3/2010 http://www.caricom.org/jsp/pressreleases/2010 Accessed 16/10/2011.

79. CARICOM (2010c), *Patterson's Statement to Donors Conference 31/3/2010* http://www.caricom.org/jsp/speeches/donor_conference_haiti_patterson.jsp Accessed 16/10/2011.

80. CARICOM (2010b) 'Failure Not an Option in Haiti Reconstruction', press release 249/2010 3/6/2010, http://www.caricom.org/jsp/pressreleases/2010 Accessed 16/10/2011.

81. CARICOM (2010a) press release 310/2010 7/7/2010 http://www.caricom.org/jsp/pressreleases/2010 Accessed 16/10/2011.

8 | *Some Perspectives on Gordon Lewis's Legacy in the Understanding of Regionalism*

Edward Greene

Introduction

This Conference is a fitting tribute to one of the most erudite scholars to have graced the Caribbean. The profundity of his thinking, the elegance of his language and the pervasiveness of his logic, wisdom, cutting wit and fearless candour are indeed essential characteristics that memorialize Gordon K. Lewis. In addition there was a humanity and compassion in his willingness to foster in others a sense of responsibility to champion the values of scholarly integrity and his dedication to lending his enviable understanding of colonialism and development and clarity of thought toward the improvement of the welfare and well-being of the Caribbean. He had a profound belief in and vision about the potential for social and economic growth of the Caribbean. He championed the processes of its growth and development. He viewed regional integration as enabling the coherence of a group of member states to compete more creditably in the globalized economic and political environments and to collectively stem the tide of international and other adversities. Accordingly, he viewed economic and political integration as being a perennial and neuralgic issue in the Caribbean agenda: 'the recognition of seminal truth that only a unified Caribbean politically and economically can save the region from fatal particularism is at least a century old.'[1]

No doubt, were he with us today he would challenge us to try to come to grips with both the seminal truth and fatal particularism of regional integration as integral to the region's competitiveness in the global economy. My contribution will focus generally on Gordon Lewis's legacy to regional thought and development and more specifically on the salient features, challenges and achievements of the integration process and the path ahead for the Caribbean Community.

Salient Features of the Integration Process

Seminal truth underscores the philosophy of regionalism in its various manifestations. The short lived West Indies Federation (1958–62), followed by the revival of the integrationist ideal in the less ambitious Caribbean Free Trade Association (1968) was a central feature of Lewis's early works. Then there is the broadening of the scope of integration through the establishment of the Caribbean Community and Common Market (CARICOM), aimed at formalizing a customs union, foreign policy coordination and functional cooperation as prescribed in the Treaty of Chaguaramas.[2] The inclusion of Suriname in the early 1990s, which signalled a move toward cultural diversity further illustrated by the inclusion of Haiti as a full member of the Community in 2003, would certainly accord with Lewis's view of expanding the linguistic-political zone of the regional enterprise. In this regard the concept of CARIFORUM which embraces the Dominican Republic in an institutionalized arrangement with CARIOCM would have thrilled his political sensitivities. The establishment of the Caribbean Court of Justice (CCJ) in 2005, the initiation of the CARICOM Single Market in 2006, and the ultimate ambitious target set to achieve, by 2015, full mobility of goods, services and people and the harmonization of economic policies in a CARICOM Single Market and Economy (CSME), are in full alignment with his call for deepening the structural arrangements for regional co-operation.

If Gordon Lewis were present with us today he would no doubt have lamented not only the slow process toward deepening the integration process but would have expressed disappointment at the lack of the Pan-Caribbean mission that he passionately advocated. But he would also have examined the reasons why, and acknowledged the challenges and the elements of the region's success before endeavouring to propose the way forward.

The Challenges of the Regional Integration Movement

The evaluations of the Caribbean Community are normally cast in the mould of the ultimate ambitious target of a CSME which not even the most acclaimed regional integration movement, the European Community, has achieved. This is mainly due to the fact that the political and economic realities are not fully appreciated based on what gains can be realistically expected from the CSME process and what policies should be explored to maximize these gains.

Recent discussions by a Think Tank on *A Strategic Plan for Regional Development in CARICOM* co-ordinated by Professor Norman Girvan seek to establish the macroeconomic context of CARICOM's development, to review its components with what is called the single development vision for CARICOM and then to match this approach with national development strategies. Of 14 Member States in the Community, 12 participate in the CSME process. Overall, there are wide differences among these countries in resource endowments, human capital, economic infrastructure, and institutional capabilities, and their associated export specializations suggest that *divergence and differentiation rather than convergence and homogeneity* will continue to be the norm in the near future.[3]

What is clear is that the traditional gains from regional integration – whether in terms of enlarged market effect or competitive/allocational gains – are bound to be limited because the Caribbean economies display a high degree of openness, the enlarged market is relatively small and countries have relatively similar factor endowments. But impediments to an accelerated approach to the CSME are compounded by failure of the region to reach agreement on several important prerequisites for a 'single economy.' Among them are the establishment of a monetary union (not totally achieved by the EU), the adoption of a CARICOM Investment Agreement, the harmonization of tax policies and provision for fiscal incentives.

At the same time, successes have been recorded with respect to the establishment and implementation of the Regional Development Fund, the replacement of the Caribbean Regional Negotiating Mechanism with the Office of Trade Negotiations within the Directorate of Trade and Economic Integration of the Caribbean Community Secretariat, and the establishment of the Caribbean Competition Commission. These are all critical to sustaining a level playing field, coordinating trade negotiations and guaranteeing the application of common criteria in trade and production in the Community – all prerequisites for a sustainable integration process. In addition, many of the standards related to free movement of certain categories of persons, such as university graduates, cultural workers, teachers, nurses, and sports persons, are in effect. Other categories, like artisans and domestics with the CARICOM Vocation Qualification (CVQ) have been approved for inclusion. Yet other standards based on contingent rights of spouses and families of 'certified' workers are in the process of being finalized.

The basic rationale for CARICOM integration is to overcome the constraints on development specially associated with small size. Hence the Think Tank identified the principal aims of integration as:

- Achieving economies of scale,
- Sharing costs in operation of common services,
- Pooling bargaining power in external relations, and
- Pursuing synergies derived from combining human, financial and other resources of member states in the development effort.

While the first, normally associated with market integration and common policies, is within the comfort zone of macroeconomic analysts, 'the last three involve functional cooperation in one way or another and therefore constitute the principal challenge for the policy researcher.'[4] This is the dilemma. At the same time, it provides a useful opportunity to fast track regional integration through functional cooperation.

Despite the trade creating reforms of the 1990s and 2000s and the possible determinants of their impacts, there is evidence that the magnitude of the gains has not been significant. At the same time, integration in the area of 'non tradables' i.e. services related to the countries' social and physical infrastructure has over the years demonstrated substantial successes that are often not recognized by focusing strictly on the outcomes of the CSME.

While acknowledging this implementation deficit, most objective analysts agree on the magnitude of the tasks designed to achieve the CSME. Considerable technical work has been done by technicians in the CARICOM Secretariat and elsewhere on the important pillars of the CSME: such as development of a CARICOM Investment Code, a CARICOM Financial Services Agreement, proposals for the reform of Community governance and the free movement of additional categories of skilled labour. The bottlenecks are by and large due to national resistance, changes in governments and delays in the facilitation of the necessary national regulations or legislation to bring these policies and programmes into effect. In a more profound sense, accelerated approaches are stymied by the sustained preoccupation with the notion that CARICOM comprises 'sovereign states' which would be eroded by the application of 'shared sovereignty'.

Yet, with very few exceptions, the importance of the Caribbean regional integration mechanism (CARICOM) has been fully grasped by people, policymakers, academics, civil society, media and advocates. The problems with CARICOM have been expressed in terms of frustrations with the slow pace of implementation of policies and programmes, tardiness in tackling its governance arrangements and concerns about its competitiveness in a changing international environment. The challenge for the regional movement is not a lack of new ideas, innovative concepts or political will, but rather the difficulty in implementing and building on simple, pragmatic, scalable solutions in a sustainable way.

Regional Achievements, in Particular the Role of Functional Cooperation as a Critical Lever of Regional Integration

It would be difficult for anyone, with an objective frame of mind, to deny that in general much economic development has been achieved in the Region. This can readily be seen in an examination of the outcomes based on universally accepted indicators of development: income, economic structure, health, education, safety-nets, governance and even perhaps quality of life. The gains have been, undoubtedly, very unevenly distributed, both across and within countries. Also, many gaps and deficits remain, and some of these are huge. Nonetheless, there have been significant development gains to the Region, despite the persistence and harsh setbacks due to the region's vulnerability to natural and other disasters. The evidence exists in the ratings of the CARICOM countries in the UN Human Development Index, UNESCO's information on rates of enrolment in tertiary education, and WHO/PAHO health indicators, especially reductions in infant mortality. Some outstanding examples of development in the region are illustrated in the most recent UNECLAC scorecard of the region's response to the Millennium Development Goals (MDGs) reported at the recently concluded UN Summit on MDGs (September 2010). It shows that this region would achieve and surpass many of the goals by 2015, a projection that so far eludes many of the other regions of the developing world.[5]

The report of the *Caribbean Commission on Health and Development*, chaired by Sir George Alleyne, further states that 'health services utilization, as measured by immunization coverage, is a success story and that health services coverage in the percentage of pregnant women attended by trained personnel during pregnancy...is virtually 100%.'[6]

Can these economic, social and political achievements be attributed to the regional integration process? The answer is yes. And the explanation, to a large extent, is to be found in the application of functional cooperation underpinning the CSME process.

Functional cooperation relates not only to non-tradable goods but also to a modality that cuts across trade and economic activity, foreign policy and human and social development, all essential features of the CSME. *The Report of the CARICOM Task Force on Functional Cooperation*[7] fully illustrates the strides that have been made through cooperation in all these areas. Among the most celebrated examples of functional cooperation are: The University of the West Indies, (established in 1948 as a college of London University and becoming a regional institution in 1962); the Caribbean Examination Council (CXC) established in 1973; the Caribbean Cooperation in Health inaugurated in 1983; the new architecture in crime and security in the post 9/11 era spearheaded by the Council for National Security and Law Enforcement (CONSLE) and the Implementation Agency for Crime and Security (IMPACS). There is also the critical role being played by the CARICOM Community Climate Change Centre, established in 2006, in advancing science policy in support of CARICOM's negotiating positions within the UN Forum on Climate Change, as well as the outstanding case of the Pan Caribbean Partnership against HIV/AIDS that has been identified by the UN as an international best practice.

The recently established unit of functional cooperation in the office of the Secretary General has spearheaded a regional work programme for 2010–2011 that highlights functional cooperation priorities in tourism and transportation and is advocating for an agro-tourism thrust in Haiti's reconstruction process. This is an interesting development that accords in the first instance with the proposals resulting from the recommendations of the 2008 Ministerial Summit on Regional Tourism.

In addition, in the area of foreign policy and diplomacy the 'sovereign states' of the Caribbean Community can identify the value of acting collectively in the international negotiating theatres. CARICOM's unified co-operation with Cuba for over 30 years and its coordinated stance that led to the first UN High level meeting on Non-communicable Diseases in September 2011, are indicative of forms of integration that help in no small way to sustain the cohesiveness and viability of the Community in the hemispheric and global systems.

Pivotal to the agenda for effective functional cooperation are the institutions that formulate regional programmes and policies in a variety of areas, including agriculture, quality and standards, meteorology, disaster management, and fisheries management. Also important are the most recently established Caribbean Agricultural Health and Food Safety Agency (CAHFSA) in Suriname and the recent agreement to establish the Caribbean Public Health Agency (CARPHA), a phased consolidation of 5 regional health institutions into one agency between 2010 and 2014.

In this regard too, the CARICOM annual meeting of approximately 25 regional institutions provides an opportunity for elevating the role of functional cooperation through a formal process of sharing information, reducing duplication, and monitoring and evaluation of the performance of these critical drivers of development.

The salient features, challenges and achievements to which reference has been made often elude the critics of the regional integration process, largely because the achievements mainly associated with functional cooperation are not perceived as 'seminal truths' of the integration process. At the same time, it is important to admit that the major impediment to achieving the ultimate goal of the CSME resides in what Gordon Lewis so aptly describes as 'fatal particularism.'[8]

The Path Ahead and the Vision of Gordon K. Lewis

Whereas the European Union has built its integration movement on the pillars of binding legal instruments, the persistence of a philosophy that posits that the principles of a 'community of sovereign states' is incompatible with 'shared sovereignty' continues to bedevil CARICOM. It has been previously argued that a mature regionalism is premised on the establishment of a system whereby Community law prevails and proscribes the privileges and the sanctions of sustainable membership in the Community. In its absence, the Caribbean Community has been engaged in a prolonged period of discussion on the most appropriate mechanisms to improve the implementation deficit for achieving the goals of the CSME. Various formulas including CARICOM Commissioners and, more recently, a Permanent Council of Ambassadors have been proposed. Whether any of the formulas can produce concrete results outside of a more rigorous commitment to a rules-based system will ultimately depend on the goodwill of the multilevel power relations that reside within and among a community of 'sovereign states'.

This situation is compounded by other developments, such as what are perceived to be competing regional strands: The OECS, The Central American Common Market, (involving Belize) UNISUR (involving Guyana and Suriname) and ALBA (involving Dominica and St Vincent and the Grenadines). However in a most persuasive article on Sovereignty, 'Tip Toeing Through the Rain Drops,'[9] Professor Denis Benn argues that the *variable geometry* of regional integration offers strengths rather than weaknesses, by permitting concentric activities to reinforce each other in the overlapping relations between CARICOM and other regional bodies. This is especially relevant in the areas of peacekeeping and conflict resolution as well as expanding trade, cultural and diplomatic relations.

Ironically, Gordon Lewis would have taken comfort from the fact that what is emerging out of the seminal truths and fatal particularism of the Region are vestiges of Pan-Caribbeanism that may yet create the dialectic required for a sustainable CARICOM region in a competitive global arena.

In the discussion on a governance structure for a viable CARICOM Region, he would have supported the need for a long neglected mechanism, the institutionalization of the Association of Caribbean Parliamentarians, as a forum that permits members of both government and opposition groups as well as civil society to participate in the discussions on regional priorities. In this way, providing opportunities for debate among critical stakeholders would no doubt bridge the gap in understanding, and reduce the setbacks to the regional process due to changes in governments in what he would have referred to as 'enlightened self-determination.' I am sure Gordon Lewis would have urged, as he did in *The Growth of the Modern West Indies*, for approaches to regional integration that would eliminate fatal particularism and opt for those that strengthen seminal truth.[10] This no doubt would be his vision for the future of the post-modern West Indies.

Notes

1. Gordon K. Lewis, *The Growth of the Modern West Indies* (New York: Monthly Review Press, 1968), 393.
2. Treaty Establishing the Caribbean Community (Chaguaramas: CARICOM Secretariat 1973) and the Revised Treaty Establishing the Caribbean Community (Georgetown: CARICOM Secretariat 1990).
3. Norman Girvan, Draft Strategic Plan for Regional Development presented to the Regional Stakeholders Conference, Port of Spain, November 29–30, 2010 (Georgetown: CARICOM Secretariat, 2010).
4. Ibid., 12.
5. UN Millenium Goals Report (New York: United Nations, July 2013).
6. Report of the Caribbean Commission on Health and Development (CARICOM/PAHO/WHO, 2006), 8.
7. Report of the Task Force on Functional Cooperation, chaired by Edward Greene (Georgetown: CARICOM Secretariat, 2008).
8. Lewis, *Growth*, 372.
9. Denis Benn, 'Tip Toeing through the Raindrops: The Exercise in Sovereignty in the Caribbean' (unpublished 2008).
10. Lewis, *Growth*, 368–88.

9 | The Reshaping of Freedom and Power in Puerto Rico: Community-based Social Change in the Era of Neoliberal Reforms

Rafael A. Boglio Martínez

I. Introduction

> For despite all the brave talk from San Juan about the birth of a 'new civilization' in the island, what is in fact emerging is a new parallelogram of socio-economic forces defined less by customary folkways than by the 'folklore of capitalism.' This is the one seminal fact from which all discussion about the Puerto Rican future must of necessity proceed.
>
> Gordon Lewis[1]

Gordon Lewis wrote his seminal book, *Puerto Rico: Freedom and Power in the Caribbean*, at a time when the island was in the midst of an ambitious development project that according to official accounts transformed Puerto Rico (PR) from a colonial agrarian society to an industrial democratic commonwealth. Between the 1940s and 1970s, local and foreign social scientists produced a number of studies that celebrated the island as an economic miracle and a showcase of democracy for the developing world.[2] Lewis witnessed first-hand these changes, but was sceptical of those celebratory accounts, scepticism articulated in his book:

> The recent history of the territory is thus presented in terms of the 'rags to riches' imagery so dear to the American imagination; a book like Ralph Hancock's *Puerto Rico: A Success Story* is a typical example. How far is this line of argument legitimate? The more one studies the Puerto Rican situation the more it seems to be an argument at once factually evasive and morally questionable.[3]

The more Lewis studied PR the more he realized that the island's so-called quiet revolution was nothing more than a restructuring of its colonial situation. Instead of uncritically accepting the official narratives, Lewis produced his own, one that substituted the metaphor of rupture, 'of the birth of a "new" civilization,' with a metaphor of reconfiguration, 'a new parallelogram of socio-economic forces.'[4]

Lewis argues that the new parallelogram was the result of dramatic alterations in Puerto Rico's class structure. The island's industrialization programme transformed segments of the rural peasantry into new urban occupational groups and marginalized classes, such as the 'rising middle class' and 'social floaters.'[5] This reorganization of classes and/or social groups contributed to the consolidation of a number of socio-economic and political features associated with so-called modern industrial societies. For example, Lewis argues that Puerto Rico witnessed an increase in class-based identification to the detriment of community-based identification. Moreover, a pattern of class polarization started to emerge, which gradually eroded existent forms of interclass relations, such as the *compadrazgo* ties common in previous decades between *hacendados* and *peones*. Under this new parallelogram of social forces, interclass relations were either absent, or characterized by a subtle paternalism exemplified by the relationship between, on the one hand, workers and peasants and, on the other, middle class civil servants, such as welfare officers, home economists and family planners.

This study builds on and updates Lewis's examination of Puerto Rico as a 'new parallelogram of socio-economic forces.' In the early twenty-first century, Puerto Rico is still contending with the neocolonial status created at the time of Lewis's writing, but within a different global framework whose reformist trends, such as neoliberalism and participatory development, are once again reconfiguring the island's social landscape. Our current globalized era has fostered the emergence of new social actors and modes of inter-class relations that have come to form part of Puerto Rico's socio-economic development field. Non-governmental organizations (NGOs) are among those social actors that have gained prominence in the island since the 1980s. To be sure, NGOs are not new to Puerto Rico's political, economic or cultural scene, but their notable absence from Lewis's analysis is a testament to their marginal role in the island's mid-twentieth century development experiment. Our moment has also witnessed the re-emergence of community as a site of vibrant political and economic activity as well as individual and group identification. A category that was being unglued by the project of industrialization during Lewis's time, community has regained its social and political significance today as a context of development interventions and a relevant civil society actor.

NGOs and community-based groups are examples of organizational forms through which the island's social classes manifest themselves publicly and politically. NGOs are associated with middle-class professionals while the community-based groups consist primarily of the island's lower classes, including the working-class and marginalized poor. For some, development NGOs promoting community-based projects have opened new possibilities for inter-class solidarity that can advance the social justice struggles of underprivileged classes. Yet, these generic claims of empowerment and social change obfuscate the fact that NGO-sponsored community development programmes can advance diverse and often competing political projects: from neoliberal reforms to social justice oriented initiatives. Their potential contribution to multiple political projects questions the assumed transparency between the empowerment claims of NGOs and their actual effects on community-based social change efforts. Therefore, the relationship between the claims and effects of NGOs' development work needs to be interrogated. Similar to Lewis's analysis of his contemporary moment, this chapter offers a critical reading of contemporary Puerto Rico, with a particular focus on the potential of NGO-promoted anti-poverty strategies to contribute to current struggles for social justice and freedom.

II. The Challenge of the Present: Puerto Rico and Capitalism's Exclusionary Tendencies

Both local and foreign social scientists who have analysed Puerto Rico's economic problems in the late twentieth and early twenty-first centuries seem to agree on two key issues: Puerto Rico's economy has been incapable of meeting the population's demand for employment and is plagued by a low labour participation rate.[6] Since the 1970s, official unemployment statistics have remained consistently over 10 per cent, reaching close to 17 per cent in July 2010 as a result of the global economic crisis, a local recession and recent massive government layoffs.[7] Interestingly, young men with a high school education or less have been among the most affected groups by the island's chronic unemployment. Moreover, the island has experienced a significant reduction in its labour participation rates: from 55 per cent in 1950 to 41.4 per cent in January 2010, the lowest rate registered during this decade.[8] The fruitless search for employment in an economy whose formal sector seems incapable of producing sufficient jobs engenders feelings of frustration and impotence that have led many people to abandon the job search process and disparage efforts to reinsert them in that process.

The island's economic struggles reflect one of the tragic ironies of the current globalized economy: While some populations and countries have prospered and increased individual and national wealth indicators, others have experienced an increase in unemployment, poverty, and the intensification of income and social inequality. Some scholars, like Jeffrey Sachs, explain this situation by arguing that certain world regions have grown at slower rates due to factors such as geographical conditions, differential access to technology and different experiences with illnesses and plagues.[9] Others, like Ankie Hoogvelt, contend that the global capitalist system is driven by a politics of exclusion that contrasts with the politics of incorporation of peripheries characteristic of its previous developmentalist phase, of which Puerto Rico was a part in the 1940s and 1950s.[10] For Hoogvelt, the pursuit of capitalist accumulation today takes place without the pressing need to incorporate regions and populations at the margins of the market economy, regardless of whether these are found in developing countries, like Bangladesh, or in developed countries, like Puerto Rico. While she agrees with Sachs that poverty and inequality are increasingly concentrated in certain regions, countries and populations, she posits that this is a direct result of the logic of late capitalism rather than the expression of a lag or differential evolution of capitalism in different places.

This politics of exclusion is a result of a number of important changes in the global economy that have been reflected in Puerto Rico. First, recent technological advances have transformed the production process and, consequently, the dynamics of surplus value generation. Today, surplus generation depends as much on technological innovation as on the expansion of the productive apparatus and the incorporation and increased exploitation of new labour and consumer markets.[11] This has been the case for all industrial sectors, including manufacturing, pharmaceuticals and electronics, which have been the backbone of Puerto Rico's economy since its mid-twentieth century industrialization programme. While technology has benefitted corporate profits, labour has been adversely affected by it, since technological innovations have led to the elimination of both blue and white collar jobs due to the automation of production tasks and the simplification and greater efficiency of supervisory processes.[12] Thus, the competition for attractive labour markets for multinational companies is being reconfigured and is intensifying and many places like Puerto Rico are losing out.

Second, this same technology has created global communication and travel networks that have facilitated the fragmentation of various types of production processes throughout the globe. This has enabled the shifting of various phases of production to countries with lower salaries, more competitive corporate tax incentives, and more flexible labour and environmental laws, resulting in job losses in many developed countries. At the time of Lewis's writing, Puerto Rico was benefitting from that process by attracting industry to the island based on its political relation with the US, which gave it open access to US markets, its generous corporate tax incentives, and low wage market.

However, neoliberal policies implemented during the 1990s in the US eliminated important corporate tax benefits and established free trade agreements that reduced tariff barriers between the US and numerous countries throughout the Americas. That these policies were implemented with little consideration for their impact on Puerto Rico's socio-economic conditions serves only to highlight the island's continued colonial relation to the US. For example, the US has signed important free trade agreements, such as the North American Free Trade Agreement (NAFTA) and the Dominican Republic-Central American Free Trade Agreement (DR-CAFTA), which have given other Latin American and Caribbean nations equal access to US markets, diminishing Puerto Rico's competitive advantage. Moreover, the US Congress approved in 1995, a ten-year phase out of section 936 of the Internal Revenue Code, which was PR's most attractive economic incentive for US corporations. Starting in 2005, no corporation could claim the tax credit against US taxes imposed on profits earned in Puerto Rico. As a result, Puerto Rico's manufacturing sector has responded by closing their production plants, generating huge job losses in this sector: from 134,000 jobs in 2003 to 88,900 jobs in

2010.[13] To make matters worse, workers who lost their jobs have entered the ranks of the unemployed masses, a sector that has become a marginal player in the formal economy. Tragically, capitalism today has dismissed this surplus labour force from even its historic role as a reserve labour pool.[14]

Third, the predominance of the financial sectors, high tech industries and the information economy has marginalized non-skilled or poorly educated workers and increased the income and job security disparity between educated and uneducated workers.[15] According to a study conducted by the Economic Commission for Latin America and the Caribbean (ECLAC), Puerto Rico exhibited a Gini index of 0,574 in 1999, which ranks the island among the most unequal countries in a region known for intense inequality.[16] The deep class polarization that income inequality has generated in other industrialized societies has been averted somewhat in PR by the island's access to US federal welfare programmes. The cash and in-kind benefits of these programmes have given artificial life to a failed colonial project by reducing the levels of social tension, subsidizing low salaries, increasing the buying power of the unemployed or underemployed, and depoliticizing social classes and groups who have been either marginalized or excluded from the benefits of Puerto Rico's formal economic sector.

Fourth, unemployment and income inequality were and still are two important factors behind the Puerto Rican migration to the US, a migration that was officially sponsored as part of the mid-twentieth century development strategy and has continued informally in recent decades.[17] Today, that outpouring of unemployable and/or not well remunerated workers confronts the Puerto Rican nation in the form of a huge diaspora community of over four million people, which exceeds the island's current population.[18] Beyond its magnitude, the impact of the diaspora on the dynamics of Puerto Rican society is such that there are serious debates about whether or not Puerto Rico should be understood as a commuter nation, one in which people circulate between political, social and cultural spaces.[19] At stake in this debate is not only acknowledging the reality of people's movement between the island and the US, but, more importantly, grappling with the social, cultural and economic complexities and challenges created by that movement. For example, demographer Raúl Figueroa-Rodriguez argues that a significant portion of current migrants to the US are young, well-educated people in their 20s and 30s.[20] This means the island is losing an important portion of its young, well-trained labour force.

Finally, besides economic problems, the island's representative democracy also faces serious problems. Jorge Benítez's study of PR's political culture exposed the persistence in the island of *caudillismo* or charismatic leadership and *la partidocracia* (party-centred regimes).[21] The dominance of the public sphere by political strongmen and party patronage has usurped the place of genuine political representation and citizen rights as the legitimate democratic principles that enable local citizens to make demands on and have access to the benefits and resources of the state. Island residents, including many of the younger generations, continue to adjust their expectations and behaviour to manipulate and meet the exigencies of this patronage system.

In all, contemporary Puerto Rico is facing serious economic and political challenges: a faltering economy whose capacity to generate formal sector jobs is severely hampered and a representative democracy whose fissures are exposed by the persistence of patronage politics. These issues frame the life of many in the island, especially young people. Unfortunately, island residents today face the challenge of having to carve out a living in PR at a moment when the island is struggling to succeed in a highly competitive global capitalist system.

III. Responses to the Current Challenges: Participatory Development, the Community-based Movement and Community Economic Development

The problems created by capitalism's global phase and democracy's current crisis of representation have generated a wide range of responses worldwide that include everything from neoliberal conservative reforms to progressive and radical alternative solutions. Most of these solutions have asserted their presence in Puerto Rico over the last couple of decades. Puerto Rico began experimenting with neoliberal reforms in the 1980s as a result of policy initiatives approved by the US federal government under President Reagan and, locally, by the last Rafael Hernández Colón administration (1988–92). The 1990s witnessed the intensification of neoliberal reforms in Puerto Rico under the pro-statehood Governor Pedro Rosselló, who shared the Clinton administration's commitment to re-inventing government and restructuring welfare assistance. Governor Rosselló appointed a 'Privatization Committee,' which eventually approved the selling of PR's cultural pavilion in Spain, the state telephone company, sugar and pineapple corporations, naval merchant fleets, and various hotels. The state also subcontracted to private for-profit companies the administration of a number of other agencies and programmes, such as the public housing agency, state bus services, correctional facilities and public hospitals.[22] These reforms sought to reinvent the local state, promote economic growth and end poverty in Puerto Rico by adopting corporate administrative models in the public sector and endorsing market initiatives and private entrepreneurship as the most efficient model of achieving both the individual and the common good.

However, the late 1990s and early 2000s witnessed the emergence of another model seeking to change the role of the Puerto Rican state and improve the economic and social well-being of the population: participatory development. In the public sector, participatory development is most strongly associated with Sila M. Calderón, who was mayor of PR's capital city, San Juan, between 1996 and 2000, and governor of Puerto Rico between 2000 and 2004. As both mayor and governor, Calderón implemented a community development programme known as *Comunidades Especiales*, or Special Needs Communities. The programme was conceived as an anti-poverty programme based on the concepts of *apoderamiento* (empowerment) and *autogestión comunitaria* (community self-management), which are key principles of participatory development.[23] The community development programme was promoted as the administration's most important policy response to the problems of persistent poverty, chronic unemployment and insufficient citizen participation in the island's democratic system.

The institutionalization of participatory development in a state programme and its recognition as the cornerstone of Calderón's administration helped consolidate it as an attractive model of development for those seeking an alternative to neoliberalism. The success or failure of the Special Needs Communities Programme notwithstanding, one of the concrete effects of the programme was to organize communities and re-energize a community-based movement in the island, which Lewis had left for dead in the 1960s as a result of industrialization.[24] This community-based movement, along with other grassroots movements and NGOs that have longer historical trajectories, has adopted the discourse, claims and solutions of participatory development as their political project since the 1990s. For example, they advocate for increased citizen participation, focalized interventions and poverty eradication. They also privilege community as both a level of development intervention and as a key actor in the development process. Some of the movement's organizations have become emblematic of participatory development's claims and possibilities, such as the Peninsula de Cantera's community development project in San Juan and the Alliance of Community Leaders, a civil society organization that groups community leaders that emerged from the Special Needs Communities Programme.[25] Undoubtedly, the last two decades have seen the consolidation of a community-based movement in PR as an important political actor voicing the social and economic demands of impoverished and marginalized populations.

A major item on the agenda of the community-based movement has been the promotion of community economic development (CED) projects. Influenced by the participatory development paradigm, CED has been advanced as an alternative to job training programmes, which ignore the central problem of the unavailability of jobs due to the shifting of plants overseas or the higher education requirements of the high tech industries that are substituting the older textile manufacturing sector. Instead of investing in the production of a cadre of well-trained but unemployed workers, CED promotes the development of local businessmen.[26]

CED is advanced as a solution to the current focalization of poverty in certain regions and communities resulting from global economic processes. It seeks to create economic enterprises in places where capital has either left for cheaper labour markets or in localities discarded as unproductive investments. Thus, CED offers what globalization and macroeconomic policies have been unable to deliver for decades: viable economic opportunities for self-employment and income generation targeted to populations that have been excluded from the formal sectors of the economy. CED also presents a production-oriented alternative to poverty. It seeks to transform the unemployed into active economic agents, either as owners or employees of community-based economic projects. In so doing, it avoids the pitfalls of consumption-oriented responses to poverty, which merely seek to improve the welfare of impoverished people by increasing their consumption capacity through cash transfers or aid programmes. Thus, CED is committed to restructuring the relationship of people to work in such a way that work results in accumulation, not the extraction of wealth from workers.

Furthermore, CED supports economic initiatives committed to elevating the community's well-being. To ensure this, CED substitutes the profit-maximizing principle of private enterprises with a mission-driven principle, which usually consists of the desire to secure a public good, such as overcoming a persistent community problem.[27] Lastly, CED promotes the participation of community members in the creation and operation of local industry as a strategy to ensure its sustainability and combat the deficits of Puerto Rico's democracy, specifically the problems of state paternalism and patronage politics.[28]

IV. NGOs, Capacity-Building and Inter-Class Relations in the Development Field

Despite the Sila M. Calderón administration's attempt to reclaim the relevance of state interventions in our current neoliberal moment, the Puerto Rican state has fallen into disrepute in the last decade as a result of the efficacy of neoliberal discourses and decades of administrative reforms, and economic policies that have depleted its tax base and policy reach.[29] In fact, there seems to be an interesting convergence today of the Puerto Rican Left and Right around an anti-state critique, which includes everything from its incapacity to redistribute wealth and protect the environment, its bureaucratic inefficiency, its fiscal bankruptcy, its lack of proper representation of minority groups, and its gigantism and corruption. This generalized critique has led to a revalorization across the political spectrum of the nongovernmental sector as a site of possible alternative socio-economic and political solutions.

As a result, NGOs have increased their presence and roles in Puerto Rico's contemporary social landscape. The data on the nongovernmental sector shows that it has blossomed in the last couple of decades. A total of 51,331 non-profit organizations were registered by 2007, but only about 6,378 were believed to have been active.[30] Most significantly, 21,042, or 64 per cent, of all registrations occurred between 1981 and 1999, which indicates that the growth of the sector is a recent trend.[31] This process has intensified even more over the last couple of years. On average 2,500 new organizations have registered in the island between 1999 and 2003.[32]

The island's non-governmental sector plays an important role in a number of social, cultural and economic areas. The majority of non-profit organizations in PR offer services in the areas of health, education and housing to a population of mostly children, adolescents and women.[33] Of those organizations devoted to the field of education, 21 per cent indicated that they offered capacity-building and training services. Interestingly, 10.2 per cent of the organizations surveyed indicated economic development as one of their service areas, which includes such activities as small business development and community-based economic development.[34]

NGOs investing in capacity-building, training and technical assistance claim to be addressing an important but frequently unacknowledged consequence of poverty: community groups often do not poses the technical knowledge or human resources necessary to develop an effective and sustainable business initiative. Therefore, NGO-sponsored capacity-building and technical assistance programmes seek to transfer knowledge and skills to grassroots groups in order to enhance their potential to transform the conditions that limit their self-development. Thus, the sector claims to be building the social capital necessary for impoverished populations to succeed in developing their local economic initiatives.

Interestingly, the whole project of capacity-building and technical assistance indexes the class differences between community groups and NGOs. The former consists of volunteer members of impoverished communities who share in the risks, costs and benefits of their social change initiatives.[35] By contrast, NGOs are self-governed organizations usually managed by middle class professionals highly educated in such areas as participatory governance models, development projects and client-centred research.[36] As such, NGOs are intermediary agents in the development field. This means NGO staff members are not directly implicated in the problems to which they attend, at least not in the same manner as members of community-based groups. Moreover, their educational background, professional jobs and income mark them as belonging to a different class than the people they assist.

The project of building social capital through NGO-sponsored capacity-building and technical assistance claims to have opened up an alternative work arena for a number of professionals who previously would have offered their service through welfare offices. NGOs today are havens for emerging socially committed professionals interested in pursuing alternative political and economic initiatives with different marginalized and impoverished groups.[37] NGOs claim to be constructing new forms of inter-class relations between social welfare professional and grassroots groups, relations established from a non-governmental sphere and mediated by the transfer of expert knowledge and technical skills relevant to the social change efforts of grassroots groups. Outside the purview of the state, these professionals claim that their relations with community-based groups are based on the principles of solidarity and shared political commitments, rather than the genteel condescension of the welfare state officer.[38]

V. Overcoming the Exclusion or Regulating the Poor?

The idea of NGOs promoting local economic development through capacity-building and technical assistance appeals to most people in contemporary Puerto Rico, from community activists to policymakers advancing neoliberal reforms. Ironically, the consensus seems to emerge from the ambiguity surrounding the concepts of empowerment and self-sufficiency, which are wielded indiscriminately by everyone today. From the perspective of community-based groups, the discourse of empowerment and self-sufficiency stands as a strong indictment of the waves of development initiatives implemented in Puerto Rico since the 1940s, specifically their incapacity to lift all boats, a fact critiqued by Gordon Lewis as early as the 1960s. Residents of impoverished communities have seen development initiatives come and go over the last 60 years from the vantage point of their persistent poverty. Thus, instead of continuing to wait for the next wave of economic reforms, community-based groups have shifted their agenda to increasing their political presence and generating income through local level initiatives.

These groups conceive of development NGOs, with their knowledgeable staff and access to public and private resources, as potential allies in this political project. Development NGOs offer them the tools and knowledge they lack to deal effectively with the overlapping social, economic and political context within which they are located. These NGOs assist them in mobilizing resources, building political power and starting local businesses. Thus, development NGOs present themselves as key allies in the struggle by community-based groups to overcome oppressive circumstances hindering their life possibilities.

On the other hand, state administrators and policy makers, including former governor Luis Fortuño (2008–12), a self-avowed US-style conservative republican, have picked up the discourse of empowerment and self-sufficiency and blended it with their conservative agenda, which is more interested in ending welfare dependence than in overcoming poverty through structural changes. They have re-signified the goals of empowerment and community self-management in order to align it with their anti-welfare state critique: impoverished individuals and communities should strive to sustain themselves without government assistance. Moreover, the model of community economic development carries a particular allure for them because they see in it the possibility of restoring communities through capitalist principles, such as owning and managing property and becoming small scale entrepreneurs. They conceive of community economic development as promoting the same market-based solutions to poverty advocated by their macroeconomic neoliberal policies.

Unsurprisingly, state administrators and policymakers have sought out collaborative partnerships with NGOs. These partnerships, which offer NGOs greater access to public funds, but also greater fiscal and administrative accountability to the state, expose NGOs to critiques that assert their alignment with the project of neoliberal reforms.[39] According to this critique, NGOs have become strategic actors carrying out social adjustment programmes designed to help impoverished populations cope with the effects of economic globalization and the 'temporary disequilibrium' of neoliberal reforms.[40] Moreover, their close contact with community groups makes them useful agents through which to carry out an important piece of the neoliberal project: the formation of citizen-subjects shaped by the ideas of entrepreneurship, self-help and personal responsibility.[41] NGOs' local reach has facilitated the co-optation of 'community' as a site of neoliberal governance in which social welfare experts work to transform impoverished populations into self-sufficient citizens not dependent on welfare aid.

So, where do NGOs fall in this contested political field? To what political project do their claims of empowerment and self-sufficiency contribute? In Puerto Rico, as elsewhere, NGOs proliferated in a political context in which both neoliberal reforms and participatory development models encouraged the incursion of nongovernmental organizations in important public service areas, especially the social welfare arena.[42] However, NGO is an umbrella term under which one finds a broad array of organizations with different purposes, expertise, scope of activities and relations to the state. This incredible diversity challenges any answer that attempts to encompass the political character of NGOs as a whole.

Some NGOs emerged in response to the limited capacity of states and markets to deliver public goods. They are institutional sites from which socially committed citizens present an organized response to the state's ineffective dealings with social, economic or cultural issues, and the market's inability to provide goods and services in an affordable or equitable manner. Their work with community-based groups is guided by a genuine commitment to grassroots social change efforts. Moreover, they are very vocal in their critique of the state and private sector. These NGOs are, without question, organizational offspring of our neoliberal moment, but they are at best illegitimate sons and daughters – agencies committed to questioning the logic of neoliberalism, not to advancing it.

Nevertheless, other NGOs claiming to be promoting social change through community-based initiatives do function as instruments of social adjustment. Such is the case of an agency I researched between 2008 and 2009: Acción Social de Puerto Rico, Inc. Acción Social was founded in 1982 by Flor de María Cacho, an established social welfare professional who held a Masters in Social Work and taught at the University of Puerto Rico's School of Social Work. She founded the agency with the intention of gaining access to and operating with funds from the US federal government's newly approved Community Service Block Grant (CSBG). CSBG was a funding package managed by state agencies, but awarded mostly to non-profit organizations for the purpose of attending to populations in poverty. CSBG was part of the Reagan administration's conservative attempts to dismantle the welfare state. It resulted in a significant reduction in public expenditure on social welfare programmes, promoted the incursion of private organizations in public interest areas, decentralized federal state functions to lower government levels, and substituted the social justice principles behind the Economic Opportunity Act with a discourse of individual responsibility under the guise of empowerment and self-sufficiency.[43]

Acción Social's history, then, is embedded in the history of the federal government's restructuring of social welfare policies, which marked the initial stages of the political reforms known today as neoliberalism.[44] The agency sought and obtained official recognition as a Community Action Agency, which are the primary agencies funded by CSBG. It also adopted CSBG's mission of developing and implementing counselling programmes and/or social welfare services that could have a tangible impact on impoverished communities. CSBG funds were and still are the agency's primary source of funding, which makes Acción Social a private contractor implementing the federal government's policy goals of ameliorating poverty. Thus, Acción Social constitutes a local response by Puerto Rican social welfare professionals to the federal government's welfare reform that created a new funding programme, CSBG, which sought collaborations with non-governmental agencies interested in dealing with poverty. Moreover, the adoption of CSBG's mission and the agency's dependence on federal funds curtail Acción Social from pursuing adversarial tactics, such as organizing protests and public campaigns by the community-based groups they service, to achieve their goal of overcoming poverty.

Acción Social's programmes, particularly its community development programme, exemplify the neoliberal shift to a social service delivery format as the preferred means of addressing poverty. The programme is structured by the Family Development Model adopted by Community Action Agencies in the 1980s. This model proposes a comprehensive service delivery approach that 'utilizes intensive case management to help families assess their barriers to self-sufficiency and then create a plan for escaping poverty.'[45] Ehida Torres, the programme's national coordinator, not only confirmed the use of this model, but went further in stating that it has substituted the more macro-oriented community development work:

> Now we work less with the community and give greater emphasis to the family and to the integration with other [agency] programs.

> We now focus more on family case management, although we still do some community work. Previously, community development focused more on common problems, streets and infrastructure. But, the problem is that people are no longer interested in getting involved. The community is not as relevant a unit as the family. That is where people's interests lie.[46]

The delivery of multiple, coordinated services to impoverished populations is an essential component of any anti-poverty programme. However, the Family Development Model makes the family, not the community, the programme's unit of intervention. It also focuses the intervention on case management rather than on community action, such as local infrastructure development, political organizing and community-based economic development. Moreover, her last statement seems paradoxical since the island has witnessed an increase in community-based groups over the last two decades.

Despite this model, in practice Acción Social's community development programme still attempts to organize communities by forming community boards and promoting local economic initiatives. The programme has demonstrated different levels of success throughout the island and across communities. In places where it has succeeded, Acción Social has made significant economic and educational contributions, such as in Las Mareas in the municipality of Salinas and Puerto Real in the municipality of Cabo Rojo. Nevertheless, even moments of relative success expose the limits of Acción Social's intervention to redress the political and economic problems impacting these communities.

Acción Social's community development staff conducts community needs assessments and facilitates workshops, lectures, and community meetings as a means to organize communities and foster greater citizen participation in issues relevant to their collective well-being. Yet, the work of producing more active citizen-subjects capable of voicing their demands and positing solutions to their problems is not complemented with interventions geared towards creating the institutional structures in which these new citizens can participate. Aside from elections every four years and public hearings, Puerto Rico's democratic system offers very few other mechanisms through which citizens can participate in public deliberations and decision-making processes. Unlike other jurisdictions, Puerto Rico does not have participatory budgets or policy advisory councils in which citizens can participate and contribute. Likewise, Acción Social's local economic initiatives are not accompanied by public policy proposals that would create new legal and financial structures more attuned to the community character of these enterprises. For example, Acción Social's financial assistance to community groups is limited to managing and adjudicating government grants. They have not contributed to the development of micro-loan institutions or pressured banks to invest in small community-based initiatives that present certain risks, such as the absence of collateral and prior administrative experience. Therefore, even if Acción Social's community development programme was to produce the type of citizen it claims to be producing, these citizens would still face the daunting task of having to create their own conditions of possibility for greater political participation and credit access.

More importantly, Acción Social's investment in community-based economic initiatives reduces poverty to income disparity. In so doing, it ignores that poverty is a social relation, one predicated on the production and reproduction of inequality, marginalization and disempowerment. Income-generation schemes, such as CED, treat poverty as an issue that can be overcome with certain inputs, such as education and financial aid. In that approach, poverty becomes a problem of needs and absences with no reference to the social relations that gave rise to those needs and absences. Put another way, Acción Social's focus on capacity-building ignores the fact that poverty is the result of political conflicts over resources and that its solution requires the reorganization of the social relations that produce that conflict.

Finally, the relationship between staff and community members does not always reflect the claims of inter-class solidarity and shared political vision. To begin, the capacity-building process on occasion fails to adequately engage community volunteers. Many of the workshops, presentations and meetings I observed exposed the educational gap between organizers and community members. The former used Powerpoint presentations and demanded written assignments as primary educational tools. However, most of the community members were over 50 years old, not computer literate and some did not know how to read or write. Moreover, organizers often used prejudiced value judgments, particularly about work ethics, to explain the behaviour of community members, referring to them as lazy and welfare dependent. They also used condescending attitudes during moments of conflict with community members, such as transferring complete responsibility for failures to community members.

Some of the organizers I observed during my research expressed strong commitment to their work with impoverished communities, but they viewed their jobs primarily as a means to secure their livelihood. Many were not willing to visit communities during the evening or at night, when community members were home and had more time to meet. Some did not participate in events they helped organize if they took place on weekends, citing the work hours specified in their contracts. Finally, Acción Social has employees who have worked for the organization for over 20 years. Therefore, many have made a career out of working with impoverished communities. This fact makes apparent the often obscured class inequalities existent in the sector. NGOs like Acción Social secure funding for developing projects in the name of the poor, but a significant portion of those funds are used to finance middle-class jobs and lifestyles.[47]

VI. Conclusion

Let us return to Gordon Lewis and his critical reading of Puerto Rico in his book *Puerto Rico: Freedom and Power in the Caribbean*. While many in the island, including social scientists, were swept by the widely circulating discourses of modernization and progress, Lewis retained a critical eye which allowed him to offer, in hindsight, a more insightful analysis of the social, political and economic change processes taking place. For example, he related the dramatic changes, including the island's class structure, to a broad colonial restructuring project that impacted all areas of Puerto Rican life. In other words, he exposed how power was reconfiguring itself through the discourse of change and progress.

Today, Puerto Rico is swept by another set of discourses and political and economic trends, mainly neoliberalism and participatory development, which claim to be promoting the necessary reforms to propel the island into economic prosperity. Some have taken these discourses and political practices at face value. In this chapter, I opted to follow Lewis's preference for applying a critical eye to Puerto Rico's contemporary moment. For some, Puerto Rico's economic problems are just one tax reform or industrial incentive law away from being solved. I assert that Puerto Rico's economic problems, which include high unemployment, low formal sector labour participation rates, and increased migration of young, educated people, are symptoms or expressions of a deeper structural problem related to global capitalism's exclusionary tendencies. The length and breadth of the island's economic struggles demand, in my estimation, explanations that look beyond the claims of missed opportunities and lack of political will by local politicians.

Participatory development, NGOs and community-based economic initiatives have been heralded today as solutions to many of the island's complex political and economic problems. In theory, I do not discard that possibility. However, my research has focused on disaggregating the category of NGO and interrogating the multiple uses of terms like empowerment and self-sufficiency by the different social actors that constitute contemporary Puerto Rico's political arena. In other words, my research has attempted to move beyond the uncritical acceptance of current catch phrases and slogans. Unsurprisingly, I found that, like in the 1940s and '50s, discourses of change have been used to reinvent venues and modalities through which power can be re-inscribed.

Despite its adherence to the discourse of participatory development and claims to be empowering communities, my research on Acción Social's mission, programmes and community organizing model exposed the agency as a grant managing, service delivery organization that functions much more as a safety net cushioning the symptoms of poverty than as a grassroots support organization committed to rattling the foundations of inequality. While it provides essential resources and services to impoverished communities, these are ultimately inadequate for the dismantling of the structural barriers separating low-income communities from income security and wealth creation. At best, their interventions help the poor survive in our current neoliberal world by making capitalism work for them too. As such, they do not question the core assumptions and practices of capitalism that result in the exclusion of certain populations from the formal sector productive processes. Moreover, the agency's staff demonstrated an adherence to middle class sensibility that was often dismissive of poverty's effects and expressed itself in value judgments about work ethics that undermined any claim to inter-class solidarity.

Finally, where do we leave the question of freedom? Can NGOs be a part of such a political project? Unlike some critics, I do not discard the possibility that development NGOs can make, and in effect are making, important contributions towards the social justice struggles of many impoverished community-groups. I think the current moment leaves enough room for development NGOs to pursue an alternative project in which concepts like self-sufficiency and empowerment are re-signified to mean something more radical in practice. In fact, I presume that current and future research on other NGOs in the island can and will reveal those contributions. However, regardless of whether or not NGOs will be part of the struggle for greater freedom in Puerto Rico, one thing is certain: impoverished populations will continue reinventing forms of struggle in order to overcome their marginalization in Puerto Rico's ever mutating parallelogram of socio-economic forces.

Notes

1. Gordon K. Lewis, *Puerto Rico: Freedom and Power in the Caribbean* (New York: Monthly Review Press, 1963), 247.
2. See, for example, Stuart Chase, *Operation Bootstrap in Puerto Rico, Report of Progress* (Washington, DC: National Planning Association, 1951); Charles T. Goodsell, *Administración de una revolución* (Río Piedras: Editorial de la Universidad de Puerto Rico, 1978); Earl Parker, *Transformation: The Story of Modern Puerto Rico* (New York: Simon and Schuster, 1955).
3. Lewis, *Puerto Rico*, 181.
4. Ibid., 247.
5. Ibid., 245.
6. See Susan Margaret Collins, Barry Bosworth and Migual A. Soto Class, *The Economy of Puerto Rico: Restoring Growth* (Washington, DC: Center for the New Economy: Brookings Institute Press, 2006); Linda Colón Reyes, *Pobreza en Puerto Rico: Radiografía del Proyecto Americano* (San Juan: Editorial Luna Nueva, 2005); Jorge Duany, '¿Sociedad del postrabajo?', *Puerto Rico en el Mundo* (2007), 22; Eduardo Kicinski, 'Un comenatario sobre la distribución de ingresos y la pobreza en Puerto Rico', *Ceteris Paribus* 5 (2005): 1–12; Jorge Mario Martínez, Jorge Mattar and Pedro Rivera, *Globalización y desarrollo: Desafíos de Puerto Rico frente al siglo XXI* (Mexico, DF: CEPAL, 2005); Orlando Sotomayor, 'Development and Income Distribution: The Case of Puerto Rico', *World Development* 32, no. 8 (2004): 1,395–1,406.
7. Official unemployment statistics from the Department of Labor and Human Resources. http://www.net-empleopr.org/almis23/index.jsp Accessed October 20, 2010.

8. Official statistics from Puerto Rico's Planning Board. http://www.jp.gobierno. pr/Portal_JP/Default.aspx?tabid =185. Accessed October 20, 2010.
9. Jeffrey Sachs, *El fin de la pobreza: Cómo conseguirlo en nuestro tiempo* (Mexico, DF: Random House Mondadori, 2006).
10. Ankie Hoogvelt, *Globalization and the Post-Colonial World: The New Political Economy of Development*, 2nd ed. (Baltimore, MD: Johns Hopkins University Press, 2001).
11. Laura Ortíz Negrón, *Al filo de la navaja: Los márgenes en Puerto Rico* (UPR Rio Piedras: Centro de Investigaciones Sociales, 1999).
12. Stanley Aronowitz and William Di Fazio, *The Jobless Future: Sci-Tech and the Dogma of Work* (Minneapolis-London: University of Minnesota Press, 1994).
13. Official numbers from the Department of Labor and Human Resources. http://www.netempleopr.org/almis23/ index.jsp Accessed October 20, 2010.
14. Laura Ortíz Negrón, *Al filo de la navaja:*
15. Ankie Hoogvelt, *Globalization and the Post-Colonial World*; Sandra Morgen and Jeff Maskovsky, 'The Anthropology of Welfare 'Reform': New Perspectives on U.S. Urban Poverty in the Post-Welfare Era', *Annual Review of Anthropology* 32 (2003): 315–38; José Juan Rique and Raul Oscar Orsi, *Cambio social, trabajo y ciudadanía* (Buenos Aires: Editorial Espacios, 2005).
16. Jorge Mario Martínez, Jorge Mattar and Pedro Rivera, *Globalización y desarrollo*,222.
17. Jorge Duany, *Puerto Rican Nation on the Move: Identities on the Island and in the United States* (Chapel Hill and London: University of North Carolina Press, 2002).
18. Preliminary figures from the 2010 census discussed in the press point out that the diaspora community has exceeded the population residing in the island, which remained virtually stagnant during the last decade. 'La isla pierde población, *El Nuevo Día*, August 4, 2010.
19. Jorge Duany, *Puerto Rican Nation on the Move*.
20. El Nuevo Día, August 4, 2010.
21. Jorge Benítez, *Reflexiones en torno a la cultura política de los puertorriqueños: Entre consideraciones teóricas y la evidencia empírica* (San Juan: Instituto de Cultura Puertorriqueña, 2000).
22. Linda Colón Reyes, *Pobreza en Puerto Rico*; Saul Pratts, *La privatizacion del pacto social* (San Juan, PR: Ediciones Porta Coeli, 1996).
23. Oficina para el Financiamiento Socioeconómico y la Autogestión, *El país posible: Modelo de apoderamiento y autogestión para las comunidades especiales del Puerto Rico* (San Juan: Oficina para el Financiamiento Socioeconómico y la Autogestión, 2003).
24. For an evaluation of the Special Needs Communities Programme see Bernard Klirksberg and Marcia Rivera, *La lucha contra la pobreza en Puerto Rico: Evaluación del impacto del proyecto de Comunidades Especiales*, http://www.ilaedes.org/informearchivos2.htm. Accessed September 15, 2008.
25. María Lourdes Rivera Grajales, 'Política social, apoderamiento y participación ciudadana', in *Política social y trabajo social: Comunidades y políticas sociales entre la academia y la práctica cotidiana*, ed. Nilsa M. Burgos Ortíz and Jorge Benítez Nazario. Serie Atlantea 4 (Río Piedras: Proyecto Atlantea, 2006), 265–78.

26. Carmen Correa Matos, 'Desarrollo Económico Comunitario y la Función de las Universidades: Un Enfoque Alternativo Al Movimiento Empresarial En Puerto Rico', www.icscaribbean.com/documents/DesarrolloEconomico Comunitario.pdf. Accessed March 15, 2007.
27. Edgardo Meléndez Vélez and Nilsa Medina Piña, *Desarrollo económico comunitario: Casos exitosos en Puerto Rico* (San Juan: Ediciones Nueva Aurora, 1999).
28. James Midgley and Michael Livermore, 'Social Capital and Local Economic Development: Implications for Community Social Work Practice', *Journal of Community Practice* 5, nos. 1/2 (2003): 29–40.
29. Argeo Quiñones Pérez, 'Ingeniería de una crisis fiscal autoinfligida', *Claridad* 15 al 21 de enero 2009.
30. Registration of corporations in Puerto Rico began in 1911. Estudios Técnicos, *Las organizaciones sin fines de lucro en 2007: Una fuerza económica* (San Juan, PR: Fundación Carvajal, Fundación Flamboyán, Fundación Banco Popular, Miranda Foundation, Fundación Ferré Rangel, Museo de Arte de Puerto Rico y Fundación José J. Pierluisi, 2007).
31. Carlos Díaz Olivo, 'Las organizaciones sin fines de lucro: Perfil del tercer sector en P.R.', *Revista Jurídica de la Universidad de Puerto Rico* 69, no. 3 (2000): 719–76.
32. ÉN·FA·SIS, 'Organizaciones sin fines de lucro incorporadas', 17 de Octubre de 2003, http://www.enfasispr.com Accessed November 26, 2005.
33. Estudios Técnicos, *Las organizaciones*, 32.
34. Ibid., 59.
35. Community-based groups could be legally incorporated as a non-profit organization. This would include them under the rubric of non-governmental organizations. However, despite having similar corporate standing, the differences identified still hold.
36. Bernardo Sorj, '¿Pueden las ONG reemplazar al Estado?: Sociedad civil y Estado en América Latina', *Nueva Sociedad* 210 (2007), 126–40.
37. Mirtha Raquel Brito, 'La cuestión social y la intervención desde una ONG', in *Trabajo social y las nuevas configuraciones de lo social*, ed. Susana del Valle Cazzaniga (Buenos Aires: Espacio Editorial, 2001), 281–88.
38. Lewis, *Puerto Rico*, 253.
39. See INCITE! Women of Color Against Violence, *The Revolution Will Not Be Funded: Beyond The Non-Profit Industrial Complex* (Cambridge, MA: South End Press, 2007); Sonia Arellano-López and James Petras, 'Non-Governmental Organizations and Poverty Alleviation in Bolivia', *Development and Change* 25 (1994): 555–68.
40. Julia Elyachar, 'Mappings of power: The state, NGOs, and international organizations in the informal economy of Cairo', *Comparative Studies in Society and History* 45, no. 3 (2003): 572; Leslie Gill, 'Power lines: the political context of nongovernmental organizations (ngo) activity in El Alto, Bolivia', *Journal of Latin American Anthropology* 2, no. 2 (1997):146.
41. Nikolas Rose, 'Governing "advanced" liberal democracies', in *Foucault and Political Reason: Liberalism, Neo-liberalism and Rationalities of Government*, ed. Andrew Barry, Thomas Osborne and Nikolas Rose, 38 (London: UCL Press, 1996).

42. For a discussion of this proliferation as a global phenomenon, see Lester Salamon, 'The global associational revolution: The rise of the third sector on the world scene', *Occasional Paper 15* (Baltimore, MD: Institute for Policy Studies, Johns Hopkins University Press, 1993).
43. See Howard Nemon, 'Community Action: Lessons from Forty Years of Federal Funding, Anti-Poverty Strategies and Participation of the Poor', *Journal of Poverty* 11, no. 1 (2007): 1–22.
44. Bob Mullaly, *Structural Social Work: Ideology, Theory, and Practice*, 2nd ed. (Ontario: Oxford University Press, 1997).
45. Howard Nemon, Community Action, 13.
46. Ehida Torres, personal interview, February 4, 2008.
47. For a similar argument in Bolivia, see Gill, Power lines, 157.

10 | *Gordon Lewis and the Mass Suicide in Jonestown, Guyana 1978*

Ralph Premdas

It has been one of the largest and most shocking events in the in the affairs of modern human history and it occurred in the Caribbean. On November 18, 1978, some 918 persons, all Americans, committed mass suicide in a remote and isolated hinterland settlement in Guyana, referred to as Jonestown. The Reverend Jim Jones, leader of this Christian religious community called the Peoples Temple, described the collective mass annihilating event as 'revolutionary suicide.' World attention was immediately riveted to this bizarre episode which witnessed men, women, and children, predominantly African Americans with a smattering of whites, willingly imbibe a deadly potion of Flavor Aid laced with cyanide. The act was in clear contradiction to the deep seated almost universal human instinct for self-preservation and survival. It flew in the face of our vaunted rationality and modern technological prowess suggesting the role of some mysterious macabre force.

What exactly was this event?[1] Occurring in the Caribbean sphere, but constituted of foreigners, in what sense could it be conceived as a Caribbean event? Apart from the mundane particularism of the event, larger existential issues were provoked which drew the intellectual attention of one of the Caribbean's finest thinkers, Gordon Lewis, a distinguished professor of history at the University of Puerto Rico. In his short but stimulating monograph titled *Gather With the Saints at the River: The Jonestown Guyana Holocaust of 1978*, Lewis sought to unravel and explain especially in relation to the Caribbean, the underlying factors that led to the mass suicide and the establishment of Jonestown in Guyana which sought to found a new Christian socialist community. In a rich text of masterly scholarship, Lewis tackled the enigma from many angles. At the outset of his effort, Lewis found it necessary to justify the position that Jonestown was a Caribbean issue that warranted his attention: 'Since Guyana, despite its South American location, is a part of the English-speaking Caribbean, it remains to discuss the wider Caribbean dimension of the Jonestown massacre.'[2] Lewis was quite aware of the typical West Indian attitude to dismiss Jonestown as 'a crazy event that happened in Guyana' and for Guyanese themselves to say that the event 'happened to a bunch of crazy Americans out there in the bush.'[3] Lewis argued however that

> ...there is indeed a Caribbean dimension. Jonestown responds to many Caribbean issues that cannot be dismissed too readily. For it is the truly symbolic meaning of an event like Jonestown that matters. Such an event as elsewhere in history brings together in one single historical moment (such as the Paris Commune of 1871 and the Battle of Little Big Horn of 1876, and the Amritsar massacre of 1919 etc.) all of the seminal problems that afflict the society where it occurs. Jonestown in this regard tells us about the relationship between the Caribbean and the outside world.[4]

Lewis reminded his audience that the Caribbean had been the site of two notable mass suicides, namely the collective suicide of the indigenous Indian people of Cuba and Hispaniola in the sixteenth century driven to their voluntary deaths by the Spanish conquistadores, and the case of the Caribs who threw themselves off the cliffs of Grenada when they met defeat from the English and French in the Carib Wars. For Lewis, these cases epitomized 'the first chapter in the history of resistance on the part of the victims of colonialism and imperialism.'[5] Lewis would take the Jonestown materials and spin from them a set of insightful commentaries not only on colonialism and imperialism in the shaping of the Caribbean, but on the impact of industrial modernity on the human condition generally and, equally significantly, on the challenges to Caribbean socialism and governance and leadership.

In this chapter, we shall critically accompany Lewis on this journey of analysis and discovery. First, it will be useful to offer a brief overview of some of the salient accepted facts about Jonestown which we present in Part I. This is followed by successive sections which look at Lewis's account of Jonestown from a religious, sociological, and socialist perspective.

Part I: The Reverend Jones, the Peoples Temple, and Jonestown

The proper name for Jonestown was 'The Peoples Temple Agricultural Project' which occupied 3,800 acres of land leased by the Government of Guyana to the Reverend Jim Jones and his congregation. Revd Jones originally established his Peoples Temple in Indianapolis, Indiana in the 1950s as a self-governing new congregation committed to 'apostolic socialism.' He applied Christian principles in advocating a society free from racism and poverty. Unable to gain acceptance from any of the mainstream Christian churches for his socialist ideals and programme, Jones established his own Christian denomination calling it 'The Peoples Temple.' Continuing to face rejection, Jones moved his church to Redwood Valley, California in 1965 and did well enough that he established many branches of which one, based in San Francisco, California, became his new headquarters. A charismatic preacher, Jones quickly developed popular visibility for his work on poverty and racism and won widespread approbation. He gained a foothold in San Francisco politics campaigning for the election of the successful new mayor, George Moscone. He was rewarded with appointment as chairman of San Francisco's Housing Commission. Soon criticisms emerged about his running of his Peoples Temple which was marked by internal factionalism leading to newspaper investigations into alleged abuses related to sexual misconduct and drugs.[6] Feeling persecuted, it was these events that drove Jones to seek a new location for his congregation and church despite the fact that he had developed many high profile political contacts and supporters in San Francisco and the USA. After exploring several alternative sites, Jones found a welcoming government in Guyana.

Guyana was chosen in part because it was led by a self-styled socialist, Prime Minister Forbes Burnham. The land lease that was granted to Revd Jones was located in an uninhabited and rather isolated hinterland region in northwest Guyana. His congregation was to be imported from San Francisco and live apart from the general Guyanese population. The site with its buildings was as yet not completed when Jones in the summer of 1977 arrived with a large contingent of his congregation. Officially, no weapons were allowed to be imported, but after ingratiating himself with Guyanese officials, a considerable amount of weapons arrived at the Peoples Temple which, in Guyana, soon came to be called 'Jonestown.' Most of the congregation were African Americans and many were women and elderly. Much funding for Jonestown came from the social security checks of these retirees. Principles of socialism were supposed to be the guiding framework for Jonestown residents. Jones openly and vigorously declared his allegiance to socialist countries of the world including the USSR and Cuba. He saw the United States as the enemy.

Even in virtual exile, Jones had his detractors and critics who accused him of irregularities and abuses. Some families and friends of Jonestown residents persuaded a US congressman, Bill Ryan, representing the electoral constituency in the San Francisco Bay Area, from which many of the Jonestown residents came, to visit Guyana and conduct an investigation into their charges. On November 14, 1978, Bill Ryan arrived in Guyana and on November 18, with a small entourage of media journalists and others including a group calling themselves 'Concerned Relatives,' visited Jonestown. Revd Jones was apprehensive and was sure that a negative report against Jonestown would lead to its disestablishment. Nevertheless they were allowed to inspect the facilities under the guidance of Jones's wife. While there were some dissidents and some 14 defectors who wanted to leave Jonestown, Ryan discovered through direct interviews with some 60 specific residents whom he wanted to see, that they had positive things to say about the settlement and did not want to leave. Nevertheless, Jones was sure that Ryan's visit was likely to destroy his community and congregation. As Ryan and his party were about to leave on a small plane, rather unexpectedly they were gunned down by Revd Jones's internal security guard called the Red Brigade. Ryan died, the first US congressman to be assassinated in the line of duty. Fearing an invasion that would enter and destroy the Jonestown congregation in retaliation, Jones persuaded nearly all of them, over 900 persons consisting of men, women and children, to take a potion of cyanide-laced Flavor Aid and commit an act of protest and resistance that Jones called 'revolutionary suicide.' Jones had actually prepared his faithful congregation for such an act, rehearsing the ritual of committing mass suicide a number of times. A few of the residents had fled into the frontier jungle to avoid death and a few who were at the time away in the capital city, Georgetown, also committed suicide. Jones himself was shot in the head.[7]

Just prior to the mass suicide, three high ranking Temple members were given a special assignment by Revd Jones to take luggage containing $550,000 in US currency, $130,000 in Guyanese currency and an envelope, to the Soviet Embassy in Georgetown. The envelope contained among other things a letter to Feodor Timofeyev of the Embassy of the Soviet Union in Guyana. It read:

> Dear Comrade Timofeyev,
>
> The following is a letter of instructions regarding all of our assets that we want to leave to the Communist Party of the Union of Soviet Socialist Republics. Enclosed in this letter are letters which instruct the banks to send the cashiers checks to you. I am doing this on behalf of Peoples Temple because we, as communists, want our money to be of benefit for help to oppressed peoples all over the world, or in any way that your decision-making body sees fit.
>
> Rev. Jim Jones

The letters included listed accounts with balances totalling in excess of $7.3 million to be transferred to the Communist Party of the Soviet Union.

Part II: Lewis's General Views on Jonestown

Before we undertake in subsequent sections a more specialized discussion of Lewis's views on Jonestown and socialism and other matters, it will be valuable to visit Lewis's general overarching views on the Jonestown episode. This would take us into Lewis's philosophical views and his ideological commitments as a scholar and citizen of the Caribbean. This is best summed up by his argument that Jonestown involved 'transcendental questions of a truly terrifying proportion that goes to the heart of the human condition.'[8] In this respect, Lewis addressed what he saw as the dark forces that inhabit the human psyche arguing that Jonestown pointed to 'a macabre example of the deep satanic evil that lies beneath the thin veneer of civilized habit in organized society.'[9] As a progressive socialist, Lewis — whose philosophical thought can be associated with the Enlightenment in celebrating human rationality and technological progress rather than with medieval religious superstition in grappling with and solving human problems — felt momentarily stumped and defeated by this mass destructive suicide at Jonestown. Its utter senselessness led him to conclude that it was Thomas Hobbes and not John Locke who was 'more prescient in his perception of the continuing character of the state of human nature' and argued that in the eighteenth century debate 'Voltaire was nearer the mark in his pessimistic view of human nature than Rousseau in his vision of the idyllic natural society based on sentiment and feeling.'[10] Jonestown for Lewis challenged the paramountcy of human rationality and reason suggesting that just below the vaunted claims of our modernity and technological triumphs prowled an irrational animal. Jonestown prompted Lewis to daub the event a 'holocaust' on the scale of the slave trade and Nazi atrocities of genocide against the Jews in the Second World War. Further, for Lewis, Jonestown challenged 'the existence of benign Divine Intelligence compelling us anew to re-examine the nature of good and evil in human destiny.'[11] Hence, Jonestown offered the occasion for deep introspective reflection on the pretences of contemporary human civilization and the human condition and human destiny, casting a dark shadow on our triumphalist claims of modernity and on optimistic plans that we habitually celebrate with godlike narcissist self-adoration. Especially, as a socialist, Lewis would try to extract from Jonestown wider lessons that were to be applied to rescue socialism from being discredited in the Caribbean and elsewhere. We shall take up at length this issue later in the chapter.

Since Jonestown was established as a religious community, the mass suicide invited reflection from the perspective of the sociology of religion, including the Marxist argument that religion was the opiate of the people. From Christian church history, Lewis underscored the salient point that Jonestown represented a rejection of mainstream orthodox institutionalized Christianity whose ecclesiastical bodies could not accommodate the Reverend Jones's radical preaching against widespread poverty and racism in American society. Jonestown represented a utopian critique and an alternative response to rejection and persecution by mainstream Christian churches, which, to Jones, had abandoned the revolutionary teachings of their founder for equality and justice, especially for the oppressed and poor. Jonestown symbolized, in the language of liberation theology, the 'preferential option for the poor' that embodied the authentic message of the Christian gospel. Lewis declared however that he was less interested in

Jonestown for its doctrinal and institutional challenge to mainstream Christianity and more as a radical protest movement. Seeking to locate Jonestown as such, in a Caribbean context, Lewis argued that it was necessary to view the Caribbean 'in its historical role as a passive instrument of all sorts of expatriate forces that used it for its own purpose.'[12] The Caribbean became a refuge for dissidents seeking escape from American society which had become a place that had lost its sense of community and had become a lonesome site of alienation. Said Lewis:

> ...America more than any other modern industrial nation is a profoundly lonely society. It is full of lonely hearts, frustrated unhappy people looking for a way out of their life of crisis. All the leading institutions of the society...have failed to answer to that emotional vacuum.[13]

It is in this regard that Lewis viewed Jonestown's location in the Caribbean as a protest frontier of escape that represented a quest for the rediscovery of community in a wilderness settlement in Guyana. Lewis emphasized that Jonestown sought 'to create a community of egalitarian fellowship' with the sharing of wealth.[14] The Reverend Jones, a white man, devoted much of his energy to the disinherited of the earth and 'the dregs of society of all races and colours' even though the overwhelming majority of Jonestown was black. Lewis described life in Jonestown thus:

> In the Guyana commune, there is a planned work day; the ethic of work by hand, so denigrated in American consumerist society, is encouraged; and it produces everything from cultivated tropical crops to hand crafted toys for sale in Georgetown stores. There is Rousseauistic call for a return to nature, turning its back on what is seen as all the evils of modern city life....[15]

Lewis noted that in Jonestown the administrative staff was constituted mainly of women, attesting to Jones as a feminist, and the fact of the overwhelming majority of black membership pointed to Jones's consistent concern with the race problem in American life. Lewis underscored that in Jones '...racist feeling was one thing he would not tolerate.'[16] For Jones, these idealized practices of Jonestown portrayed a protest against the loss of community in American life and the pervasive sense of helplessness. In effect, Jonestown symbolized a scorching critique of acquisitiveness in American society. For Lewis, the Jonestown mass suicide served to symbolize 'as no other single event could have managed to do so (sic) the moral emptiness and spiritual vacuity' of American civilization, condemning it for its obsession with material possessions.[17] Further, Jonestown challenged American claims of equality by its commitment to 'economic individualism and domination of corporate capitalism.'[18]

Lewis however, was not an uncritical defender of Jonestown promise and practices. He was particularly concerned by the claims of Reverend Jones that the settlement was socialist. Lewis had noted that a number of commentators had argued that Jonestown attested to the failure of socialism. Lewis felt that Jonestown, while it might have had good socialist intentions and was probably genuinely socialist in the beginning, lost its way to the ego of Reverend Jones who assumed personalistic authoritarian control of the settlement. He said:

> The evidence of witnesses is just too overwhelming and proves that, as time passed, the original socialist idealism of the cult gave way to a personalistic authoritarianism based on the adoration of the leader, so much so that at the end Jonestown, almost certainly, was not so much a socialist commune as an armed camp many of whose members were held against their will.[19]

Things quickly deteriorated in Jonestown and the settlement assumed the aura of a living nightmare. Lewis continued:

> The loud public address harangues, frequently in the middle of the night, the public humiliations of offenders, the barbarous physical punishment of the same offenders, the sexual coercion, the blackmail involved in compelling members to sign letters confessing to non-existent offenses, to be used against them should they defect, even the invention of a 'hit list' of enemies to be murdered by hired gunmen: the grim catalogue testifies to a dream turned sour.[20]

Lewis said that the Reverend Jones had become paranoid and a drug addict and came to believe that he was an incarnation of Jesus and Lenin.[21] Something had gone badly wrong. Jonestown had become not a place of socialist renewal but a concentration camp, leading Lewis to conclude that 'the most tragic figure of Jonestown was Jones himself.'[22] Jones was totally convinced that outside evil powers were descending on the settlement to destroy him and it. He responded with what he deemed an act of 'revolutionary suicide' in which he decided to take his congregation with him to death rather than to be taken captive and eventually killed. He had rehearsed the collective suicide act as a practised ritual and had reduced the community to a 'childlike dependency upon the father figure' and thus they accepted suicide in the same way 'as a trusting child will obey a parent's command even when he does not understand the reason for the command.'[23]

Lewis summed up the psychosocial rationale of Jones's so-called 'revolutionary suicide' explaining why the suicide took place thus:

> As this Manichean vision grows, the cult member becomes slowly enveloped in a world of hate and fear. He sees the world outside as a vast conspiracy seeking to destroy him. He inhabits a universe of discourse in which all is filled with enemies, spies, conspirators, false friends. Inevitably, there comes breaking point where he comes to believe, with full conviction, that it is better to kill himself than to be killed by all of those alien forces; and indeed, that by killing himself he takes his ultimate revenge on them. Even more: as he kills himself he kills his enemies, for they thereby learn that it is a noble thing to die with dignity than for the sake of a great cause.[24]

Lewis subscribed to the view, then, that a paranoid Revd Jones resorted to mass suicide as 'a defensible act' and, as well, a calculated way to retaliate against the intrusion into his domain in Jonestown.[25] The paranoia was palpable and literally drove Revd Jones to the edge of insanity. Lewis observed that:

> Jonestown, as a group, really did come to believe that all kinds of alien forces were moving deliberately to destroy it: the US Central Intelligence Agency, the Ku-Klux Klan, the American mainstream churches, even the host Guyanese government itself. Mercenaries hired by the relatives who wanted to reclaim their loved ones and Guyanese soldiers who would slaughter the commune members to avenge the death of Congressman Ryan, figured in the conviction of the Jonestown community that they were going to die anyway. Perceiving themselves involved in a suicidal struggle they could not

hope to win, they elected to end it themselves by suicide. They saw it as a heroic sacrificial act.[26]

The outcome was the collective suicide with Lewis concluding that: 'All the available evidence suggests that it was all this that finally drove the Jonestown cultists to their ultimate sacrifice of the death ceremony.'[27]

If the paranoia of Revd Jones is regarded as the precipitating cause of the Jonestown affair, then there were deeper structural reasons behind the event. To discover this, Lewis examined the theoretical literature from the European school of classical sociology including the work of Karl Marx, Emile Durkheim, Simmel and Max Weber. Lewis noted that all these thinkers tended to focus on the repercussions of the new capitalist industrial economy upon European society. They examined in particular the new mode of production in private property, industrial technology, urbanization, and commodity exchange and how this reshaped the relationship between the person and society. The result was that while unprecedented material wealth was created, it was acquired at the cost of the destruction of community and creation of alienation and meaninglessness in life. Thus Lewis concluded that while 'all those aspects are in turn present in the Jonestown event', it is unsatisfactory to regard 'Jones as some kind of Frankenstein monster or to see the Temple as manufactured creatures out of H.G. Wells *Island of Dr. Moreau*.'[28] Rather, Lewis argued that instead Jonestown must be explained 'as a violent expression of the internal contradictions of the modern industrial capitalist culture with which all the great names of European classical sociology were concerned in one way or another.'[29] In effect, Lewis was unwilling to lay the onus of any valid explanation entirely on the precipitating factors such as paranoia, and perversion of the socialist aims of Jonestown by the personalistic quest for power by a charismatic drug addict. Rather, the true source resided in the anomie and loss of community that industrial society had created in the wake of its economic and technological success.

Part III: Socialism: What lessons Jonestown taught for the Caribbean

Lewis had assigned himself another task in undertaking an examination of Jonestown. That is, the relationship between

Jonestown and socialism — especially in the light of the fact that some commentators had chosen to denigrate socialism as a whole because of the mass suicide. Lewis was not willing to see the socialist experiments in Cuba and elsewhere in the Caribbean tarnished by Jonestown's claim to be socialist. More specifically, however, on a broader canvas, Jonestown as a self-described Christian socialist experiment offered an opportunity for Lewis to address the issue of constructing a socialist society generally and in the Caribbean in particular. To begin with, in the light of leadership in the Caribbean tending towards personalism and its abuses, Lewis suggested a number of safeguards and institutions to promote the survival of socialism. Lewis took aim at the emergence of authoritarianism and the loss of accountability and democratic consultation as Jonestown descended into chaos and resembled a concentration camp.

The lessons for the Caribbean were many. First, Lewis points to the vital requirement that a democratic structure be maintained at all times as the antidote against personalism and tyranny. To assist the poor and oppressed, the Revd Jones at the beginning of his ministry did enact practices that offered 'substantial autonomy for each congregation to select its own pastor...and a liberal theology' but in a few years thereafter especially at the Peoples Temple in Jonestown, 'all of this was transformed into abusive anti-democratic and personalistic leadership.'[30] For Lewis the lesson was clear: 'For socialists everywhere, the lesson is clear: only a solid and genuinely democratic structure can prevent the emergence of corrupted leadership.'[31] In support, Lewis cited Marx who said that 'it is only the democratic, revolutionary instinct of the masses and not the charisma of leaders that makes for real social change.'[32]

Second, Lewis underscored the critical demand to eschew 'socialist sloganeering' and static organizational forms as well as blind faith in charismatic leadership, all of which pretend to represent the essence of socialism. Lewis described the tendency to reduce socialism to intolerant dogmatism, rhetorical and static formulas and slogans, and in the process forget the foundation principles and critical thinking that ground authentic socialist practice.[33] Lewis weighed in on these typical patterns of abuse:

> For socialists concerned with the democratic meaning of socialism the lesson again is self evident...the fascination with organizational techniques at the sacrifice of clearly stated and publicly debated first principles; reducing socialist thought to sloganeering and static formulas, and thus cutting it off from studying the historical world as it really exists.[34]

In particular, Lewis was concerned with the loss of critical thought that became victim to conformism thereby crushing creativity and variability in free expression. He pointed to this tendency to stifle critical thinking, and noted

> ...the perversion of collectivism and self-criticism from true collegiality based on honest exchange of views, and the encouragement of diversity in the search for knowledge into a methodology that subordinates the individual critical judgment to mass conformity and blind faith in charismatic leaders; perversion of the idea that 'the personal is the political' from a reasonable understanding of the social character of personality into an authoritarian weapon against privacy, dissent, variability, personal judgment and critical thought.[35]

For Lewis, then, socialism requires for its authentic existence a community which engages in free open critical exchanges of ideas and that cultivates this as a sustaining cultural value that eliminates empty sloganeering, mindless formalism, group conformity, and personalistic tyranny. Socialism is therefore democracy thriving on open dialogue and self-criticism.

Finally, Lewis turned his guns against the tendency for the opportunistic usage of the term 'socialism' itself, where the label is promiscuously traded and false prophets are manufactured. He observed that:

> ...there is the lesson that the socialist movement everywhere, to use a biblical term, must beware of false prophets. We live in a region, in the Caribbean, where socialism as an ideology is in the air. In Third World countries like Guyana...it is the official label of society. That naturally leads to loose usage of the term. It leads even worse to opportunistic exploitation of the term.[36]

Clearly, the loose invocation of the socialist label needed some form of cross checking which in turn must be submitted to careful and thorough understanding of socialist doctrines in the context of open inquiry. Quoting Cheddi Jagan, Lewis said; '...not everyone who cries Comrade, Comrade shall enter into the kingdom of Socialism.'[37] To be a socialist, in part, calls for practical engagement with the world. Socialist practice should not be simply self-labelling but should demonstrate sustained involvement with the real world in the struggle against the forces of capitalism. This led Lewis to castigate Jonestown for isolating itself in a self-contained utopia instead of struggling with capitalist society:

> The Jonestown holocaust teaches us that any socialist movement that takes itself seriously cannot hope to defeat the capitalist world by retreating from it. As Marx himself made clear in the famous arguments with men like Fourier and St. Simon, there are no socialist utopias that exist outside of historical time and place. The only reality is the class struggle situated within the conditions of capitalist society.[38]

Part IV: Jonestown, Guyana and the Caribbean: Connections

In this part, we shall examine how Lewis located Jonestown within the Caribbean context and within Guyana's politics and society in particular. It may be useful to ask why Prime Minister Burnham permitted Jonestown to be located legally in Guyana.

First is the ethno-demographic factor pertaining in particular to the African-Indian proportion in the population.[39] Because of the tight bi-polar ethnic struggle that has characterized modern Guyana politics with a plurality of the population in favour of Indo-Guyanese, Burnham calculated that the predominant black congregation of Jonestown would offset in however small a way, the smaller Afro-Guyanese section. Said Lewis:

> ...the Burnham acceptance of the Peoples Temple was used as a pawn presumably in the intramural Negro-Indian struggle. The acceptance of a North American exile group, overwhelmingly Black, could be seen as something that would redress, in however a small way, the demographic balance of the races.[40]

That apart, Black Jonestown members were recruited to campaign for Burnham's ruling party as well as to participate in other supportive political activities. Lewis again:

> In response to that welcome, the Jonestown group became a new support group for the ruling Peoples National Congress: the small echelon of Jonestown members resident in Georgetown itself undertook house-to-house canvassing for the party in the controversial referendum election of 1978. Government and party functionaries were handsomely feted whenever they visited the settlement in gratitude no doubt for all of the help received from Georgetown.[41]

A second reason for the invitation by Burnham concerned the ongoing inflamed border dispute between Guyana and Venezuela.[42] Venezuela had reopened the old settled border dispute and now claimed up to two-thirds of Guyana's territory adjacent to the northwest part of the country. That claimed area was largely uninhabited and that fact seemed to have invited Venezuela to make its claim which would also give it a new Atlantic port. Inviting Revd Jones to settle his community within the disputed area not only underscored Guyana's sovereign right to do so but enabled Guyana to secure the border and reaffirm its claim to its territory.[43]

A third reason for the invitation concerns the ideological affinity between the socialist ideology of the ruling Peoples National Congress (PNC) and the socialist ideals of Jonestown. Remarked Lewis: 'The Peoples Temple preached a socialist doctrine and a pattern of cooperative living based on self-reliance corresponding to the Marxist ideology of the Guyana government....'[44]

A fourth reason seemed to suggest that the Jonestown settlement would have assisted the government in luring Guyanese to settle in the hinterland interior of the country. Successive governments had attempted this project but failed. Somehow it was figured that Jonestown would be worth emulating if it succeeded in establishing a viable settlement. These reasons account for the Guyana connection for Jonestown but a separate reason had to be adduced to point to the larger Caribbean connection. Lewis posited that the fact that the Caribbean has been the home of many religious faiths, several of which were new syncretistic religious formations in their own right,[45] as well as the site of missionizing activities, seemed to account substantially for yet another group in Jonestown to add to this landscape of religious diversity and tolerance. Whether this was regarded as 'religious imperialism' by external missionaries or new experiments in religious frontier life, the Caribbean, it seemed to Lewis, was simply re-enacting an old role as a recipient of foreign faiths as it had always done in its history by accepting Jonestown in its midst. He noted:

> As every student of Caribbean culture and society knows, the Caribbean folk peoples, for a variety of reasons, are deeply religious. Over the centuries they have shaped mass popular religions that have been the outcome of a syncretising process, mingling the European forms with African forms of the slave populations and out of that admixture grew up the rich and vital cults, sects, and churches of the region.[46]

But, asks Lewis, how does Jonestown fit into all this? In two ways, he postulated. First, positively, 'the Peoples Temple benefitted from Caribbean religious hospitality. The Caribbean has always been open rather than closed, ready to welcome and assimilate new doctrinal elements from outside.'[47] Second, but negatively, Jonestown underscored that the Caribbean was the victim of religious re-colonization. Said Lewis: 'All over the region…you can hear the American evangelists bellowing their simplistic born again message… the entire region is seen as a vast new mission field….' [48] He argued that Jonestown was arrogant in assuming that it could contribute either socialism or a new religion to the Caribbean.

Finally, apart from Jonestown having an unwelcome intrusive entry into the Caribbean space and to some extent lending credence to those critics of Caribbean socialism because of the atrocities of Jonestown, Lewis felt that Jonestown gave the Caribbean a bad rap in its image to the world. He said, 'It is not too much to say that Jonestown places the image of the whole Caribbean in jeopardy.'[49] But Guyana fared worse: 'distorted image or not, the Guyanese people will have to learn to live with the image of Jonestown.'

Conclusion

In the Jonestown case, Lewis discovered a great opportunity to take on several topical issues related to the Caribbean. Probably, the most significant concerned the socialist experiment that several Caribbean countries had embarked upon to grapple with persistent poverty and the remnants of colonial exploitation. The modern Caribbean, as a relatively recent human settlement created by European imperialism, bore as part of its legacy deep scars on its social and cultural fabric as well as on its economic and political structures. Jonestown bears an indirect relationship to its postcolonial underdevelopment and dependency and in particular to its continuous struggle to attain autonomy and dignity. It seemed for a moment that the Jonestown experiment offered the potential for establishing an autonomous socialist community as a model. Instead, it became an anti-model in its betrayal of socialist ideals at the hands of a maniac who was obsessed with his own glory and ego. While, to some, Jonestown discredited socialism, Lewis sought valiantly to extract from its failure critical lessons for Caribbean socialism.

As an anti-model, Jonestown in effect pointed *de negativa* to valuable guidelines towards socialist reconstruction that Lewis eked out of the collapse of the Jonestown experiment. Jonestown offered sombre lessons for Caribbean experiment in social engineering towards creating a more equal and just society. In this regard, Lewis articulated some salient ideas that have challenged the evolution of critical Caribbean social and political thought.[50] Lewis wanted to tell Caribbean leaders and peoples that socialism was a worthy project but that it needed certain critical ingredients to survive. Lewis tackled head on the problem of personalistic leadership and sloppy socialist sloganeering which bedevil socialist and liberal reform in left wing movements in the Caribbean. For Lewis, socialism is a way of life that is sustained on free open critical exchanges of ideas and eschews vacuous sloganeering, rigid formalism and formulas, social conformity, and personalistic dictatorship. Socialism is therefore constituted of democratic practices that creatively strive on open dialogue and self-criticism. Further, Lewis argues that, unlike Jonestown isolationism and escapism, the building of socialism calls for engagement with the capitalist world in struggle, reminding socialist aspirants that Marx himself warned against seeking to construct socialist utopias outside of historical time and place. According to Marx, 'The only reality is the class struggle situated within the conditions of capitalist society.'[51]

While arguing for all these changes, it could be argued that Lewis did not go far enough for the fundamental reform of Caribbean society towards socialist reconstruction. Caribbean social structure remains a main obstacle in the hierarchies that are found everywhere in the family, work places, churches, etc. Clearly, democracy and equality must begin at home. The Caribbean household continues to challenge the flourishing of these values. While reforms in governance at the macro level of political structures are relatively easy to formulate and implement, the reform of Caribbean society at the grassroots in cultural values and daily practices must remain the primary challenge. To Lewis, the solution seems to reside in the ideology of socialism as the best promise for establishing equality and fraternity.

Notes

1. Ethan Feinsod, *Awake in a Nightmare: Jonestown: The Only Eyewitness Account* (New York: W.W. Norton & Co., 1981). [Based on interviews with Odell Rhodes]; Wilson Harris, *Jonestown* (London: Faber and Faber. 1996); Shiva Naipaul, *Journey to Nowhere: A New World Tragedy* (New York: Simon and Schuster, 1981). Published in the UK as *Black and White* (London: Hamish Hamilton, 1980); Rebecca Moore, *A Sympathetic History of Jonestown* (Lewison, NY: Edwin Mellen Press, 1985); Marshall Kilduff and Ron Javers, *The Suicide Cult: The Inside Story of the Peoples Temple Sect and the Massacre in Guyana* (New York: Bantam Books, 1978).
2. Gordon Lewis. *Gather With The Saints At The River: The Jonestown Guyana Holocaust of 1978* (Rio Piedras, Puerto Rico: Institute of Caribbean Studies, University of Puerto Rico, 1979), 30.
3. Ibid.
4. Ibid., 30–31.
5. Ibid., 31.
6. Tim Reiterman with John Jacobs, *Raven: The Untold Story of Rev. Jim Jones and His People* (New York: E.P. Dutton, 1982).
7. Charles A Krause, with Laurence M. Stern, Richard Harwood and the staff of the *Washington Post, Guyana Massacre: The Eyewitness Account* (New York: Berkley Pub. Corp., 1978).
8. Lewis, *Gather with the Saints*, 1.
9. Ibid.
10. Ibid.
11. Ibid.
12. Ibid., 3.
13. Ibid., 9.
14. Ibid., 7.
15. Ibid., 8.
16. Ibid., 9.
17. Ibid., 10.
18. Ibid.

19. Ibid., 14.
20. Ibid.
21. Ibid., 17.
22. Ibid., 18.
23. Ibid., 14.
24. Ibid., 19–20.
25. Ibid.
26. Ibid., 20.
27. Ibid.
28. Ibid., 22.
29. Ibid.
30. Ibid., 42–43.
31. Ibid., 43.
32. Ibid.
33. Ibid.
34. Ibid., 44.
35. Ibid.
36. Ibid., 45.
37. Ibid., 46.
38. Ibid.
39. Ralph Premdas, *Ethnic Identity in the Caribbean: Decentering a Myth*. Harney Seminar and Lectures Monograph Series on Multiculturalism and Migration (University of Toronto, 1995. Re-issued by the Center for Latin American Studies, Yale University, 1996); R.S. Milne, *Politics in Ethnically Bi-Polar States* (Vancouver: University of British Columbia Press, 1982); Leo A. Despres, *Cultural Pluralism and Nationalist Politics in British Guiana* (Chicago: Rand McNally, 1967); Leo A. Despres, and Ralph Premdas, 'Ethnicity, the State and Economic Development', in *Identity, Ethnicity, and Culture in the Caribbean*, ed. R. Premdas (Trinidad: School of Continuing Studies, University of the West Indies, 1996); R.T. Smith, *British Guiana* (London: Oxford University Press, 1962); Andrew Morrison, *Justice: The Struggle for Democracy in Guyana 1952–1992* (Georgetown: Red Thread Women's Press, 1998); Thomas Spinner, Jr., *A Political and Social History of Guyana, 1945–1983* (Boulder, CO: Westview Press, 1984).
40. Lewis, *Gather With the Saints*, 28.
41. Ibid., 28–29.
42. Premdas, *Ethnic Identity in the Caribbean*, 157–67.
43. Ibid., 24–25.
44. Ibid., 24.
45. Premdas, *Ethnic Identity in the Caribbean*; M. Galanter, *Cults: Faith, Healing, and Coercion* (New York: Oxford University Press, 1999); David Chidester, *Salvation and Suicide* (Bloomington: Indiana University Press, 1988).
46. Lewis, *Gather With the Saints*, 35–36.
47. Ibid., 36.
48. Ibid., 37.
49. Ibid., 39.
50. See Brian Meeks and Folke Lindahl, eds., *New Caribbean Thought* (Kingston: UWI Press, 2001).
51. Cited in Lewis, *Gather With The Saints*, 46.

Bibliography

Abrams, E. 'The Shiprider Solution: Policing the Caribbean.' *The National Interest*, Spring issue (1996) 86–92.
Allen, R.M. 'The Complexity of National Identity Construction in Curaçao, Dutch Caribbean.' *European Review of Latin American and Caribbean Studies* 89, 2010.
———. 'Cultural Identity in a Curaçaoan Mirror: A Critical View on René Römer's Contribution.' In *René Römer als Inspirator: Actualisering van zijn Gedachtegoed*, edited by R.M. Allen, Jurriaan de Haan and Goretti Narain. Willemstad: University of the Netherlands Antilles, 2006.
———. 'Music in Diasporic Context: The Case of Curaçao and Intra-Caribbean Migration.' *Black Music Research Journal* 32, No. 1, (Spring 2012): 2.
———. 'National identities, Belonging and citizenship in Curaçao: the Complexity of Changing Nationhood Narratives and Performances in a Caribbean Small Island Context.' In *Multiplex Cultures and Citizenships: Multiple Perspectives on Language, Literature, Education, and Society in the ABC-Islands and Beyond*, edited by Nicholas Faraclas, Ronald Severing, Christa Weijer and Elisabeth Echteld, Curaçao: FPI &UNA, 2012.
———. 'Twentieth Century Migration from the English-speaking Caribbean Discursive Inclusion and Exclusion.' In *Researching the Rhizome: Studies of transcultural Language, Literature, Education, and Society in the ABC-Islands and Beyond*, edited by Nicholas Faraclas, Ronald Severing, Christa Weijer and Elisabeth Echteld. Curaçao: FPI & UNA. 2013.
Allen, R.M., Jurriaan de Haan and Goretti Narain, eds. *René Römer als Inspirator: Actualisering van zijn Gedachtegoed*. Willemstad: University of the Netherlands Antilles, 2006.
Ani, Marimba. *Yurugu: An African-Centered Critique of European Cultural Thought and Behavior*. New Jersey: Africa World Press, 1994.
Ansano, R. 'To Question Identity: Public Discourse and Transpersonal Ethics in Curaçao.' In *Multiplex Cultures and Citizenships: Multiple perspectives on Language, Literature, Education, and Society in the ABC-Islands and Beyond*, edited by Nicholas Faraclas, Ronald Severing, Christa Weijer and Elisabeth Echteld, 55–68. Curaçao : FPI & UNA. 2012.
Anyanwu, U.D. 'Erima: Towards a Theory of Igbo Political tradition.' In *The Igbo and the tradition of Politics*, edited by U.D Anyanwu and J.C Aguwa. Uturu. Nigeria: Center for Igbo Studies, 1993.
Arellano-López, Sonia and James Petras. 'Non-Governmental Organizations and Poverty Alleviation in Bolivia.' *Development and Change* 25 (1994): 555–68.
Aronowitz, Stanley and William Di Fazio. *The Jobless Future: Sci-Tech and the Dogma of Work*. Minneapolis-London: University of Minnesota Press, 1994.

Artaraz, Kepa. *Cuba and Western Intellectuals Since 1959*. NY: Macmillan Palgrave, 2009.
Barrow, E. Speech to United Nations General Assembly September 12, 1960. www.foreign.gov.bb/pageselect.cfm?page=90. Accessed 18/7/2011.
Barrow-Giles, C. *Regional Trends in Constitutional Developments in the Commonwealth Caribbean*. Briefing Paper, SSRC Conflict Prevention and Peace Forum, January 2010.
———. 'Dangerous Waters: Sovereignty, Self-Determinism and Resistance.' In *Living at the Borderlines: Issues in Caribbean Sovereignty and Development*, edited by Cynthia Barrow-Giles and Don Marshall, 51–62. Kingston: Ian Randle Publishers, 2010.
Bartilow, H. *The Debt Dilemma: IMF Negotiations in Jamaica, Grenada and Guyana*. London: Macmillan Press, 1997.
Belle, George. 'Against Colonialism: Political Theory and Re-Colonisation in the Caribbean.' Unpublished Paper presented at the *Conference on Caribbean Culture*, Mona, Jamaica, March 3–5, 1996. Later published as 'Against Colonialism: Political Theory and Re:Colonization in the Caribbean' in *Caribbean Political Thought: Theories of the Post Colonial State*, edited by Aaron Kamugisha. Kingston: Ian Randle Publishers, 2013.
Benítez, Jorge. *Reflexiones en torno a la cultura política de los puertorriqueños: Entre consideraciones teóricas y la evidencia empírica*. San Juan: Instituto de Cultura Puertorriqueña, 2000.
Benítez-Rojo, Antonio. *The Repeating Island: The Caribbean and the Postmodern Perspective*. Trans. James E. Maraniss. Durham, NC: Duke University Press, 1996.
Benjamin, A. *Jews of the Dutch Caribbean. Exploring Ethnic Identity on Curaçao*. London and New York: Routlegde Harwood Anthropology, 2002.
Benn, Denis. *The Caribbean: An Intellectual History, 1774–2003*. Kingston: Ian Randle Publishers, 2004.
———. *The Growth and Development of Political Ideas in the Caribbean 1774–1983*. Mona: Institute of Social and Economic Research, 1987.
———. 'Tip Toeing through the Raindrops: The Exercise in Sovereignty in the Caribbean' (unpublished, 2008).
Bernal, Martin. *Black Athena: The Afro-Asiatic Roots of Classical Civilisation. Vol. 1 – The Fabrication of Ancient Greece 1785–1985*. New Brunswick, New Jersey: Rutgers University Press, 1987.
Bevan, Ruth A. *Marx and Burke: A Revisionist View*. La Salle, II: Open Court Publishing Company, 1973.
Biersteker, T. 'State, Sovereignty and Territory.' In *Handbook of International Relations*, edited by W. Carlsnaes, T. Risse and B. Simmons. London: Sage Publications, 2005.
Bishop, M. Speech to United Nations 34th General Assembly, September 1979. www.assatashakur.org. Accessed July 1, 2011.
Bisnauth, Dale. *History of Religions in the Caribbean*. Kingston: LMH Publishing Limited, 1998.
Bodin, Jean, *Six Books of the Republic*. Paris: Du Puys, 1576.
Bogues, Anthony. *Black Heretics, Black Prophets*. New York: Routledge, 2003.

Bolland, Nigel. *The Birth of Caribbean Civilisation: A Century of Ideas about Culture and Identity, Nation and Society.* Kingston: Ian Randle Publishers, 2004.

Bottomore, T. B., ed., *Karl Marx: Early Writings.* New York: McGraw, 1963.

Brathwaite, E. *The Development of Creole Society in Jamaica, 1770–1820.* Oxford: Clarendon Press, 1971. Re-issued Kingston: Ian Randle Publishers, 2005.

Brereton, Bridget. *From Imperial College of the West Indies: A History of the St. Augustine Campus, Trinidad and Tobago.* Kingston: Ian Randle Publishers, 2010.

Brevold, Louis I. and Ralph G. Ross, eds. *The Philosophy of Edmund Burke.* Ann Arbor, Michigan: University of Michigan Press, 1961.

Brito, Mirtha Raquel. 'La cuestión social y la intervención desde una ONG.' In *Trabajo social y las nuevas configuraciones de lo social,* edited by Susana del Valle Cazzaniga, 281–88. Buenos Aires: Espacio Editorial, 2001.

Brown, K.A. 'The Shiprider Model: An Analysis of the US Proposed Agreement concerning Maritime Counter-Drug Operations in its Wider Legal Context.' *Contemporary Caribbean Legal Issues* no. 1. Cave Hill, Barbados: Faculty of Law, UWI (1997): 80.

Bull, H. *The Anarchical Society: A Study of Order in World Politics.* London: Macmillan Press, 1977.

Burke, Edmund. 'Opening Speech at the Impeachment of Warren Hastings.' 16 February, 1788. Cited in *Edmund Burke: Prerevolutionary Writings,* edited by Ian Harris. Cambridge: Cambridge University Press, 1993.

———. *Letters on a Regicide Peace* (1776) cited in Gordon K. Lewis. *Grenada: The Jewel Despoiled.* Baltimore, MD: Johns Hopkins University Press, 1987.

Byron, J. 'The Caribbean Community's "Fourth Pillar": The Evolution of Regional Security Governance.' In *The Security Governance of Regional Organizations,* edited by E. Kirchner and R. Dominguez. New York: Routledge, 2011.

Calcagno, Francisco. *Romualdo: uno de tantos.* 1869. Reprinted in *Noveletas Cubanas,* edited by Imeldo Alvarez, 279–388. Havana: Editorial de Arte y Literatura, 1977.

Callender, L. 'IMF: Friend or Foe, Partner or Prison Warder? 2011. www.sknvibes. com/news/newsdetails.cfm/28667. Accessed 20/9/2011.

———. 'What happens when we become 'Asset Poor' and are still indebted?' 18/6/2011 www.kittivisianlife.com.articles/06-2011/. Accessed 20/9/2011.

Caribbean Contact, 7–8. July 1984.

CARICOM. 'Haitians must be at the centre of their development.' Press Release 101/2010 11/3/2010. http://www.caricom.org/jsp/pressreleases/2010. Accessed 16/10/2011.

CARICOM. 'Failure not an option in Haiti reconstruction'. Press Release 249/2010 3/6/2010. http://www.caricom.org/jsp/pressreleases/2010. Accessed 16/10/2011.

CARICOM. *Patterson's Statement to Donors Conference 31/3/2010.* http://www.caricom.org/jsp/speeches/donor_conference_haiti_patterson.jsp. Accessed 16/10/2011.

CARICOM. *Statement on the Situation in the Turks and Caicos Islands, an Associate member of the Community.* Press Release 96/2009 24/03/2009. http://www.caricom.org/jsp/pressreleases/2009. Accessed 29/9/2011.

CARICOM. *Statement on the Situation in the Turks and Caicos Islands issued at the Conclusion of the 30th Regular Meeting of the Conference of Heads of Government* of *CARICOM 2–5 July 2009 Georgetown Guyana*. Press Release 270/2009 4/07/2009. www.caricom.org/jsp/pressreleases/2009. Accessed 29/9/2011.

CARICOM. Press Release 310/2010 7/7/2010 http://www.caricom.org/jsp/pressreleases/2010. Accessed 16/10/2011.

Carruthers, Jacob. *MDW NTR: Divine Speech – A Historiographical Reflection of African Deep Thought From the Time of the Pharaohs to the Present*. London: Karnak House, 1995.

Cassidy, Laurie M., and Alex Mikulich, eds. *Interrupting White Privilege: Catholic Theologians Break the Silence*. New York: Orbis Books, 2007.

Chase, Stuart. *Operation Bootstrap in Puerto Rico, Report of Progress*. Washington, DC: National Planning Association, 1951.

Chevannes, Barry. *Betwixt and Between: Explorations in an African-Caribbean Mindscape*. Kingston: Ian Randle Publishers, 2006.

Chidester, David. *Salvation and Suicide*. Bloomington: Indiana University Press, 1988.

Clark, Steve. 'The Second Assassination of Maurice Bishop.' *New International, A Magazine of Marxist Politics and Theory*, no. 6 (1987): 13.

Clegg, P. 'The Commonwealth Caribbean and the Challenges of Institutional Exclusion.' *The Round Table* 97, no. 395 (2008): 227–41.

Clegg, P. and E. Pantojas-García, eds. *Governance in the Non-Independent Caribbean: Challenges and Opportunities in the Twenty-First Century*. Kingston: Ian Randle Publishers, 2009.

Collins, Susan Margaret, Barry Bosworth and Migual A. Soto Class. *The Economy of Puerto Rico: Restoring Growth*. Washington, DC: Center for the New Economy: Brookings Institute Press, 2006.

Cone, James. *Black Theology & Black Power*. 20th Anniversary Edition New York: Harper & Row Publishers, 1989.

———. *God of the Oppressed*. New York: Seabury Press, 1975.

Corbin, C. 'Constitutional Reform and Political Identity in the Non-Independent Caribbean.' *Overseas Territories Review* 31/01/2010. http://overseasreview.blogspot.com/2010/01/constitutional-reform-and-political.html. Accessed 2/10/2011.

Cornet, F. 'Decolonizing Transnational Subaltern Women: The Case of Kurasolenas and New York Dominicanas.' PhD thesis, University of South Carolina, 2012.

Correa Matos, Carmen. 'Desarrollo Económico Comunitario y la Función de las Universidades: Un Enfoque Alternativo Al Movimiento Empresarial En Puerto Rico.' www.icscaribbean.com/documents/DesarrolloEconomico Comunitario.pdf Accessed March 15, 2007.

Cox Alomar, R. *Revisiting the Transatlantic Triangle: The Constitutional Decolonization of the Eastern Caribbean*. Kingston: Ian Randle Publishers, 2009.

Cudjoe, S. ed. *Eric Williams Speaks*. Wellesley, MA: Calaloux Publishers, 1993.

Cugoano, Ottobah. *Thoughts and Sentiments on the Evil of Slavery*. New York: Penguin Books, 1999.

Curtin, Philip. *Two Jamaicas: The Role of Ideas in a Tropical Colony*. New York: Atheneum, Press, 1970.

Davidson, Basil. *Africa in History*. New York: Collier Books, 1974.

Davis, Kortright. *Emancipation Still Comin': Explorations in Caribbean Emancipatory Theology.* New York: Orbis Books, 1990.

Deere-Birkbeck, C., E. Jones and N.Woods. *Manoeuvring at the Margins: Constraints faced by Small States in International Trade Negotiations.* London: Commonwealth Secretariat, 2010.

Despres, Leo A. *Cultural Pluralism and Nationalist Politics in British Guiana.* Chicago: Rand McNally, 1967.

Despres, Leo A. and Ralph Premdas. 'Ethnicity, the State and Economic Development.' In *Identity, Ethnicity, and Culture in the Caribbean,* edited by Ralph Premdas. Trinidad: School of Continuing Studies, University of the West Indies, 1996.

Díaz Olivo, Carlos. 'Las organizaciones sin fines de lucro: Perfil del tercer sector en P.R.' *Revista Jurídica de la Universidad de Puerto Rico* 69, no. 3 (2000): 719–76.

Diop, Cheikh Anta. *Civilization or Barbarism: An Authentic Anthropology.* New York: Lawrence Hill Books, 1991.

Do Rego, C. *The Portuguese Immigrant in Curaçao: Immigration, Participation and Integration in 20th Century.* Amsterdam: SWP, 2012.

Du Bois, W.E.B. *Black Reconstruction in America.* New York: Free Press, 1998.

Duany, Jorge. *Puerto Rican Nation on the Move: Identities on the Island and in the United States.* Chapel Hill and London: University of North Carolina Press, 2002.

———. '¿Sociedad del postrabajo?' *Puerto Rico en el Mundo* (2007): 22.

Edmonds, Ennis B., and Michelle A. Gonzalez. *Caribbean Religious History: An Introduction.* New York: New York University Press, 2010.

Eikrem, O. 'Contested Identities: A Study of Ethnicity in Curaçao, the Netherlands Antilles.' PhD Thesis, Norwegian University of Natural Science and Technology (NTNU), 1999.

El Nuevo Día. 'La isla pierde población.' August 4, 2010.

Elyachar, Julia. 'Mappings of Power: The State, NGOs, and International Organizations in the Informal Economy of Cairo.' *Comparative Studies in Society and History* 45, no. 3 (2003): 572.

ÉN·FA·SIS. 'Organizaciones sin fines de lucro incorporadas.' 17 de octubre de 2003. http://www.enfasispr.com Accessed November 26, 2005.

Engels, Friedrich. 'Socialism: Utopian and Scientific.' In *The Marx-Engels Reader,* edited by Robert Tucker, 688. New York: Norton, 1972.

Erskine, Noel. *Decolonizing Theology: A Caribbean Perspective.* New York: Obis Books, 1981.

———. *From Garvey to Marley.* Gainsville: University of Florida Press, 2005.

———. 'The Making of a Caribbean Intellectual.' In *Ministry Perspectives from the Caribbean,* edited by Eron Henry. New York: Caribbean Diaspora Baptist Clergy Association, 2010.

Estudios Técnicos. *Las organizaciones sin fines de lucro en 2007: Una fuerza económica.* San Juan, P.R.: Fundación Carvajal, Fundación Flamboyán, Fundación Banco Popular, Miranda Foundation, Fundación Ferré Rangel, Museo de Arte de Puerto Rico y Fundación José J. Pierluisi, 2007.

European Commission. *Joint Annual Report 2006 Delegation of the European Commission in Barbados and the Eastern Commission and the Office of the NAO in Dominica,* (2007). C1*4D(2007)5889 http://ec.europa.eu/development/icenter/repository/jar06_dm_en.pdf

Feinsod, Ethan. *Awake in a Nightmare: Jonestown: The Only Eyewitness Account*. New York: W.W. Norton & Co., 1981.
Fenton, A. 'Haiti and the Dangers of Responsibility to Protect.' January 3, 2009. www.haitianalysis.com/2009/1/3/haiti-and-the-dangers-of-responsibility-to-protect. Accessed July 12 2011.
Ferguson, T. *To Survive Sensibly or to Court Heroic Death: Management of Guyana's Political Economy 1965–1985*. Georgetown: Public Affairs Consulting Enterprise, 1999.
Firmin, Antenor. *The Equality of the Human Races*. New York: Garland Publishing, 2000.
Fischer, Sibylle. *Modernity Disavowed*. Mona: University of the West Indies Press, 2004.
Fontaine, T. 'Dominica and the IMF.' www.thedominican.net 1, no. 42, May 7, 2003. Accessed July 20, 2011.
Francis Brown, Suzanne. *Mona, Past and Present: The History and Heritage of the Mona Campus, University of the West Indies*. Kingston: University of the West Indies Press, 2004.
Galanter, M. *Cults: Faith, Healing, and Coercion*. New York: Oxford University Press, 1999.
García, Gloria. *La esclavitud desde la esclavitud*. Havana: Instituto Cubano del Libro, 1996.
Gaspar, David Barry. *Bondmen & Rebels*. Baltimore: Johns Hopkins University Press, 1985.
Giddens, Anthony. *Capitalism and Modern Social Theory*. Cambridge: Cambridge University Press, 1971.
Gill, Leslie. 'Power Lines: The Political Context of Nongovernmental Organizations (NGO) Activity in El Alto, Bolivia.' *Journal of Latin American Anthropology* 2, no. 2 (1997):146.
Girigori, S. 'Pasado, Presente I Future. Curaçao's Cultural Expression Revised.' In *Multiplex Cultures and Citizenships: Multiple Perspectives on Language, Literature, Education, and Society in the ABC-Islands and Beyond*, edited by Nicholas Faraclas, Ronald Severing, Christa Weijer and Elisabeth Echteld, 77–82. Curaçao: FPI & UNA, 2012.
Girvan, Norman. Draft Strategic Plan for Regional Development presented to the Regional Stakeholders Conference, Port of Spain, November 29–30 2010. Georgetown: CARICOM Secretariat, 2010.
Glissant, Édouard. *Le Discours Antillais*, ed. Du Seuil, Paris: Edition Caribenes, 1981.
de Gobineau, Joseph Arthur. *Essai sur l' Inegalite des Races Humaines*, 4 volumes, Paris: Libraire de Firmin Didot Freres, 1853–55.
Gómez de Avellaneda, Gertrudis. *Sab*. 1841. Reprinted Havana: Instituto Cubano del Libro, 1973.
Goodsell, Charles T. *Administración de una revolución*. Río Piedras: Editorial de la Universidad de Puerto Rico, 1978.
Goulbourne, Harry. 'The Institutional Contribution of the University of the West Indies to the Intellectual Life of the Anglophone Caribbean.' In *Intellectuals in Twentieth-Century Caribbean Volume I: Spectre of a New Class: The Commonwealth Caribbean*, edited by Alistair Hennessy. London: Macmillan Press, 1992.

Granderson, C. 'The CARICOM Initiative towards Haiti: A Case of Small State Diplomacy.' *Focal Point* 3, no. 6 (2004): 1–4.

Griffith, I. *Drugs and Security in the Caribbean: Sovereignty under Siege*. University Park PA.: Pennsylvania State University Press, 1997.

———. 'Security and Sovereignty in the Contemporary Caribbean: Probing Elements of the Local-Global Nexus.' In *Living at the Borderlines: Issues in Caribbean Sovereignty and Development*, edited by Cynthia Barrow-Giles and Don Marshall, 209–25. Kingston: Ian Randle Publishers, 2003.

Grynberg, R, ed. *WTO at the Margins: Small States and the Multilateral Trading System*. Cambridge: Cambridge University Press, 2006.

Gutierrez, Gustavo. *A Theology of Liberation*, rev. ed. New York: Orbis Books, 1988.

Hall, John R. *Gone from the Promised Land: Jonestown in American Cultural History*. New Brunswick, New Jersey: Transaction Publishers, 1987.

Hall, Kenneth and Denis Benn, eds. *Contending with Destiny: The Caribbean in the 21st Century*. Kingston: Ian Randle Publishers, 2000.

Hambuch, D. 'Rereading the Caribbean through *Dubbelspel* by Frank Martinus Arion.' *World Literature Today* 72.1 (1998): 55–58.

Hamid, Idris. *Troubling of the Waters*. San Fernando: Rahaman Printers Ltd., 1973.

Harris, Ian, ed. *Edmund Burke: Prerevolutionary Writings*. Cambridge: Cambridge University Press, 1993.

Harris, Wilson. *Jonestown*. London: Faber and Faber, 1996.

Henke, H. 'Drugs in the Caribbean: The Shiprider Controversy and the Question of Sovereignty.' *European Review of Latin American and Caribbean Studies* 64 (1998): 27–47.

Hennessy, Alistair, ed. *Intellectuals in Twentieth-Century Caribbean Volume I: Spectre of a New Class: the Commonwealth Caribbean*. London: Macmillan Press, 1992.

Henriquez, J. 'Embracing National Culture through a Policy of Difference.' In *Multiplex Cultures and Citizenships: Multiple Perspectives on Language, Literature, Education, and Society in the ABC-Islands and Beyond*, edited by Nicholas Faraclas, Ronald Severing, Christa Weijer and Elisabeth Echteld, 99–106. Curaçao: FPI and UNA, 2012.

Henry, Paget. 'Africana Political Philosophy and the Crisis of the Postcolony.' *Socialism and Democracy* 21, no. 3 (2007).

———. 'Between Hume and Cugoano: Race, Ethnicity and Philosophical Entrapment.' *The Journal of Speculative Philosophy* 18, no.2 (2004).

———. *Caliban's Reason: Introducing Afro-Caribbean Philosophy*. London and New York: Routledge, 2000.

———. 'Rastafarianism and the Politics of Dread.' In *Existence in Black: An Anthology of Black Existential Philosophy*, edited by Lewis R. Gordon. New York: Routledge, 1997.

Heywood, A. *Key Concepts in Politics*. London: Macmillan Press, 2000.

Hillman, Richard S. and Thomas J. D'Agostino, eds. *Understanding the Contemporary Caribbean*. Kingston: Ian Randle Publishers, 2003.

Hoetink, H. *Het patroon van de oude Curaçaose samenleving: Een sociologische studie*. Assen: Van Gorcum, 1958.

Hood, Robert. *Must God Remain Greek: Afro Cultures and God Talk*. Minneapolis: Fortress Press, 1990.

Hoogvelt, Ankie. *Globalization and the Post-Colonial World: The New Political Economy of Development*, 2nd ed. Balitimore, MD: Johns Hopkins University Press, 2001.
Hooker, James R. *Henry Sylvester Williams: Imperial Pan-Africanist*. London: Rex Collings, 1975.
Hutton, Clinton. *The Logic and Historical Significance of the Haitian Revolution*. Kingston: Arawak Publications, 2005.
INCITE! Women of Color Against Violence. *The Revolution Will Not Be Funded: Beyond The Non-Profit Industrial Complex*. Cambridge, MA: South End Press, 2007.
International Monetary Fund. *IMF Country Report No. 11/270 St. Kitts and Nevis Article IV Consultation and Request for Stand-By Agreement*. September 2, 2011. www.imf.org/external/country/kna/index.htm?pn=0 Accessed 20/9/2011.
Jackson, Richard. *The Black Image in Latin American Literature*. Albuquerque, NM: University of New Mexico Press, 1976.
Jackson-Miller, D. 'Jamaica welcomes Aristide, new Haiti government protests.' www.albionmonitor.com/0403a/copyright/2004. Accessed October 17, 2011.
Jagessar, Michael N. *Full Life All: The Work and Theology of Philip Potter: A Historical Survey and Systematic of Major Themes*. Zoetermeer: Uitegeverij Boekencentrum, 1997.
Jamaica Gleaner. 'Barbados yields to Shiprider.' *Jamaica Gleaner* June 24, 1997.
———. 'Bird defends Countries which signed Shiprider Agreement.' *Jamaica Gleaner* March 6, 1997.
———. 'JA/US high-level maritime talks open.' *Jamaica Gleaner*, October 17, 1996.
———. 'No Option – Jamaica returning to IMF – Shaw – No immediate effect on public sector' http://jamaica-gleaner.com/gleaner/20090722/lead/lead1.html. Accessed 11/9/2011.
———. 'T&T, UK sign Crime Treaty.' *Jamaica Gleaner*, May 16, 1997.
———.'This sets a dangerous precedent.' http://jamaica-gleaner.com/gleaner/20040301/lead/lead1/html. Accessed October 17, 2011.
Jamaica Observer. 'The IMF cannot escape its responsibility.' www.jamaicaobserver.com/editorial/imf-cannot-escape-its-responsibility_948660. 2011. Accessed 11/9/2011.
———. 'US, Jamaica to sign new Shiprider Agreement.' February 5, 2004. www.jamaicaobserver.com/news/55324_US--Jamaica-to-sign-new-Shiprider-Agreement. Accessed October 10, 2011.
James, C.L.R. *The Black Jacobins*. New York, Vintage Books, 1989.
Janga, L. '*Géni: Taal van Verzet*.' *Het Nationaal Museum vormen we tezamen*. Curaçao: NAAM, 2011.
Jennings, Theodore W. Jr., ed. *The Vocation of the Theologian*. Philadelphia, PA: Fortress Press, 1985.
Jones, W.T., ed. *Masters of Political Thought Volume Two: Machiavelli to Bentham*. London: Harrap, 1980.
de Jong, Lammert. *Being Dutch, More or Less*. Amsterdam: Rozenberg Publishers, 2010.

Kamugisha, Aaron, ed. *Caribbean Political Thought: Theories of the Post-Colonial State* and *Caribbean Political Thought: The Colonial State to Caribbean Internationalisms*. Kingston: Ian Randle Publishers, 2013.

Karenga, Maulana. 'Towards a Sociology of Ma'atian Ethics.' In *Egypt Revisited*, edited by Ivan Van Sertima. New Brunswick: Transaction Publishers, 1993.

Kent, R.K. 'Palmares: An African State in Brazil.' In *Maroon Societies*, edited by Richard Price. Baltimore, MD: Johns Hopkins University Press, 1979.

Kicinski, Eduardo. 'Un comenatario sobre la distribución de ingresos y la pobreza en Puerto Rico.' *Ceteris Paribus* 5 (2005):1–12.

Kilduff, Marshall and Ron Javers. *The Suicide Cult: The Inside Story of the Peoples Temple Sect and the Massacre in Guyana*. New York: Bantam Books, 1978.

Klirksberg, Bernard and Marcia Rivera. *La lucha contra la pobreza en Puerto Rico: Evaluación del impacto del proyecto de Comunidades Especiales*, http://www.ilaedes.org/informearchivos2.htm. Accessed September 15, 2008.

Kramnick, Isaac, ed. *The Portable Enlightenment Reader.* New York: Penguin Books, 1995.

Krasner, S. 'Rethinking the Sovereign State Model.' *Review of International Studies* no. 27 (2001):17–48.

———. 'Sharing Sovereignty: New Institutions for Collapsed and Failing States.' *International Security* 29, no. 2 (2004):85–120.

Krause, Charles A. with Laurence M. Stern, Richard Harwood and the staff of the *Washington Post. Guyana Massacre: The Eyewitness Account.* New York: Berkley Pub. Corp., 1978.

Lampe, Armando. *Christianity in the Caribbean: Essay on Church History.* Kingston: University of the West Indies Press, 2001.

Lancashire, Robert and Kenneth Magnus. *The Department of Chemistry UWI, Mona: With Emphasis on the Early Years.* Kingston: Ian Randle Publishers, 2010.

Laski, Harold J. *The Communist Manifesto: An Introduction.* New York: New American Library, 1982.

Lawson, Winston. *Religion and Race: African and European Roots in Conflict – A Jamaican Testament.* New York: Peter Lang, 1996.

Layton, Deborah. *Seductive Poison.* New York: Anchor Books 1998.

Leonora, L. 'Will the real Yu di Korsou please stand up. The double-bind cultural identity of the citizens of Curaçao.' In *Multiplex Cultures and Citizenships: Multiple Perspectives on Language, Literature, Education, and Society in the ABC-Islands and Beyond*, edited by Nicholas Faraclas, Ronald Severing, Christa Weijer and Elisabeth Echteld, 127–44. Curaçao: FPI &UNA, 2012.

Lewis, Gordon. *Gather With The Saints At The River: The Jonestown Guyana Holocaust of 1978.* Rio Piedras, Puerto Rico: Institute of Caribbean Studies, University of Puerto Rico, 1979.

———. *Grenada: The Jewel Despoiled.* Baltimore, MD: Johns Hopkins University Press, 1987.

———. *Main Currents in Caribbean Thought: The Historical Evolution of Caribbean Society in Its Ideological Aspects, 1492–1900.* Baltimore, MD: Johns Hopkins University Press, 1983.

———. *Notes on the Puerto Rican Revolution.* New York: Monthly Review Press, 1974.

———. *Puerto Rico: Freedom and Power in the Caribbean*. New York: Monthly Review Press, 1963. Rpt. New York, Harper & Row, 1968. Reissued, Kingston: Ian Randle Publishers, 2004.

———. Review of José Luís González's work. *Sunday San Juan Star Magazine*. November 28, 1976, 7–8.

———. *The Growth of the Modern West Indies*. New York: Monthly Review Press, 1968. Reissued, Kingston: Ian Randle Publishers, 2004.

———. 'The Making of a Caribbeanist,' San German, Puerto Rico: Caribbean Institute and Study Center for Latin America, Working Paper No.10, 1983.

———. 'The Modern Caribbean: A New Voyage of Discovery.' See David Lewis's Foreword in *Gordon K. Lewis On Race, Class and Ideology in the Caribbean*, edited by Anthony Maingot, vii–xiv. Kingston: Ian Randle Publishers, 2010.

———. *The Virgin Islands: A Caribbean Lilliput*. Evanston: Northwestern University Press, 1972.

Lewis, Rupert. 'The Writing of Caribbean Political Thought.' Review of *Main Currents in Caribbean Thought – The Historical Evolution of Caribbean Society in its Ideological Aspects, 1492–1900*, by Gordon K. Lewis and *The Growth and Development of Political Ideas in the Caribbean 1774–1983*, by Denis Benn. *Caribbean Quarterly* 36, nos. 1 & 2 (1990) 153–65.

Lewis, V. 'Small States in the International Society with Special Reference to the Associated States.' *Caribbean Quarterly* 18, no. 2, (1972): 36–47.

Ling, Trevor. *Karl Marx and Religion in Europe and India*. London: Macmillan, 1980.

Locke, John. 'A Letter Concerning Toleration.' In *The Portable Enlightenment Reader*, edited by Isaac Kramnick. New York: Penguin Books, 1995.

Maaga, Mary McCormick. *Hearing the Voices of Jonestown*. Syracuse: Syracuse University Press, 1998.

Maingot, Anthony P. 'Requiem for a Utopia.' *Miami Herald*, October 30, 1983, 10, 60.

———. *The Passionate Advocate: Gordon K. Lewis and Caribbean Studies*. Coventry: Centre for Caribbean Studies, University of Warwick, 1991.

———, ed. *Gordon K. Lewis on Race, Class and Ideology in the Caribbean*. Kingston: Ian Randle Publishers, 2010.

———. 'Gordon K. Lewis: The Engaged Scholar as Passionate Advocate' Introduction to *Gordon K. Lewis On Race, Class and Ideology in the Caribbean*, edited by Anthony Maingot. Kingston: Ian Randle Publishers, 2010.

Manley, M. *Jamaica: Struggle in the Periphery*. London: Third World Media Ltd., 1982.

———. 'Not for Sale.' Speech at 38th Annual PNP Conference, September 19, 1977. San Francisco, CA: Editorial Consultants Inc., 1977.

Marcha V. and Paul Verveel. *De cultuur van angst: Paradoxale ketenen van angst en zwijgen op Curaçao*. Amsterdam: SWP. 2003.

Martínez, Jorge Mario, Jorge Mattar and Pedro Rivera. *Globalización y desarrollo: Desafíos de Puerto Rico frente al siglo XXI*. Mexico, D.F.: CEPAL, 2005.

Martinus, F. 'The Guene Kriole of the Netherlands Antilles. Its Theoretical and Practical Consequences for Better Understanding Papiamentu and Other Portuguese Based Creoles.' *Annales del Caribe* 4–5 (1984): 335–50.

———. *The Kiss of a Slave. Papiamentu's West-African Connections.* PhD thesis, University of Amsterdam, 1996. Curaçao: De Curaçaose Courant, 1997.

———. 'The Victory of the Concubines and the Nannies'. In *Caribbean Creolization. Reflections on the Cultural Dynamics of Language, Literature and Identity,* edited by K. Balutansky and Marie-Agnès Sourieau. Gainesville, FL: University Press of Florida, 1998.

Marx, Karl. *Capital.* New York: Modern Library, 1906.

———. 'On the Jewish Question.' In *The Marx-Engels Reader,* edited by Robert C. Tucker. New York: Norton, 1972.

Mazrui, Ali, and Michael Tidy. *Nationalism and New States in Africa.* London: Heinemann, 1987.

McLellan, David. *Marxism After Marx.* London: The Macmillan Press, 1980.

Meeks, Brian, and Folke Lindahl, eds. *New Caribbean Thought.* Kingston: UWI Press, 2001.

Meléndez Vélez, Edgardo, and Nilsa Medina Piña. *Desarrollo económico comunitario: Casos exitosos en Puerto Rico.* San Juan: Ediciones Nueva Aurora, 1999.

Meyerowitz, Eva. *The Sacred State of the Akan.* London: Faber & Faber, 1951.

Mibiti, John S. *Concepts of God in Africa.* London: SPCK, 1970.

Midgley, James, and Michael Livermore. 'Social Capital and Local Economic Development: Implications for Community Social Work Practice.' *Journal of Community Practice* 5, nos. 1/2 (2003): 29–40.

Migliore, Daniel L. *Faith Seeking Understanding.* 2nd ed. Grand Rapids, MI: William B. Eerdmans, 2004.

Milne, R.S. *Politics in Ethnically Bi-Polar States.* Vancouver: University of British Columbia Press, 1982.

Mintz, Sidney. 'Gordon K. Lewis 1919–1991.' *Caribbean Studies Newsletter* 19 (1992): 2–24.

Moltmann, Jurgen. *Experiences in Theology: Ways and Forms of Christian Theology* Minneapolis: Fortress Press, 2000.

Moore, Rebecca. *A Sympathetic History of Jonestown.* Lewison, NY: Edwin Mellen Press, 1985.

Morgen, Sandra and Jeff Maskovsky. 'The Anthropology of Welfare 'Reform': New Perspectives on U.S. Urban Poverty in the Post-Welfare Era'. *Annual Review of Anthropology* 32 (2003): 315–38.

Morrison, Andrew. *Justice: The Struggle for Democracy in Guyana 1952–1992.* Georgetown: Red Thread Women's Press, 1998.

Mullaly, Bob. *Structural Social Work: Ideology, Theory, and Practice.* 2nd ed. Ontario: Oxford University Press, 1997.

Naipaul, Shiva. *Black and White.* London: Hamish Hamilton, 1980.

———. *Journey to Nowhere: A New World Tragedy.* New York: Simon & Schuster, 1981.

Nemon, Howard. 'Community Action: Lessons from Forty Years of Federal Funding, Anti-Poverty Strategies and Participation of the Poor.' *Journal of Poverty* 11, no. 1 (2007): 1–22.

Nettleford, R. *Caribbean Cultural Identity: The Case of Jamaica: An Essay in Cultural Dynamics.* Kingston: Ian Randle Publishers, 2003.

———. *Inward Stretch, Outward Reach: A Voice from the Caribbean.* London: Macmillan Press, 1993; New York: Caribbean Diaspora Press, 1995.

Nettleford, R., and Philip Sherlock. *The University of the West Indies.* London: Macmillan Caribbean Press, 1990.

Obenga, Theophile. 'African philosophy of the Pharonic Period.' In *Egypt Revisited*, edited by Ivan Van Sertima, 286–324. New Brunswick: Transaction Publishers, 1993.

Official numbers from the Department of Labor and Human Resources. Puerto Rico http://www.netempleopr.org/almis23/ index.jsp. Accessed October 20, 2010.

Official statistics from Puerto Rico's Planning Board. http://www.jp.gobierno.pr/Portal_JP/Default.aspx?tabid =185. Accessed October 20, 2010.

Official unemployment statistics from the Department of Labor and Human Resources. Puerto Rico http://www.net-empleopr.org/almis23/index.jsp. Accessed October 20, 2010.

Oficina para el Financiamiento Socioeconómico y la Autogestión. *El país posible: Modelo de apoderamiento y autogestión para las comunidades especiales del Puerto Rico.* San Juan: Oficina para el Financiamiento Socioeconómico y la Autogestión, 2003.

Oostindie, G. and Peter Verton. *Ki Sorto di Reino?- What Kind of Kingdom?: Visies en Verwachtingen van Antillianen en Arubanen omtrent het Koninkrijk.* Den Haag: Sdu Uitgevers, 1998.

Oostindie, Gert and Inge Klinkers, *Decolonising the Caribbean: Dutch Policies in Comparative Perspectives.* Amsterdam: Amsterdam University Press, 2003.

Ortíz Negrón, Laura. *Al filo de la navaja: Los márgenes en Puerto Rico.* UPR Rio Piedras: Centro de Investigaciones Sociales, 1999.

Paris, Peter. *The Spirituality of African Peoples: The Search for a Common Moral Discourse.* Minneapolis, MN: Fortress Press, 1995.

Parker, Earl. *Transformation: The Story of Modern Puerto Rico.* New York: Simon & Schuster, 1955.

Patterson, Orlando. *The Sociology of Slavery.* London: Granada Publishing Ltd., 1973.

Paul, Annie. 'No Space for Race? The Bleaching of the Nation in Postcolonial Jamaica.' In *The African-Caribbean Worldview and the Making of Caribbean Society*, edited by Horace Levy. Kingston: The University of the West Indies Press, 2009.

Paula, A. *The Cry of My Life: Bitterzoete herinneringen aan een levensweg vol kronkels.* Curaçao: Curaçaosche Courant, 2005.

———. *From Objective To Subjective Social Barriers: A Historico-Philosophical Analysis of Certain Negative Attitudes Among the Negroid Population of Curaçao.* Willemstad: Curaçao, 1967.

Payne, A., and M. Bishop. 'Caribbean Regional Governance and the Sovereignty/Statehood Problem.' *Caribbean Paper No. 8*, (2010). Centre for International Governance Innovation. www.cigionline.org. Accessed 1/9/2010.

Payne, A., and P. Sutton. *Charting Caribbean Development.* London: Macmillan Press, 2001.

Perkinson, James. *Shamanism, Racism and Hip Hop Culture: Essay on White Supremacy and Black Subversion.* New York: Palgrave Macmillan, 2005.

———. *White Theology: Outing Supremacy in Modernity.* New York: Palgrave Macmillan, 2004.

Phaf, Ineke. 'Women Writers of the Dutch-Speaking Caribbean: Life Long Poem in the Tradition of Surinamese Granmorgu (New Dawn).' In *Caribbean Women Writers: Essays from the First International Conference,* edited by Selwyn Reginald Cudjoe. Wellesley, MA: Calaloux, 1990.

Plato. *The Essential Plato.* Edited by Alain De Botton and Translated by Benjamin Jowett. London: The Softback Preview, 1999.

Plumb, J. H. *The Making of An Historian: The Collected Essays of J. H. Plumb.* Athens, GA: The University of Georgia Press, 1988.

Pratts, Saul. *La privatizacion del pacto social.* San Juan, PR: Ediciones Porta Coeli, 1996.

Premdas, R. *Ethnic Identity in the Caribbean: Decentering a Myth.* Harney Seminar and Lectures Monograph Series on Multiculturalism and Migration. University of Toronto, 1995. Re-issued by the Center for Latin American Studies, Yale University, 1996.

———. *Ethnicity and Development: The Case of Guyana.* Ashgate: Avebury Press, 1995.

———. 'Guyana.' *The South American Handbook,* edited by Patrick Henan and M. Lamontagne. London: Fitzroy Dearborn Publishers, 2002.

———. 'Self-Determination and Sovereignty in the Caribbean: Migration, Transnational Identities and Deterritorialisation of the State.' In *Caribbean Survival and the Global Challenge,* edited by Ramesh Ramsaran. Kingston: Ian Randle Publishers, 2002, 49–64.

Price, Richard. *Alabi's World.* Baltimore: Johns Hopkins University Press, 1990.

———, ed. *Maroon Societies.* Baltimore: Johns Hopkins University Press, 1979.

Quiñones Pérez, Argeo. 'Ingeniería de una crisis fiscal autoinfligida.' *Claridad* 15 al 21 de enero 2009.

Raddatz, Fritz J., ed. *Karl Marx-Friedrich Engels: Selected Letters.* Boston: Little, Brown, 1980.

Ramoutar, R. 'The Dark Side of Security Intelligence,' *Trinidad and Tobago Guardian* December 12, 2010. http://test.guardian.co.tt/index.php?q=commentary/editorial/2010/12/12/dark-side-security-intelligence Accessed 17/10/2011.

Rapley, J. 'The New Middle Ages.' *Foreign Affairs,* May–June 2006.

Reddie, Anthony G. *Is God Color-Blind? Insights From Black Theology for Ministry.* Great Britain: SPCK, 2009.

———. *Working Against the Grain: Re-imaging Black Theology in the 21st Century.* London: Equinox Publishing, 2008.

Reid-Salmon, Delroy A. *Home Away From Home: The Caribbean Diasporan Church in the Black Atlantic Tradition.* London: Equinox Publishing Ltd., 2008.

Reiterman, Tim with John Jacobs. *Raven: The Untold Story of Rev. Jim Jones and His People.* New York, NY: Dutton, 1982.

Report of the Caribbean Commission on Health and Development, (CARICOM/PAHO/WHO, 2006), 8.

Report of the Task Force on Functional Cooperation, Chaired by Edward Greene. Georgetown: CARICOM Secretariat, 2008.

Reyes, Linda Colón. *Pobreza en Puerto Rico: Radiografía del Proyecto Americano.* San Juan: Editorial Luna Nueva, 2005.

Rique, José Juan and Raul Oscar Orsi. *Cambio social, trabajo y ciudadanía.* Buenos Aires: Editorial Espacios, 2005.

Rivera Grajales, María Lourdes. 'Política social, apoderamiento y participación ciudadana.' In *Política social y trabajo social: Comunidades y políticas sociales entre la academia y la práctica cotidiana*, edited by Nilsa M. Burgos Ortíz and Jorge Benítez Nazario. Serie Atlantea 4. Río Piedras: Proyecto Atlantea, 2006, 265–78.

Römer, Louis Philippe. Making Empire Safe for Consumption: the Politics of the Colonial 'Past' in Non sovereign Curaçao. *Paper presented at the AES Spring Conference*, New York, NY, 2012.

Römer, René. Cultuurbehoud en cultuurverandering: Een Caribisch Dilemma. *Kristof* 8, no.3 (1993):5–21.

———. *Een volk op weg. Un pueblo na kaminda. Een sociologisch historische studie van de Curaçaose samenleving.* PhD thesis,University of Leiden, 1977. Zutphen: De Walburg Pers, 1979.

———. *Het Caribisch gebied, een terreinverkenning.* Curaçao: Universiteit van de Nederlandse Antillen, 1982.

———. 'Het wij van de Curaçaoënaar. *Kristof* 1 no. 2 (1974): 49–60.

Rosalia, R. *Rumbo pa independensia mental: 'Konosé bo historia i kultura pa bo konosé bo mes:' plan di maneho i akshon di kultura pa Kòrsou Kòrsou.* Willemstad, Curaçao: 2001. s.n.

———. *Tambú, de legale en kerkelijke repressie van Afro-Curaçaose volksuitingen.* Zutphen: Walburg Pers, 1997.

Rose, Nikolas. 'Governing "advanced" liberal democracies.' In *Foucault and Political Reason: Liberalism, Neo-Liberalism and Rationalities of Government*, edited by Andrew Barry, Thomas Osborne and Nikolas Rose, 38. London: UCL Press, 1996.

Rupert, L.M. *Creolization and Contraband: Curaçao in the Early Modern Atlantic World.* Athens, GA: University of Georgia Press, 2012.

———. *Inter Imperial Trade and Local Identity: Curaçao in the Colonial Atlantic World.* PhD Thesis, Duke University, 2006.

Russell, Horace. 'The Emergence of the Christian Black: The Making of a Stereotype.' *Jamaica Journal* vol. 16, no. 2 (1983): 58.

Sachs, Jeffrey. *El fin de la pobreza: Cómo conseguirlo en nuestro tiempo.* Mexico, D.F.: Random House Mondadori, 2006.

Salamon, Lester. 'The global associational revolution: the rise of the third sector on the world scene.' *Occasional Paper 15*. Baltimore: Institute for Policy Studies, Johns Hopkins University Press, 1993.

Sanders, R. *Crumbled Small: The Commonwealth Caribbean in World Politics.* London: Hansib Publications, 2005.

Scholes, Theophilus. *Glimpses of the Ages.* 2 vols. London: John Long, 1905 and 1907.

Schwarz, Bill, ed. *West Indian Intellectuals in Britain.* Manchester: Manchester University Press, 2003.

Searle, C., ed. *In Nobody's Backyard: Maurice Bishop's Speeches 1979–1983.* London: Zed Books, 1984.

Shillington, Kevin. *History of Africa.* New York: Palgrave Macmillan, 2005.

Singh, R. 'Frank Talking at Drugs Summit.' *Jamaica Gleaner*, December 23, 1996.

Smith, Ashley. *Emergence From Innocence: Religion, Theology and Development.* Mandeville: Eureka Press, 1991.

Smith, M. 'An Island among Islands: Haiti's Strange Relationship with the Caribbean Community.' *Social and Economic Studies* 54, no. 3 (2005): 176–95.
Smith, M.G. *The Plural Society in the British West Indies*. Berkeley, CA: University of California Press, 1965.
Smith, R.T. *British Guiana*. London: Oxford University Press, 1962.
Sorj, Bernardo. 'Pueden las ONG reemplazar al Estado?: Sociedad civil y Estado en América Latina.' *Nueva Sociedad* 210 (2007): 126–40.
Sotomayor, Orlando. 'Development and Income Distribution: The Case of Puerto Rico.' *World Development* 32, no. 8 (2004): 1395–1406.
Spinner, Jr., Thomas. *A Political and Social History of Guyana, 1945–1983*. Boulder, CO: Westview Press, 1984.
St. Kitts-Nevis Observer. 'IMF says St. Kitts and Nevis has the World's Second Highest National Debt.' No. 867, June 10, 2011. www.thestkittsnevisobserver.com/2011/06/10/national-debt.html. Accessed September 1, 2011.
Stewart, Dianne. *Three Eyes for the Journey*. New York: Oxford University Press, 2005.
Stewart, Robert J. *Religion and Society in Post-Emancipation Jamaica*. Knoxville, TN: University of Tennessee Press, 1992.
Suárez y Romero, Anselmo. *Francisco*. 1839. Rpt., Havana: Publicaciones del Ministerio de Educación, Dirección de Cultura, 1947.
Tanco y Bosmeniel, Félix. *Petrona y Rosalía*. 1838. Rpt. Havana: Editorial Letras Cubanas, 1980.
Taylor, Burchell. *Free For All – A Question of Morality and Community*. Kingston: Grace Kennedy Foundation, 1983.
———. 'The Theology of Liberation.' *Caribbean Quarterly* 37, no. 1 (1991): 19–34.
The Sunday Gleaner (Jamaica), March 2, 1958.
Thomas, C.Y. *The Poor and the Powerless: Economic Policy and Change in the Caribbean*. London: Latin American Bureau, 1988.
Tillich, Paul. *Systematic Theology* vol. 1, 11–15. Chicago: The University of Chicago Press, 1951.
Torres-Saillant, Silvio. *An Intellectual History of the Caribbean*. New York: Palgrave Macmillan, 2006.
Tracy, David. *Analogical Imagination: Christian Theology and the Culture of Pluralism*. New York: Crossroad, 1981.
Treaty Establishing the Caribbean Community. Chaguaramas: CARICOM Secretariat 1973; and the Revised Treaty Establishing the Caribbean Community. Georgetown: CARICOM Secretariat 1990
Tuchman, Barbara W. *The First Salute*. New York: Ballentine Books, 1988.
Tucker, Robert C., ed. *The Marx-Engels Reader*. New York: Norton, 1972.
Turner, Mary. *Slaves and Missionaries: The Disintegration of Jamaican Slave Society, 1787–1834*. Urbana, IL: University of Illinois Press, 1982.
UN Millenium Goals Report. NY: United Nations, July 2013.
Van der Dijs, N. *The Nature of Ethnic Identity among the People of Curaçao*. Curaçao: Curaçaosche Courant, 2011.
Van Lier, R.A.J. De sociale wetenschappen van de neger in Amerika. *Bijdragen tot de taal-, land-, en volkenkunde*, 107, no. 2 (1951): 279–303.
———. *Frontier Society: A Social Analysis of the History of Surinam*. Translated from the Dutch by M.J.L. van Yperen. The Hague: Martinus Nijhoff, 1971.

———. *Samenleving in een Grensgebied: een Sociaal-historische Studie van Suriname.* Den Haag: Nijhoff, 1949.
Van Sertima, Ivan, ed. *Egypt Revisited.* New Brunswick: Transaction Publishers, 1993.
Vasciannie, S. 'No Longer at Sea.' *Jamaica Gleaner,* October 28, 1996.
———. 'Shiprider Sails Home.' *Jamaica Gleaner,* May 19, 1997.
Villaverde, Cirilo. *Cecilia Valdés.*1839 and 1882. Rpt., Havana: Editorial Letras Cubanas, 2002.
Wagley, Charles. 'Plantation Americas, a Cultural Sphere.' In *Caribbean Studies: a Symposium,* edited by Vera Rubin. Institute of Social and Economic Research, University College of the West Indies, 1957.
Walker, Corey. *A Noble Fight.* Urbana, IL: University of Illinois Press, 2008.
Watson, H. 'The 'Shiprider Solution' and Post-Cold War Imperialism: Beyond Ontologies of State Sovereignty in the Caribbean.' In *Living on the Borderlines: Issues in Caribbean Sovereignty and Development,* edited by Cynthia Barrow-Giles and Don Marshall. Kingston: Ian Randle Publishers, 2003.
Wearne, P. 'Guadeloupe – History.' In *Europa Regional Surveys of the World: South America, Central America and the Caribbean 2009.* 17th ed. London: Routledge, 2008, 481–83.
———. 'Martinique – History.' In *Europa Regional Surveys of the World: South America, Central America and the Caribbean 2009.* 17th ed. London: Routledge, 2008, 594–95.
West, Cornel, and Eddie S. Glaude, Jr., eds. *African American Religious Thought: An Anthology.* Louisville: Westminster John Knox Press, 2003.
Williams, G. *Statement by the Hon. Galmo Williams, Premier of the Turks and Caicos Islands,* CRS/2009/CRP.12, United Nations Caribbean Regional Seminar on the Implementation of the Second International Decade for the Eradication of Colonialism. Frigate Bay, St. Kitts, 12 – 14 May 2009. www.un.org/en/decolonization/pdf/crp_2009_08_williams.pdf. Accessed 2/10/2011.
Williams, Lewin. *Caribbean Theology.* New York: Peter Lang Publishing, 1994.
Wilmore, Gayraud S. *African American Religious Studies.* Durham, NC: Duke University Press, 1989.
Witteveen, I and L. Weeber, *Kultura, Base pa Desaroyo Propio.* Nota di Diskushon pa Dia di Estudio, 20–21 di Mart. *Rapòrt Integral pa Barionan di Kòrsou; Plan di Urgensha i Kontinuidat/Integrale Ontwikkeling van de Curaçaose Buurten: Urgentieplan en voor Continuïteit.* Curaçao: IPK (Inisiativa Partikular Kòrsou)/Grupo di Trabou/Universiteit van de Nederlandse Antillen, 1993.

Contributors

Rose Mary Allen, PhD, is a consultant and visiting lecturer at the University of the Netherlands Antilles, where she teaches Caribbean Studies. She has published, co-published and edited several books and articles on the cultural and social history of the Dutch Caribbean islands with special attention to cultural traditions, migration, gender studies and cultural diversity.

Rafael A. Boglio Martínez has a Joint PhD in Social Work and Anthropology from the University of Michigan. He is an Assistant Professor in the Social Sciences Department at the University of Puerto Rico, Mayagüez Campus. His research focuses on the political ambiguity of participatory development in our current neoliberal era. This he explores through his ethnographic study of contemporary community-based, anti-poverty initiatives in Puerto Rico, specifically, capacity-building efforts by grassroots non-profit organizations.

Jessica Byron is a Senior Lecturer in International Relations and former Head of the Department of Government, University of the West Indies, Mona, Jamaica. She coordinates a tripartite BSc/MSc programme in Politics and International Cooperation involving the UWI, Universite Antilles-Guyane and the University of Bordeaux IV. A member of the Executive Board of the Institute of International Relations, UWI, St Augustine, her recent publications include *The Caribbean Community's Fourth Pillar: The Evolution of Regional Security Governance* (2011) and *Regional Integration and Caribbean Civilization: Continuing the Debate* (2012).

Edward Greene, currently UN Secretary General Special Envoy for HIV in the Caribbean, was previously Assistant Secretary General, Human and Social Development, CARICOM Secretariat 2000–2010 and Senior Adviser, Health and Human Development, PAHO/WHO 1995–99. At the UWI, he was appointed Professor in 1988 and served as Pro Vice Chancellor, Development and Alumni Relations 1989–93; University Director, Institute of Social and Economic Relations, 1982–89; and was inaugural Professorial ISER Fellow in 1994. He has authored ten books and over 60 articles and is Professor Emeritus of UWI.

Paget Henry is professor of sociology and Africana Studies at Brown University, the editor of the *C.L.R. James Journal* and also of the *Antigua and Barbuda Review of Books*. He is the author of *Peripheral Capitalism and Underdevelopment in Antigua* (1985); *Caliban's Reason: Introducing Afro-Caribbean Philosophy* (2000); and *Shouldering Antigua and Barbuda: The Life of V.C. Bird* (2009).

Tennyson S. D. Joseph holds a PhD from the University of Cambridge and is a Lecturer in Political Science at the University of the West Indies, Cave Hill (Barbados) Campus. His research interests revolve around Caribbean Political Thought, Globalization and Anti-colonialism, Sovereignty and Decolonization and the Post-1945 Political History of Saint Lucia. His publications include *At the Rainbow's Edge: Collected Speeches of Kenny D. Anthony* (co-edited with Didacus Jules), *General Elections and Voting in the English-Speaking Caribbean 1992–2005* (co-authored with Cynthia Barrow-Giles), and *Decolonization in St. Lucia: Politics and Global Neo-Liberalism 1945–2010*.

Anthony Maingot was born in Trinidad, raised in Costa Rica and formally educated in Curaçao. He received his undergraduate and doctoral degrees from the University of Florida, Gainesville. His work has focused on the history and geopolitics of the Greater Caribbean and the broader patterns of US-Caribbean relations. He has published eight books, numerous monographs and over 100 refereed journal articles. He was President of the Caribbean Studies Association in 1982–83 and received the 'Distinguished Service Medallion' from Florida International University upon his retirement in 2004.

CONTRIBUTORS

Jermaine McCalpin is currently Lecturer in Transitional Justice in the Department of Government, University of the West Indies, Mona. He specializes in Africana political philosophy, Caribbean political thought, and transitional justice. His research interests include truth commissions and political accountability, as well as reparations for slavery, Native American extermination, and the Armenian Genocide. He has written on the South African, Grenadian and Haitian truth commissions.

Brian Meeks is Professor of Social and Political Change at UWI Mona and Director of the Sir Arthur Lewis Institute of Social and Economic Studies. He has taught at Michigan State University, Florida International University and Anton de Kom University of Suriname and served as Visiting Scholar at Cambridge University, Stanford University and Brown University. He has authored or edited nine books including *Caribbean Revolutions and Revolutionary Theory*; *Envisioning Caribbean Futures: Jamaican Perspectives*; *The Thought of New World: The Quest for Decolonisation* (with Norman Girvan); and *M.G. Smith: Social Theory and Anthropology in the Caribbean and Beyond*. His novel, *Paint the Town Red* was published in 2003.

Ralph R. Premdas is Professor in the Sir Arthur Lewis Institute of Social and Economic Studies (SALISES) at the University of the West Indies, St Augustine, Trinidad and Tobago. He holds PhDs in Political Science (Illinois, 1970) and Comparative Religion (McGill, 1991). His research focuses on issues of democratic governance and public policy in ethnically divided states. His publications include many books among which are *Identity, Ethnicity and Culture in the Caribbean* (2000); *Ethnic Conflict and Development: The Case of Guyana* (1997) *and Trinidad and Tobago: Identity and Ethnicity in Public Sector Governance* (2007).

Delroy A. Reid-Salmon is pastor of Grace Baptist Chapel, New York, and Research Fellow at the Oxford Centre for Christianity and Culture, Regent's Park College. He is a graduate of Long Island University, Harvard Divinity School and the University of Birmingham, UK. His publications include *Burning for Freedom: A Theology of the Black Atlantic Struggle for Liberation*, and *Home Away from Home: The Caribbean Diasporan Church in the Black Atlantic Tradition*.

Claudette Williams is Professor of Hispanic Caribbean Literature in the Department of Modern Languages and Literatures, UWI Mona Campus. Her essays have appeared in various international journals. With her first book, *Charcoal and Cinnamon: The Politics of Color in Spanish Caribbean Literature* (2000) she broke new ground in the study of gender and racial politics in the Caribbean and Latin America. Her second book, *The Devil in the Details: Cuban Antislavery Narrative in the Postmodern Age*, was published in 2010.

Index

Acción social, 167–72
African cosmology, 58
African slaves, 25, 51
African world view, 59
Afrocentric, 48, 69
Allen, Rose Mary, xii
Alleyne, George, 150
American Revolution, 3, 4
Ancient Egyptian Thought, 48
Anglophone Caribbean, xi, 98
Ani, Marimba, 48, 54, 59, 60–62, 65
Ansano, Richenel, 105
Antigua and Barbuda, 6, 33–35, 133
Antillanité, 95
Anti-slavery narratives, xiii
Aristide, Jean Bertrand, 135, 136
Aristotle, 57
Asylum, 136

Banda ‹Bou, 104
Bangladesh, 157
Barbados, 24, 80, 122, 129, 132, 133, 139
Barrow-Giles, Cynthia, 113
Battle of Little Big Horn, 178
Belle, George, 47, 49, 56, 58
Benítez, Jorge, 160
Benítez-Rojo, Antonio, 71, 75, 105
Benn, Denis, xiii, 48, 49, 52–56, 65, 152
Bernal, Martin, 57
Biersteker, Thomas, 119
Bishop, Mathew, 127, 136
Bishop, Maurice, 127, 128, 129, 139
Black Athena, 57

Black nationalist, 25, 69
Blanchard, Paul, 95
Blyden, Edward, 40
Bodin, Jean, 116
Boglio Martínez, Rafael, xiv
Brenneker, Paul, 103
Brievengat, 104
Brown University, vii, ix, xv,
Bull, Hedley, 117
Burke, Edmund, xiii, 1–3
Burnham, Forbes, 129, 179, 189–90
Bush, Barbara, 71
Byron, Jessica, xiv,

Calderon, Sila M., 161, 163
Caliban's Reason: Introducing Afro-Caribbean Philosophy, xiii, 54, 55
Capacity building, 134, 163–65, 170
Capitalism, xii, 2, 10, 22, 84, 154, 156, 157, 159, 160, 172, 184, 189
Caribbean Agricultural Health and Food Safety Agency, 151
Caribbean Commission on Health and Development, 150
Caribbean Competition Commission, 147
Caribbean Cultural Identity: The Case of Jamaica - An Essay in Cultural Dynamics, 105
Caribbean Examination Council, 150
Caribbean Graduate School of Theology, 79
Caribbean Intellectual Thought, xiii, 79, 81–85, 87, 89

Caribbean Political Thought, ix, 13,
    22–24, 26, 37, 40, 41, 46, 48, 49,
    55, 58, 62, 63
Caribbean Public Health Agency, 151
Caribbean Reasonings, vii, ix
Caribbean Regional Negotiation
    Mechanism, 147
Caribbean slavery, xiii, 71
Caribbean Theology, 85
Caribbean Thought, vii, viii, xi, xiii,
    14, 19, 20, 41, 46–59, 62–66, 85,
    88, 95, 134
Caribbeanness, 95, 105
CARICOM Community Climate
    Change Centre, 150
CARICOM Financial Services
    Agreement, 148
CARICOM Investment Code, 148
CARICOM Secretariat, 148
CARICOM Single Market and
    Economy, 115, 146
CARICOM Strategic Plan for
    Regional Development, 147
CARICOM Vocation Qualification,
    147
CARIFORUM, 146
Caudillismo, 159
Central African Republic, 135
Centre for Caribbean Thought, vii,
    ix, xv
Chaguaramas Declaration, 127
Christian socialist, x, 177, 187
Clinton administration, 160
Codrington College, 80
Colonialism, ix, x, 2, 18, 41, 53, 59,
    89, 99, 100, 103, 120, 145, 178
Commonwealth Status, x, 154
Community Action Agency, 168
Community Economic Development
    Projects (CED), 160, 162, 163,
    166, 170,
Community Service Block Grant
    (CSBG), 167, 168

Compadrazgo, 155
Cornet, Florencia, 105
Council for National Security and
    Law Enforcement, 150
Covert rebellion, 76
Creolization, 16, 20, 21, 32, 35, 38,
    43, 49, 50, 51, 55, 56, 63, 64, 65,
    95, 98, 99 - 101
*Creolization and Contraband: Curacao in
    the Modern Atlantic World*, 99
*Cry of My Life, The: Bittersweet
    Memories of a Life Full of Twists*, 100
*Cry of My Life, The: Bitterzoete
    herinneringen aan een leevensweg vol
    kronkels*, 100
Cuba, xii, xiii, 7, 32, 51, 69, 70, 75,
    76, 77, 113, 123, 124, 151, 178,
    180, 187
Cuban bourgeoisie, 75
Cuban war of independence, 114
Curaçao, 94–106

Davis, Kortright, 88
*Decolonising the Caribbean: Dutch
    Policies in Comparative perspectives*,
    96
*Decolonizing Theology: A Caribbean
    Perspective*, 85
del Monte, Domingo, 70, 71, 73
Democracy, xiv, 10, 35, 38, 84, 135,
    144, 153, 160, 163, 188, 193
Diop, Cheikh Anta, 54, 61, 62, 65
Directorate of Trade and Economic
    Integration, 147
Dominica, 24, 131, 136, 142, 152
Dominican Republic, 32, 123, 124,
    146
Dominican Republic - Central
    American Free Trade Agreement
    (DR-CAFTA), 158
Dubbelspel, 95
Dutch Caribbean, xiii, xiv, 94–97,
    102Earthquake disaster, 135,
    136

INDEX

Eastern Caribbean Central Bank, 130
Eastern Caribbean Currency Union, 130
Economic Commission for Latin America and the Caribbean (ECLAC), 149, 159
Economic sovereignty, 123, 128
Edwards, Bryan, 24, 53
Een volk op weg: Un Pueblo na Kaminda, 97
Elections, 1980, xii
Emergence of the Christian Black, The: The Making of a Stereotype, 86
English humanitarianism, 50
Epistemology, 48, 55, 60–64, 141
Erasure, 23, 43, 96,
Erskine, Noel, 85
Estado libre asociado, 2, 121
European hegemony, 51, 52–55, 57, 59, 63, 65

Farrell, Sybil, vii, x
Fatal particularism, 145, 151–53
Figueroa-Rodriguez, Raúl, 159
Fortuño, Luis, 166
Francisco, 75
Free movement, 147, 148
Free Villages, 86, 126
French Caribbean, 120
French Enlightenment, 50
French Revolution, 3, 50
From Objective to Subjective Social Barriers, 99
Froude, James Anthony, 51

Garvey, Marcus, 41, 53, 54
Gather with the Saints at the River: The Jonestown Guyana Holocaust of 1978, xiv, 177
Girigori, Su, 105
Girvan, Norman, 146
Glissant, Edouard, 95
Globalization, 84, 104, 105, 113–15, 117, 125, 127, 136, 162, 166

God, 1, 4, 8, 9, 28, 30, 31, 81, 82, 84, 88, 89
Goulbourne, Harry, 80
Goveia, Elsa, 95
Greene, Edward, xiv
Grenada, xii, xiv, 1, 10, 11, 36, 37, 115, 137, 139, 178
Grenada: The Jewel Despoiled xii, 9, 16, 124
Griffith, Ivelaw, 134, 135
Growth and Development of Political Ideas in the Caribbean 1774–1983, The, 52
Growth of the Modern West Indies, The, xi, 16, 18, 21, 122, 152
Guyana, xii, xiv, 129, 130, 152, 177, 178, 179, 180, 181, 183, 188–91

Haitian crises, 135
Haitian Revolution, 38, 39, 42, 47
Hall, Patricia, 132
Hall, Stuart, ix
Hambuch, Doris, 95
Hamid, Idris, 85
Hancock, Ralph, 154
Hart, Richard, ix
Harvard, x, 14
Henriquez, Jeanne, 105
Henry, Paget, xiii, 47–49, 54–57, 62, 63, 65
Hernández Colón, Rafael, 160
Hispaniola, 178
Hobbes, Thomas, 116, 117, 126, 138, 182
Hoetink, Harmannus ‹Harry›, 94, 97
Hoogvelt, Ankie, 157
Human existence, 84, 87

Iberian culture, 99
IMF Programmes, 130, 131
Imperialism, 2, 6, 7, 15, 16, 61, 84, 89, 178, 191, 192
Implementation Agency for Crime and Security, 150

International Monetary Fund, 129–31, 137
Irish Question, ix
Island of Dr. Moreau, 186

Jackson, Richard, 73
Jagan, Cheddi, 189
Jamaica, 35, 36, 39, 105, 129, 133, 136, 139, 142–44
Jamaica Theological Seminary, 79
James, C.L.R., xv, 37, 39, 41, 95
Jesus, 184
Jones, Jim, xiv, 177, 179, 181–87, 190
Jonestown, xii, xiv, 177–87, 189–93
Joseph, Tennyson, xiii
Juliana, Elis, 103

Kas di Kultura, 103
Kingdom of the Netherlands, 95, 96, 101, 102, 104, 109
Kiss of a Slave, The: Papiamentu's West African Connections, 100
Klinkers, Inge, 96
Knight, Franklin, 71
Krasner, Stephen, 117–19, 125
Kultura Propio, 104

La partidocracia, 160
Lamming, George, ix
Latortue, Gerard, 136
Le Discours Antillais, 95
Leewards, 122, 123
Lenin, 2, 184
Leonora, Lianne, 105
Leviathan, 116
Lewis, Gordon K., ix - xv, 1–11, 14–27, 33, 36, 37, 40, 41, 46–57, 64, 65, 69, 71, 73–75, 77, 82–84, 94, 95, 100, 103, 105, 113, 115, 120–25, 132, 137, 145, 146, 151, 152, 154–56, 158, 161, 165, 171, 177, 178, 181–93
Lewis, Rupert, vii, 49, 56–58
Lewis, Vaughan, 122

Liberation, xii, 2, 4, 83, 88, 89, 122, 128, 182
Long, Edward, 24, 53, 77

Maharaj, Ramesh, 133
Main Currents in Caribbean Thought, 52, 56, 69, 73, 82, 83, 94, 123
Maingot, Anthony, xiii, 121
Manley Government, xii
Manley, Michael, 128, 129
Manners, Robert, 95
Marcha, Valdemar, 94, 102
Martha, Guiselle, 105
Marti, Jose, 124
Martinus Arion, Frank, 94, 95, 100, 101
Marx, 57, 186, 187, 189, 192
Mintz, Sidney, 95
Monetary union, 147
Moscone, George, 179
Muñoz Marín, Luis, xi, 121

Nature of Ethnic Identity Among the People of Curacao, The, 101
Negrophobia, 57, 70
Neoliberal policies, 158, 166
Nettleford, Rex, 32, 42, 105
New World Group, ix
Non Governmental Organizations (ngos), 155, 164, 165–67, 171–73
Non-independent Caribbean territories, 144
North American Free Trade Agreement (NAFTA), 158
Northern Caribbean University, 79
Northern Cradle, 61, 62

OECS, 122, 123, 130, 133, 152
Office of Trade Negotiations, 147
Old representative system, 53
Oostindie, Gert, 96, 102
Operation bootstrap, 121
Oxford University, x, 14

Papiamentu, 96, 99–101
Paris commune, 178
Patterson, H. Orlando, 71, 72
Patterson, P.J., 136, 143
Paul, 88
Paula, Alejandro 'Jandie', 94, 96, 99, 100
Payne, Anthony, 127, 137
Peoples Temple, 177, 179, 181, 187, 189, 190, 191, 193
Peoples Temple agricultural project, 179
Petit marronage, 74
Phaf, Ineke, 96
Plato, 48, 54, 57, 59–65
Post abolition Caribbean, 98
Postmodernity, 71
Premdas, Ralph, xiv, 126, 127, 138
President Reagan, 160
Puerto Rico: A Success Story, 154
Puerto Rico: Freedom and Power in the Caribbean, x, 15, 154, 171
Pythagoras, 57

Ramphal, Shridath, 113
Rapley, John, 117
Rastafari, 3, 39, 42, 58, 63
Red brigade, 180
Regional Development Fund, 147
Reid-Salmon, Delroy, xiii
Religion, 4, 5, 18, 21, 24–26, 43, 54, 57, 79–81, 83, 97, 182, 191
Religious studies, 81
Repeating Island, The: The Caribbean and the Postmodern Perspective, 71
Report of the CARICOM Task Force on Functional Cooperation, 150
Rodney, Walter, xii, xv
Römer, Louis Philippe, 105
Römer, René A., 94, 96–101
Rosalia, René V., 94, 103
Roselló, Pedro, 160, 161
Rousseau, Jean Jacques, 116, 138, 182

Rupert, Linda, 99
Russell, Horace, 85–87
Ryan, Bill, 180, 185

Sachs, Jeffrey, 157
San Francisco, 179, 180
San Juan, 154, 161, 162
Sanders, Ronald, 128
Scott, Rebecca, 71
Self determination, 113–15, 120–22, 125, 128, 152
Sephardic Jews, 99
Sharp, Granville, 77
Shiprider agreements, 132–34
Skerrit, Roosevelt, 136
Smith, M.G., ix, 16
Socialism, xii - xiv, 1, 7, 9, 178–82, 184, 186–89, 191–93
Socialist, x, xiv, 1, 2, 7–10, 15, 17, 40, 47, 50, 177–82, 184–90, 192, 193
Socialist thought, 47, 50, 188
Sophists, 3, 60, 61
South Africa, vii, 136
Southern Cradle, 61
Sovereignty, xiv, 32, 35, 113–20, 122–29, 131–38, 149, 151, 152
Soviet Embassy, 181
Soviet State, ix
Special Needs Communities Programme, 161, 162
St. Domingue, 113
St. John Vianney, 80
St. Michael's Seminary, 79
Suárez y Romero, Anselmo, 75
Suriname, 98, 101, 102, 146, 151, 152

Tambú, 103
Taylor, Burchell, 84
Theology, xiii, 3, 79–89, 182, 187
Thomas, C.Y., 130
Thomas, J.J., 51
Torres, Ehida, 168

Treaty of Eastern Caribbean Union, 123
Trinidad, xi, 80, 123, 133
Troubling the Waters, 85
Turks and Caicos Islands, 133

United Kingdom, ix
United Theological College, 79
University of California Los Angeles, x
University of Chicago, x
University of Curaçao, 96
University of Puerto Rico Rio Piedras, ix, x
University of the West Indies, ix, 79, 80, 150

Van der Dijs, Natasha, 101
van Lier, Rudolph, 97, 98
Vattelian sovereignty, 118
Venezuela, 140, 190
Verweel, Paul, 102

Wagley, Charles, 96
Wales, ix, 14
Watson, Hilbourne, 134
Weeber, Leon, 104
Wells, H.G., 186
West European culture, 99
West Indies Federation, xi, 122, 146
Western Philosophy, 58, 59
Westphalian, 117, 118, 128
Williams, Claudette, xiii
Williams, Eric, 16, 40, 88, 95, 128
Williams, Lewin, 85
Windwards, 122, 123
Witteveen, Ieteke, 104
Wolf, Eric, 95
World Trade Organization, 132
Wynter, Sylvia, ix

Yu di Kòrsou, 99, 101
Yurugu, 48

www.ingramcontent.com/pod-product-compliance
Lightning Source LLC
Chambersburg PA
CBHW032040150426
43194CB00006B/365